The ADVENTUROUS READER'S Guide to the Epic Worlds of ALFRED DÖBLIN

A MEDLEY of THEMES

Selected & Translated by

Chris Godwin

G

GALILEO PUBLISHERS, CAMBRIDGE

Published by
Galileo Publishers
16 Woodlands Road, Great Shelford
Cambridge CB22 5LW

www.galileopublishing.co.uk

Distributed in the USA by SCB Distributors
& in Australia by Peribo Pty Ltd

First Edition

ISBN: 9781915530578

Printed in the EU

Alfred Döblin's epic novels in English:

Translated by C D Godwin:

The Three Leaps of Wang Lun. 2nd ed., NY Review Books/CUHK Press 2015.

Wallenstein. PDF download at https://beyond-alexanderplatz.com

Mountains Oceans Giants. Galileo 2021.

Manas. Galileo 2021.

Citizens & Soldiers (Vol. 1 of *November 1918*). Galileo 2024.

The Babylonian Exile. PDF download at https://beyond-alexanderplatz.com

The Land without Death. Galileo 2022.

The two passages from *Berlin Alexanderplatz* in this book are adapted by C. D. Godwin from Eugene Jolas' 1931 translation.

Translated by others:

Berlin Alexanderplatz. Tr. Michael Hofmann. NY Review Books/Penguin 2018 / Tr. Eugene Jolas, Viking 1931.

November 1918: A German Revolution.

Vols 2/3 *A People Betrayed / The Troops Return*. Tr. John E Woods. Fromm 1983

Vol 4: *Karl & Rosa*. Tr. John E Woods. Fromm 1983.

Tales of a Long Night. Tr. R & R Kimber. Fromm 1984.

In Döblin's novels, Nature is no describable reality, but a locus of forces, a magnetic field, electricity. Only from this standpoint can the essence of this writer be discerned: he is the Energiser, whose noisy, colourful, tough energies overleap every life form and sweep in a wild flood over cosily descriptive narrative art. His language does not follow the contours of inner and outward reality, but blooms like an organism.

– Rudolf Keyser, *Das Kunstblatt*, 1925

... As a writer he outstripped himself, he created characters whose fullness of experience, powers of thought, sceptical acumen were endlessly bigger than his "own"; in philosophical terms: ***his creations outshone the creator****; in psychological terms: in* ***a post-hypnotic amnesia he betrayed no sign of his actual depths,*** *and to some extent had no notion of those depths, had no understanding of them at all. A schizo-condition, as must be the rule with musicians who converse in trivialities but compose profoundly; but I have never encountered it among writers.*

- Günther Anders, *Mensch ohne Welt*, 1984

CONTENTS

INTRODUCTION

If you have navigated your way to this page, then you are, by definition, an Adventurous Reader!

Of the three great German word-artists of the first half of the 20th century, Alfred Döblin remains the least known. (The other two are Thomas Mann, whose attitude towards Döblin ranged from cautious admiration to intense frustration; and Berthold Brecht, who learned much from the ideas of his friend Döblin. NB: We're not concerned here with their great Austrian contemporaries.) Anglophone readers have almost no source of information about Döblin, or about those works of his already published in English (*Berlin Alexanderplatz* perhaps excepted).

In Germany, reliable editions of Döblin trickled out between the 1980s (decades after his death in 1957) and the 2010s. Academic lit. crit. scholars enjoy tackling aspects of his life and output in ways attractive to other scholars. But little has been done to promote Döblin to a wider pool of readers. Instead he is acknowledged, with a sigh, to be "difficult", of interest only to a select minority.

Since 2018 my website <https://beyond-alexanderplatz.com> has sought to remedy this neglect; and more recently the podcast "The Epic Worlds of Alfred Döblin" explores his work in the context of his life and the social and political background. Also, Döblin's Wikipedia page in English has expanded usefully in recent years; there you can find basic biographic information.

The "official" view of Döblin is grievously misconceived. Yes, his major works fill weighty tomes – but so do Thomas

Mann's! Yes, he tackles profound questions about the world and human existence, but so do Mann and Brecht! The issue with Döblin, I believe, is summed up in an acute observation by an old school friend, Moritz Goldstein, in his review of *Wallenstein:*

> *A severely short-sighted writer, who has to bring objects really close to his eyes, has created a colossal wall-painting for short-sighted people.*

Goldstein's remark offers a way into Döblin's epic worlds: provide Adventurous Readers with map and compass and rations to sustain them, as they proceed through vividly imagined exotic landscapes.

All nine of Döblin's epic works are now available in English: seven titles as books. The other two can be found on my website, which attracted attention not only from readers hungry for more Döblin, but also from Galileo Publishers, who brought out two epics in 2021 (*Mountains Oceans Giants* and *Manas*), a third in 2022 (*The Land without Death*), a fourth in 2024 (*Citizens & Soldiers*, the missing first volume of *November 1918*), and who leaped at the chance to publish this thematic selection.

Since Döblin is still so little known in English, these publications have so far attracted only a few (but enthusiastic) reviews. Journal editors seem reluctant to find space for reviews; competent reviewers may be few and far between; hence bookshops don't stock Döblin and the wider literate public remains unaware of his work. *Because Döblin is so little known, he shall remain unknown.*

Döblin famously declared: If a novel can't be cut up into ten pieces like a worm, and each piece lives by itself, it is worthless. The themed excerpts presented here show how he put this maxim into practice. Each deserves close reading, for each brings to life its own vivid world.

At the start of his writing career, Döblin was already reflecting on a new kind of fiction as a way out of the moribund 19th century German novel. He sharpened his views over the next three decades, alongside his practice as a writer. Critics have noted how the first five epics from *Wang Lun* to *Berlin Alexanderplatz* show a clear line of development, in particular an increasing intensity and economy of language: maximum meaning from precisely targeted words, phrases, sentences, scenes and voices. In his most neglected work, *Manas*, immediately preceding the much-dissected *Berlin Alexanderplatz*, the intensity required a breakout from normal prose to a kind of free verse. Critics responded positively (and really the format of *Manas* should present the open-minded reader with little difficulty) but many German readers were baffled, and scholars are still reluctant to engage with this remarkable work. (Literary scholars seem to feel safer when they can quote lots of preceding scholarship.)

The epics after *Berlin Alexanderplatz* were produced under difficult conditions of exile. Döblin had lost his medical career, most of his German-reading public, and the lively sardonic vernacular of working-class Berlin (a veritable treasure, he believed, absurdly despised by the educated). The major works of exile should not lightly be dismissed as below the standard set by *Berlin Alexanderplatz*, but considered respectfully on their own merits.

SEQUENCE OF THE EPIC NOVELS:

The Three Leaps of Wang Lun. Written 1911-12, published 1916.
Wallenstein. Written 1917-19, published 1920.
Mountains Oceans Giants. Written 1921-23, published 1924.
Manas. Written 1926, published 1927.
Berlin Alexanderplatz. Written 1927-28, published 1929.

1933-45: twelve years in exile

The Babylonian Exile. Written 1933 in Switzerland/France, published 1934.

The Land without Death (the Amazonas Trilogy):

Vol 1: *Journey to the Land without Death.* Written 1935-36 in France, published 1937.

Vol. 2: *The Blue Jaguar.* Written 1937 in France, published 1938. These two titles were not obviously linked. For the postwar edition of 1947-48, Vol. 2 was split into two volumes, thus forming a Trilogy.

November 1918: a German Revolution:

Vol 1 *Citizens & Soldiers.* Written 1938-39 in France, published October 1939: very limited circulation.

Vol. 2 later split into two volumes *A People Betrayed* and *The Troops Return.* Written 1939-40 in France, typed up and revised in the USA, published 1948/1949 in Germany.

Vol. 3[4] *Karl and Rosa.* Written 1942-43 in the USA, published 1950 in Germany.

Tales of a Long Night. Written 1945-46 in West Germany, published 1956 in East Germany.

THE EPICS:

The Three Leaps of Wang Lun – Döblin's first venture into long-form fiction astonished reviewers with its vivid recreation of an 18th century China untouched by the West. The theme: individual fates against the implacable force of the world/the State. Language and structure show Modernist and Expressionist features, alongside extensive narrative sequences.

Wallenstein – a 900-page tapestry of the Thirty Years War in central Europe, covering almost every main personality and event. The total absence of dates disoriented German readers. The theme: power. It springs seemingly from nowhere in the case of the war-entrepreneur Wallenstein; and evaporates into ever more tawdry pretending in the case of Emperor Ferdinand. Passages just as intense as the opening scene are scattered throughout, amid vivid narratives of war, popular suffering, and characters presented with Dickensian gusto.

Mountains Oceans Giants – from trying to understand the past, Döblin now seeks to understand the future that awaits if current trends of technological hubris continue. The intensity of his imaginative effort almost led to a nervous breakdown. The first half, said a critic in *The LA Review of Books*, reads like "a demented 27th century edition of *The Economist*". The Greenland-Iceland venture in the second half and its horrific aftermath are unparalleled anywhere in Science Fiction.

Manas – The first three epics featured humans *en masse* (religious sects, armies, crowds). In *Manas* the focus is on one man (a war hero) and his beloved wife, who rescues him from Shiva's Field of the Dead. The theme: how to reconcile the human Ego with the world of Nature. Imaginative intensity demanded an unconventional style of presentation: Robert Musil called it "a kind of primal verse, raw and passionate, conjured as if for the first time from the fabric of prose".

Berlin Alexanderplatz - the only Döblin epic known to any sizeable number of Anglophone readers. Ex-con Biberkopf finds it hard to live decently amid economic challenges and dangerous acquaintances in the unforgiving world of Weimar Berlin. The sights and sounds of the city and unfolding events are presented with relentless vigour and linguistic skill.

The Babylonian Exile – Amid the hysterical angst and turmoil of the dying Weimar Republic, Döblin envisioned a Babylonian god, cursed by Jeremiah, who descends to Earth to atone for his sins. (The first chapters accompanied Döblin across the Swiss border in February 1933; he completed the text in Zurich's Central Library.) But Conrad will not atone. Shocked to find Ancient Babylon a forsaken ruin, he takes a Grand Tour through 1920s Europe, and life as a human. The many comical scenes are interspersed with historical vignettes of war and massacre; the loose structure and many digressions invite comparison with *Tristram Shandy*.

The Land without Death – In the Bibliothèque Nationale in Paris, Döblin constructed a convincing tapestry of yet another alien time and place. The first volume lands the reader straight in the world of The Other (Amazonian Indians and Inca refugees); follows three bands of European marauders up into the Andean highlands; and shows the priest Las Casas hopelessly trying to persuade an Indian tribe that Christianity means more than enslavement and plunder. Volume 2 covers two centuries of Jesuit activity culminating in sanctuaries where Guarani Indians develop their own blend of native and European religion. Volume 3 is set largely in 1930s Europe, where a reckoning is sought between the promises of the Enlightenment and the reality of human misery in a mechanical age.

November 1918: a German Revolution – a 2200-page, five year effort to understand the calamity of the First World War and its aftermath, focusing on the two months between the Kaiser's abdication and the murders of Karl Liebknecht and Rosa Luxemburg. Volume 1 (*Citizens & Soldiers*) is a deftly fictionalised narrative based on Döblin's own experience of the war's end in and around Strasbourg. Seemingly disparate characters and scenes gradually reveal a fascinating picture of players negotiating a game without rules. The French Occupation Authority in 1946 vetoed republication of vol. 1 fearing it would stir up Franco-German resentments; it was left out of the 1980s English translation.

THE THEMES:

1. Overtures – These four opening passages, written between 1918 and 1933, show great mastery of language and musical architecture. Each sets the reader down *in media res*, without the authorial scene-setting usual in conventional fiction. Try reading "A Feast" or the opening of *Manas* out loud a few times, to savour the vigour, the rhythms, the brutally accurate adjectives and verbs, the musical structure. (The Conrad excerpt, bursting with comedy, is closer to standard narrative style.)

The 30 opening lines of *Manas* present the epic theme with admirable concision and clarity. The first 15 lines are set in our physical world: weather, mountains, vegetation, cliffs, rivers, plains. But in the second half, this natural environment turns out to be an alien, sentient reality: Shiva's realm, where benign shrubbery becomes grasping thorns, dying souls bob like boats in the wind of Shiva's breath, the iceheads are Shiva's crystal palace. The language is, without doubt, poetry; such dense meaning would be hard to package so neatly as prose. As the story proceeds, every transition between the mundane world and Shiva's realm is signalled by echoes from these opening lines.

The first pages of *Berlin Alexanderplatz* largely present Franz's stream of consciousness, with occasional interjections by an observing Narrator. Surreal imagery ("lifeless" crowds surging; roofs about to topple) renders the city doubly present.

2. Spirits – Here we see Döblin's urge to dig beneath surface reality, to the unconscious and demonic layers beneath. It may resonate with readers of Nietzsche ("Do not gaze too long into the abyss, lest the abyss gaze back at you") and Carl Jung (the Collective Unconscious, and the Shadow). You will spot relevant passages under some other Themes.

3. Nature – By the early 1920s Döblin was increasingly occupied with Nature, and the inadequacy of scientific explanations of the world and the place of human beings in it. This interest, as well as his training as a neurologist and psychiatrist, informs the excerpts here and in some other Themes. Be alert for allegories: e.g. invisible microbes lurking to undermine apparently healthy organisms.

The other headings are fairly self-explanatory, though in a few cases you may wonder: how does this excerpt fit here? Some excerpts highlight the Promethean hubris of people striving to surmount the limits of their humanity, just like our lovely 21st century trans- and post-humanists. (The ghastly conclusion of such efforts was graphically portrayed in a notable but neglected 1935 novel by Döblin's contemporary Paul Gurk: *ToZoB-37: The Myth of Grey Humanity, or of the Number 1* which unaccountably slipped past Nazi censors. You can find it in English on my website. So far even publishers of historical Science Fiction have shown no interest!)

The excerpts have been chosen (from many possible candidates) for their power to entertain, provoke, amuse, cause shudders, and showcase Döblin's mastery of styles, moods, and expressive possibilities. After reading through the selection, or even just dipping in, you should be well prepared to tackle a whole epic novel.

Please find time to listen to the podcast "The Epic Worlds

of Alfred Döblin", and spread word of this great writer, who is still to be properly discovered by the wider public!

Chris Godwin
Stroud, U.K.
Summer 2024

THEME 1. OVERTURES

A Feast (from *Wallenstein*)
No more rain (from *Manas*)
Tram 41 into town (from *Berlin Alexanderplatz*,
Tr. Eugene Jolas, amended by C. D. Godwin)
Conrad awakes (from *Babylonian Exile*)

★★★

A Feast

WHEN THE BOHEMIANS were defeated no one was better pleased than the Emperor. Never had his teeth worked away so nimbly at a pheasant, never had his little eyes in their wrinkled setting flashed so wolfishly from sideboard to plate, plate to sideboard. Had it been feasible between the ponderous droopheaded ox on his left – grey Prince of Carafa, Girolamo – and the haughty guzzling slurping representative of his Holiness in torrid Rome – shimmering red his buttoned-up silk soutane, purple socks and shoes on the legs beneath the table alongside the German Emperor's fidgety snow-white feet – then Ferdinand would have greeted every one of the serving-lads order-takers carving-men hastening through the curtains, the august looming black-staffed Privy Purse, with a "Halloo" and a wave: "This way! Closer! No dawdling, my good fellows, haha. Here he is." Chew, nibble, bite, tear, grind, crunch. The High Steward of the Kitchen moved over the yellow silk carpet, glanced with a sly smile through the poles of the baldachin at Ferdinand's muscular lips: pirates boarding oncoming men o' war, cheeks bulging left and right, seizing booty, emptying like sluices, abetted by the squeezing tongue.

A harp strummed softly, the German flute droned. Leap this way, that way, look lively, bring more jugs; the guzzler is no friend of pauses; must wash down what he's swallowed. Ferdinand's lips wanted wet, his throat wet, they'd earned it, threshed their corn.

In the Empire – what need to say it – in the Empire there was satisfaction. The Bohemians defeated, the saints Ludmilla and Wenzel had withdrawn their hands from their deranged worshippers: now they sat in the dust, haha, along with Hus, all their fraternities, their forest witch Libuše, the Elector Palatine Frederick. The Palatine – what need to say it – the Palatine now hauled his princely garb in a sack on a rope behind him, at his heels through winter mud, crying through the streets, unskilled balladeer in marketplaces, villages: "Will no one here provide a bite to eat? Ten children and no end in sight, will no one fill our stomachs? Wife the daughter of the English king, I once was king in Bohemia; that 'once' rings not well in poor Jack's ears." Who could say a word at such a time.

Let him toddle on, sweet bold forked creature, they'll delouse him till his pelt is scoured hairless. Ah, but Malvasier. But Alicante. Ah, Bohemian wine from Podskali. And green Bisamberger, Traminer from Tyrol; and Bacharach and Braubach, moist tinkling pointy-shoed from the banks of Rhine. Apples on the pressed boar's head: but Molsheimer and Andlauer to chase it down; Alsace, wonderful Alsace.

Who is bewitched by ginger, ginger in the haunch of venison, so that he cannot resist? Hens have been slaughtered, borne in on silver platters, lit by slim white candles. The adoring gaze of twenty tyrants and princes directed their way: rumps and little legs and necks wobble in almond milk, raisins for nibbling scattered around, stuffed into the candied beaks. Mouths pouting, lips salved with spittle, it flowed in streams, bucketed from every spring.

Here comes young wine from the Palatinate. Fire-spewing musket, splendid allegory for a wine-decanter: easy to find the hellhound who thinks to die here. Even the Elected Roman

Emperor, say: a shot must come now, this minute, from the great musket resting on the shoulder of the head cup-bearer; the Emperor readies aims fires, straight into the gorge of the capering Fool, prancing laughing goblin in drab cap and bells, while His Majesty gives his white cuffs a shake, sinks back in his chair, calls for a napkin almost swooning in his fervour: "More!"

Trumpets, a half dozen, blared down from the choir, the balcony's golden cage; the war-drum beat *boom*. The Emperor sat amid the music behind a wild boar roast in pepper, white hat with heron's feather on his balding head, ears not hindered by his crunching teeth from following the tune. Sansoni, cornettist, performed his high-pitched duty; unseen falsettos castrati piped and trilled and warbled, played around the steady calm of the bass and the low voice answering, imploring.

To the left of the melancholy Spaniard Carafa is a narrow cheekless goat's face, crab-red satin scarf above a bulky leather cape-collar, spidery reaching from tight green sleeves towards the millefiori glass: Karl of Liechtenstein, castellan-in-chief, governor in Prague, was speaking of Heidelberg and the fugitive Winter King, how the weather was still frosty, changeable, and all the roads a heavy going, especially for one in a hurry. An abbot chewed a leg off his capon, and as he crunched totted up the abandoned Palatine silver plate delivered to him in Bohemia by pious Walloons. And even old Harrach nibbling at his fieldfare, rocking benignly in his chair, gracious, bald-headed, held forth on trials and confiscations in the defeated land, they were good as dead now, Peter von Schwanberg, Ulrich Vchynský, Albrecht von Smiřický, fled away, would not dream of coming back.

Lusty trumpet blasts. All the nobles glanced up for a moment, those in Spanish ruffs, those in embroidered pointed collars from the Netherlands on bright fur-trimmed jackets, those in tight-laced doublets of Hungary-green, in frilly

French waistcoats and purple capes, cardinals, abbots, generals and princes, and a shiver went through them as if what they heard was a clarion call to battle. At once the music and the mood relented. Every heated nerve experienced a delicious thrill as the ghostly armies of defeated gorgeous blond-curled Frederick marched through the hall, rode through the clink and roar of voices cups plates, down from the tapestries hanging from the choir on towards the two blazing chandeliers, thundered against curtains that flapped with the comings and goings of marshals and guards: splendidly dismembered Palatine corpses, headless torsos, sightless eyes, wagons, wagons laden with corpses, pulled by donkeys, enveloped in a fog of powder and stink, jammed into caskets like limbs from trees, teetering tottering hup! hup! through the air.

Oh how good they taste, the baked mussels tartlets and conserves of His Imperial Majesty. Shame and scandal if an earl prince archduke becomes Roman Emperor and his stomach fails to match his rise; throat can't swallow more than it can hold; that goes for all of them: sly abbot of Krems-minster and Emperor alike, Prince Eggenberg, Liechtenstein and Emperor alike, High Steward of the Plate oratory server seneschal carver custodian of carpets doorkeeper of the kitchen and Emperor alike, Marquis Hyacinto di Malaspina, Ugolino di Maneggio, Thomas Bucella, Christoph Teuffel, organist Platzer and His supreme anointed Imperial Majesty of the Holy Roman Empire – all alike, all crunching in unison on their waffle.

Oh how the Tokay in its Venetian glass delighted the Emperor under his white plumed hat. How he smacked his thigh, buried himself deeper in his chair; his face, betrayed by laughter, hidden in his lap.

★★★

Manas

THERE WAS NO MORE RAIN.
Storms shredded the black clouds hither and down
From the eastern iceheads of Himalaya,
Blew them onto mountains and cedar forests,
Onto blooming meadows, southerly slopes,
This bedlam of beasts and trees –
Euphorbia acacia stands of bamboo; –
Tossed them, torrents and ice-needles,
Over sheer rockwalls, seething hills and spates,
Over rivers, --
They raced thundering down deep valleys,
Kosi, Alaknanda, Yamuna,
Surged onto the radiant plains of India! --
Storms shredded the black clouds away,
Howled.

And ravines meadows rockwalls awoke to the drumming of waters,
Began howling like seas.
And ships rode on the seas.
What sort of ships were they that rode the sea,
Boats bobbing, darting under sail, capsizing, coming aright?
In the pattering of the waters
Souls, pale misty souls,
Came gliding by nooses of vine, stretched themselves past grasping thorns:
Shimmers of silence in the turbulent tumultuous hubbub!
They clumped in white masses,
Waited motionless under the downpour,
Wind whirled them high, breath from the mouth of Shiva,

Three-eyed God on crystal Kailash,
Whirled them high, spun them like a wheel,

Spilled them, mist onto water.

★★★

Tram 41 into town

HE STOOD outside the Tegel Prison gate and was free now. Yesterday he'd been hoeing potatoes with the others in the fields behind the blocks, wearing convict stripes, now here he was in a tan summer coat, and they were still hoeing back there and he was free. He let tram after tram go by, pressed his back against the red wall, and didn't budge. The gate guard walked past several times, pointed him to the right tram; he didn't budge. The terrible moment had come (terrible, Franze, why terrible?), the four years were over. The black iron gates he'd been regarding with growing disgust for a year now (disgust, why disgust?) had closed behind him. He'd been released. Inside, the others sat at their carpentering, varnishing, sorting, gluing, had two years, five years more to do. He was at the tram stop.

The punishment has begun.

He shook himself and gulped. He stepped on his own foot. Then with a run he took a seat on the tram. In among people. Off we go. At first it was like being at the dentist's, when he's grabbed a root with the forceps and pulls; the pain grows, your head's about to burst. He turned his head back towards the red wall, but the tram had dashed ahead with him along its track, so now only his head was oriented to the prison. The tram took a bend; trees and houses blocked the view. Busy streets flashed by, Seestrasse, people got on and off. Something inside him screamed in terror: Look out, look out, now it's starting. The tip of his nose was cold as ice; something tickled his cheek. *Zwölf Uhr Mittagszeitung, B.Z., Berliner Illustrierte, Die Funkstunde.* "Any more fares?" The cops wear blue uniforms now. He got off undetected, and was back among people again. So what? Nothing. Hoy, you skinny swine, watch where you're going or I'll give you a knuckle sandwich! Crowds, what a swarm! Hustle and bustle! My brain needs oiling, it must've dried up. What was all this? Shoe shops, hat shops, electric lamps, schnaps bars. Course they need shoes to run around so much, we used to have a cobbler's shop, don't forget! Hundreds of shiny windowpanes, let em dazzle, they won't frighten you, why, you can smash em, can't you, what's wrong with em, they're wiped clean, that's all. The roadway on Rosenthaler Platz was being torn up, he walked on duckboards with all the rest. Just mix in with people, let it all wash past you, then you won't notice anything, dummy. Wax mannequins in the show windows, in suits, overcoats, with skirts, with shoes and stockings. Outside it was all in motion, but – there was nothing behind it! It – wasn't – alive! It had happy faces, it laughed, waited in twos and threes on the traffic island opposite Aschinger's, smoked cigarettes, turned the pages of newspapers. It stood there just like the street lamps – and became ever more rigid. They belonged with the buildings, all white, all wooden.

Terror rose in him as he walked down Rosenthaler Strasse and saw a man and a woman in a little bar right by the window: they poured big mugs of beer down their gullets, what else were they doing, they'd had a drink, they had forks and stabbed lumps of meat into their mouths, then they pulled the forks out and didn't bleed. Oh, how his body cramped, I can't come free of it, where can I go? The answer came: punishment.

He can't turn back, he's come this far on the tram, he's been released from prison and must go into this thing, deeper and deeper into it.

I know, he groaned to himself, I have to go into this thing and I've been released from prison. They had to release me, the punishment was over, that's as it should be, the bureaucrat does his duty. So I shall go into it, but I don't want to, oh God, I can't.

He wandered down Rosenthaler Strasse past Wertheim's department store, turned right into narrow Sophienstrasse. He thought, this street is darker, it's probably better where it's darker. Prisoners are housed in isolation, solitary confinement, and general confinement. In isolation the prisoner is segregated from others night and day. In solitary confinement the prisoner is housed in an individual cell, but during open air exercise, instruction or religious service he is brought together with others. Traffic roared and jangled, lines of buildings rolled away into the distance, never ending. And roofs were on the buildings, they hovered over the buildings, his eyes drifted up to them: if only the roofs don't come sliding down, but the buildings stood erect. I'm such a sad sack, where can I go? He shuffled along a wall, there was no end to it. I'm a great big booby, a fellow should be able to weave his way through this, five minutes, ten minutes, then drink a cognac and sit down. At the appropriate bell, work must begin immediately. It may be interrupted only at times allotted for eating, exercise, and instruction. During exercise the prisoners must hold their arms straight and swing them back and forth.

***

Conrad wakes up and wonders: where's breakfast

CONRAD was a Babylonian-Chaldean-Assyrian god and was sitting, knees drawn up, on his great royal seat of stone. The hairy old bandit was propped on thick cushions, rubbing his nose and chin. He sat scrunched in a corner of the throne like a little old monkey, and struggled with the dreadful torpor that would not let him go. His head drooped, and he snored.

On his head was a bonnet with two horns. It rolled into his lap. So he thought someone was kissing his hand. He made a gesture of blessing, knocked the bonnet off his lap onto his bare feet. He twitched, opened his eyes wide, yawned: "What's the time?" The bonnet, of course, made no reply. Conrad sat up and commanded: "My bonnet's fallen off."

The bonnet made no move. Nothing else moved either. Puzzling silence.

Now the old hero was wide awake, sucked his teeth, clutched at his beard, shouted full of wrath: "Hey, hollo, no one there, who'll retrieve my bonnet? My bonnet's on the floor. I want breakfast."

Whereat nothing moved.

He turned his head, looked down at himself. His fingernails had grown horribly long, curved like sabre-sheaths. He must have been asleep a considerable time. His red, gold-braided overgown with the embroidered animal figures was crumpled, torn, faded. It sagged on him, he was tucked inside as in a shell. He unfolded his skinny legs. A poplar-wood staff, one of his insignia of power, was leaning in the prescribed location against his seat. He reached for it, banged on the stone floor, cawed murderously: "My bonnet's fallen off. I want breakfast!" Yes, Conrad the Pasha, the superannuated Lion, wanted his routine.

And then one after another they rose up from the flagstones. Their condition was even more ruinous and shrivelled than his. They lay scattered like dry twigs, like petrified snakes higgledy-piggledy across the floor, and now they rose to their feet. The scene was so absurd that Conrad up there on his seat of stone kept his mouth open and forgot to curse. He rammed the bonnet back in place, closed his eyes, opened them, appalled. They were ancient, ancient men, about sixty all told, a whole mouldy forest of white hair flowed from heads and beards, long arms fumbled in wide overgowns. Conrad was speechless with bewilderment.

The ragged mob below began to cough, gather its gowns, throw beards over shoulders, bow down to him, uncoordinated, crooked as rain-battered corn. They tried to bend but couldn't, they were doing physical jerks. The old robber up above raged. The choir stood there mute.

At this point Conrad grew thoughtful, sniffed about him, took in all the ruination and growled: "What's been going on here? Doesn't it seem we've all been asleep?" They were well placed to affirm this. "A fine state of affairs!" roared Conrad. "So why were you all asleep? Hey, what? Who's been on duty here? How were tasks apportioned? Who fetched up the sun, led it down? Where is it anyway? And when will I have my breakfast?"

They bowed in silence, joints cracked, it came easier now. Conrad glared angrily at the rabble. There was nothing to be got from this lot, you had to be patient. After a while he cawed at them again, already they looked a bit smarter: "Who's the doorkeeper? Who had the task of feeding the sun-horses, who?" And when they all stared at one another, the full horror fell on him: "The horses, the horses have starved to death." And this business and the whole situation was so monstrous he burst into peals of laughter. He laughed and cried in his chair. He wept shiny tears. The wretches have let the horses starve, doesn't bear thinking about, what else has happened.

He wiped away the tears. "But," he said quietly to himself, approaching the central question, "but am I not Conrad, and did I not create the world?" (We use the modern name Conrad, because we won't allow him to hide behind the old bombastic names.)

Two of the longbeards regarded him humbly. It seemed they understood him. "But did I not, I myself, create the world?" They nodded. He sighed, sniffed about again. "Show it me!" Whereupon two men between the pillars lifted a pair of curtains. Mortar trickled. Tiles came loose, fell crashing into the hall. Conrad roared: "Enough!" They said: "That's the world." Conrad sniffed: "No it's not."

He could smell the roast already, but he wanted to pin the blame on them, it was his way. When the trembling dolts began to lift more curtains, he clapped his hands.

He sat in his chair. Yes, this was his throne, even if one arm had broken off. When he shouted, he was concerned to note, no thunder came. Where were his lightning bolts? There, two on the floor. He stretched out a hand, stealthily let them drop. All they did was clatter: scrap iron. He sat up.

★★★

THEME 2. SPIRITS

Madam Pei (from *Wang Lun*)
A Circus (from *Wallenstein*)
Demons (from *Manas*)
The Spider's Web (from *The Land without Death*)
Tauler (from *Citizens & Soldiers*)

***

Madam Pei

AND SO Madam Pei, ensnared in this manner, was only a little startled when the monstrous man bent towards her, weapons clanking, to whisper in her ear, having pushed aside the string of pearls that dangled from her headdress: it was the Emperor she was to bewitch.

The trust accorded her in this circle had excited her before now. Now a passion coursed through her head, her eyes were dazzled. She made up her mind to succeed, to hold power.

A lapidary was brought in into the plot, a friend of the eunuch who often worked in the palaces of the Vermilion City. He was given four thousand taels by Prince Mien and a golden amulet representing the God of Longevity. Madam Pei commissioned him to carve a jade statue of the Emperor as big as an arm; he was to depict the Emperor lying down, wearing only a linen nightshirt. The further decking out of the doll she would take care of herself.

It was more than five weeks later when the lapidary, working of necessity in secret, finished his task and one evening lifted a finely carved and stained booktrunk from his cart and carried it on his shoulder into the house occupied by Madam Pei.

The doll of green nephrite was alarmingly like the Son of Heaven. The sleeping head lay on its right side; the mouth breathed slightly open; a flimsy garment flowed down to the bare feet and in restless sleep had slipped from the right shoulder, revealed a strong left ankle; the hands fell thickveined and heavy at either side. The glassy green stone was the image of a near-corpse, and at the same time had an unearthly animation that welled from deep within the stone, almost speaking, fending off death.

The conspirators stood around the statue. Mien, sure of triumph, embraced the simple young lapidary, who looked proudly over his botched effort and wondered if a fold shouldn't have been placed a little differently.

Mrs Ying cried out, slunk into a corner where they could hear her sniffling; even Madam Pei, who at first had stared at the doll in feigned calm, felt unwell. She sobbed, ran in fear from the room and had to be fetched back by Mrs Ying at the prince's bidding.

The next stage of the work fell to Madam Pei. Once she had got rid of her guests it took several days before she was able to approach the doll with equanimity. Then the prince gave her the chance to observe Ch'ien-lung as he strolled among the magnolias and lily ponds of the Forbidden City. And little by little, with incantatory gestures, she absorbed from the man, as he pottered about, some part of his soul; today the spirit of the five viscera: liver, spleen, lungs, heart, kidneys; then the spirit of his eyes, brain. Every time she carried a little object in her closed left hand, the organ whose spirit she was bewitching: liver of blue wood, lungs of white metal, heart of flame-red silk. At home she squeezed the oval of material over the dreaming doll's body, breast, forehead; incense smouldered, the windows were curtained. Like a sponge the doll absorbed the spirits, the stone began to darken, the figure lost its translucency, brown nodules formed within it, from which fine lines and fissures extended like veins into the limbs and sprouted over the skin.

After Madam Pei, with one last painful burst of

concentration, had brought home the Emperor's life spirit, she locked up for five times five days the trunk in which the statue lay. Towards the end of this period perceptible groans and knocks emanated from within. Dark Prince Mien, the lapidary, and pretty Mrs Ying leaned over the box as Madam Pei, knees now under control, dressed in a wu-costume of red flames, tensed her arms and heaved open the lid. Warm vapour with a foul musty smell drifted from the trunk. Over her face Madam Pei wore a snaketongued gilded god-mask; her lively rouged hands grasped the doll, which abruptly, like a wild cat, she pressed to her bosom.

They all saw, as they stood in a circle about the sorceress, that the head of the statue was turned slightly to the front,; the right eyelid was drawn down in a wink, the folds of the gown lay smooth; the doll had stretched. Carefully the woman laid the figure onto the black felt of the table by the oil lamp, one finger always on it. Trembling, hiccuping nervously, Mrs Ying, frequently whimpering unawares, brought a delicate white mourning costume in which the sorceress quickly dressed the object.

It was nighttime; thick mist flowed over the silent palaces of the Forbidden City. In front of the Hall of Felicity, where the Emperor slept, the four conspirators felt their way to the ancient thuya tree under which Ch'ien-lung liked to sit. Quickly the prince and the lapidary dug a shallow hole, placed the doll into it, clamped between two boards. The sorceress muttered a few words; a scratching came from the hole; earth was thrown over it.

They separated. it was done. The doll would overpower the last remnants of Ch'ien-lung's soul in a choking struggle. The Emperor must die; the doll was bound tight, was unable to rise.

These events took place in the year of the Broken Melon. The Emperor seldom resided in the Forbidden City; the affair made little progress. Madam Pei returned to her apartments in the town. Prince Mien was a not infrequent visitor; before long he became loud and threatening towards her, convinced that for fear of the Emperor she had not given her powers full rein. Once he struck the indignant woman so hard on the head that a doctor had to attend to the swelling.

She complained of her ill treatment to Mrs Ying and the lapidary, both of whom came and went often. Ying was visibly pleased at her misfortune, for she had grown jealous of Madam Pei.

The lapidary, a sly avaricious man, extorted large sums from the prince in this affair. When realization dawned how difficult it was, he began to doubt the success of the enterprise, looked on Pei as a moneygrubber like himself, and attempted to secure his own safety in good time. Madam Pei doubled up in fury at his suggestion that both of them ought to touch the prince for all he was worth, then he'd marry her and take her to his home town in Shansi. Rejected and offended, he plotted revenge.

While he was working on a stone garland on the façade of a pavilion by the southern lotus lake, he claimed one day to have mislaid a piece of jade of appreciable size. He made a report to the Supervisor of Building Works, who instituted an energetic search. The lapidary explained that the jade could have disappeared months ago. He was flogged for his carelessness, and seeing how stupidly he'd managed the affair to be punished right at the beginning, he shouted a confession of the entire plot.

The jade doll was unearthed by horrified Court officials, who sought to hush the matter up.

The soil beneath the thuya was found to be loose. Penetrating a little deeper they came upon a curious hollow like an air bubble, at the bottom of which the doll lay. The boards had burst apart tin the middle and bulged upwards; the doll, its hands thrown up to its face, sat bending forwards. It was covered in white maggots as if it was a corpse.

A hunt ensued for Mesdames Pei and Ying. Both had fled. Prince Mien was found in his palace. He too tried to escape. Foiled by the palace guard, he inhaled gold leaf, and suffocated.

★★★

A Circus

The Bohemians, traumatized by the Habsburg clampdown following their defeat at White Mountain, experience demonic incursions. Here, a circus troupe at the seat of newly ennobled Wallenstein performs a grotesque parody of the incomprehensible events unfolding in the Empire.

TO THE village of Bubna near Prague, where the Duke had a dairy farm, came a troupe of players conjurers quacksalvers. They first cried their skills fit to be heard all the way to Prague, then built a fence of boards, a deep stage. Invited by the Duke to his little summer lodge, some of them one afternoon performed, under the strictest secrecy, a special entertainment.

A large hall was placed at their disposal. Elegant ladies and gentlemen occupied the balconies and galleries, servants clustered at the open doors. Spiral stairs wound down into the hall. At the start of the performance a masked player shouted from the door – he wore Greek-style buskins strapped around the calf, a loose white Greek toga, his right hand grasped a hammer from which a lightning-bolt projected; had the imperious dour expression of a Zeus: Somehow the troupe neglected to include me in the play. You may come down into the hall, if you please; there'll be such jolly fun.

It was dreadfully hot in the hall. If you looked down, the air roiled and curled over the polished floorboards as if from an oven or a blaze. But those who went down noticed no heat, felt no constriction in the chest. Standing tall and oversized, two tawny chimpanzees strayed over the boards, dropped now and then onto their hands and ran about. They clambered up pillars, gazed and spat across at the galleries, came back down, flaunted high rumps as they scampered on all fours. No one knew where they had sprung from.

More and more figures appeared down below, from where was a mystery. A young lady pulled free of her chaperone, she wanted to see the funny monkeys close to. As her foot touched the lowest step and the heated air of the hall assailed her, she rushed forward: a naked figure was running about, jumping up and down in high spirits, ran rings around her, yelped. Slowly and without embarrassment she betook her plump pink limbs, buxom body up to one of the brown-furred chimpanzees; it slid across the floorboards as if on ice. A black tail long as an arm, whip-thick, had grown from her spine; she flicked the creature on the nose with it; she still wore her silver shoes and bright dangling garters, her excessively large breasts shook, blond curls swayed like a cowl over the amused snub-nosed face. The two apes romped behind her, then flung their arms around each other and started to dog her steps.

Close by the stairs a serious little man lay still on the floor, having turned unhappily this way and that, began crawling on hands and knees. People stepped on him, scolded him; he begged their pardon, kept crawling between their legs, under their feet. Now and then he raised himself, caught his breath, looked grave and sad directly into faces, went again about his work. None were puzzled by any others. All were intent solely on themselves.

An elderly lady joined in. She wore an expensive sable stole, kept it on even in the heat; she observed everything eagerly, but from time to time her uneasy hands fiddled under the chin with the clasp of the stole. Suddenly she emitted a horrible scream, tore the stole from her as if suffocating.

And now she stood on the spot bare-throated, feet apart; bent back her head, took a deep breath, and from the florid face overtopped by a tall grey wobbling wig came a donkey-like trumpet blast, lips turned blue, the waving arms trembled and dropped the fan. She quickly walked on, retrieved the fan with a swish of silken skirts, breathed heavily, seemed somewhat relieved. Only to emit as if inspired, after a few turns that grew slower, more hesitant and with much stroking of the fur, the same harsh bray. It at once drew loud laughs from all around, including the spectators; she responded by turning pale and indignant.

An officer who braved the descent to the hall met with a serious mishap. He had intended, with his sword and muscular prowess, to put on a special show for the gallery. He crept unnoticed down the staircase, slipped on the last few steps and bounced across the floor. And now he could not stop moving. He looked like a little carved wooden manikin, legs tight together, hands clasped, thick neck, thick head; now he stood on his hands, now jumped upright; fell on his back, now whipped over on his belly, back on his feet in a flash, stood still, took a step. But the leading foot pushed him up, he had a struggle to bring the other foot along, and in this way he hurried about the hall, rising a yard high at each step, always striving to cast a friendly smile at those below and up in the galleries, show them his sword, his mighty arm muscles. At once the hall turned to him, threw him to his knees, hurried him along.

Many more came; it was evident to all that the situation harboured the seeds of uproar and discord, that they faced an evil entity. This became clear when a priest dared enter the fray with a determined expression, prayer-book under his arm. On the stair he pressed the book to his chest with his left hand, with the right he held aloft a silver crucifix. He meant to exorcise the hall. In fact, as soon as he stepped down a furious tumult erupted, screams everywhere, figures tumbling madly about. At the same time the hot vapour swirled around him in curious swaying spirals, thickened like smoke; as he brandished the crucifix, flames flickered at the tips; with challenging composure he opened the prayer book, the pages crumpled, turned yellow, deep brown along the edges. And suddenly the book was ablaze; the shocked man dropped it, the book lay smouldering on the floor. When he dropped the melting blue-flaming crucifix and blew on his burned hand, he gave a sigh from his inmost being; the black-haired long-gowned man closed his eyes, lifted his arms in a yearning gesture; the cassock with its wide sleeves was already fading in waves of acrid air. He could dance a jig like nobody in the hall, a slender youthful body on long legs in linen hose. He gazed out from artless big blue eyes, sang what sounded like hymns. His voice, a bright trill, sounded triumphant above all the noise; belted out so prettily and joyfully that up in the galleries they looked shyly at one another from little eyes, spoke of trivialities and had to suppress tremors within. He had a slightly foolish young man's face, with a stub nose. Soon one of the chimpanzees came and dragged him by the ears; the people watched anxiously, the song was interrupted by little frightened squeals.

It made a seductive impact on the servants thronging the doorways. Doorkeepers barred the way with staffs, but it was too enticing. As the vapour swirled thicker in the hall, little groups of people ran in, a moment ago they could only stretch out their hands, now they were in a Tower of Babel, limbs asprawl, tongues hanging, making odd faces, strangers to one another, filled with unfamiliar restlessness and content. They bumped each other as if dreaming, rebounded away, collided again, could never have enough of it. They leapt, under some impetus shoved each other into the hall, and were then suddenly deflated, strangely lost and confused. A few noblemen went gravely among the throng, raised their arms, cried with a flourish of the hat: "Here is the renowned So-and-so, praise him, honour him;" went on with a solemn grimace. If someone asked: "What can you do, sir?" he answered: "Anything you like; nothing is obscure to us. Praise us, honour us!" They spread out their arms, nodded respect.

Horses pranced among the people, each with a man on its back. Dogs leapt wolfishly; no dog had entered the hall. A number of gentlemen stared around after making loud noises, then befouled the floor, there was a stink, they pointed, seemed delighted, neighed laughter. One man, tears dripping from his eyes, presented a dreadful sight: his jaw hung down to his knees; the gaping lips of the mouth full of arm-long teeth smacked monstrously; the skull and upper part of the face rose glum behind; unseeing goggle eyes and shrivelled little belly trip-trapped on little legs like stalks. He clung lamentably to a pillar; stepped on from time to time, slurped snorted snarled horribly. Snuffling he would approach someone, grab the frozen shrieking fellow tight by the hands, the jaws loomed like pincers; he wrestled the twisting flailing man into his maw, sucking, turning blue. Under the horrified gaze of the onlookers he swallowed the creature into his swelling body. They beat at him, spat at him, he howled, sobbed; tears and drool trickled disgustingly. A few short minutes later, the bustle around the unspeaking fellow resumed as before. Only bluish transparent shadows of people stood close to him; these were ones he had swallowed earlier: from time to time they tried to force a way into his mouth to fetch their bodies, but he closed the jaws with some difficulty, teeth snapped angrily at them.

Breathless, drenched in sweat, several tried in distraught confusion to reach the stairs, hall doors; now their former figure was restored; they grinned, lisped timidly. They made puzzled queries, a trembling was in them, burst out laughing when people told them what was happening below, pushed their way roughly outside. Some, almost beside themselves, were seized by a melancholy, sat helpless, hid their faces.

Amid the hall's heat, the growing press of people, the tumult grew. People hit out; gradually they noticed one another. Any who did not slink away found this new home congenial. Suddenly the leaping man, the unhappy officer, sprang with this woman, then with that, up into the air; she screamed, he whooped, and although not entirely master of his legs improvised a preposterous clacking dance over the heads of the throng. Once he pulled a half-choked victim from the giant-mouthed man's teeth; roars from the frustrated fellow, wheezes from the rescued victim sailing limp through the room on the leaper's arm. The dogs kept up a running battle with the apes, now here, now there across the floor. An impetuous decision caused the hymn-singing youth, suddenly fallen silent, to assault the young horse-tailed lady; she flung the tail around his throat, he upended her; she shrieked pathetically.

A voice called out as animals milled about the hall in frightful numbers, horses, cows, boars, as various apparitions changed shape in the blink of an eye, tumbled head over heels; called: "The Duke, the Duke," the cries ever more piercing. A pillar of fire went through the hall; hissed like a waterspout, stretched slowly up to the ceiling; as it meandered turned to ashes people and animals who failed to move out of the way. Acrid smoke billowed.

Now those in the galleries and outside broke windows. Shattering screams rose from the hall and down from the galleries. The pillar of fire stood still. As if cut off at the knees, it collapsed suddenly. Smoke swirled across the floor, lay thick on the creatures screaming singing helplessly in the tumult. Draughts of fresh air blew in.

★★★

Demons

SWOOPING down over the mountains, three devils,
Wicked gods subjugated by Shiva.
And when they saw Manas they faltered, clutched at each other:
'Who is it. Who is it. A human.'
They swished aloft. Alarmed, horribly alarmed, coiling flouncing billows.
'A human of flesh and bone. With limbs and clothing.
He has broken through the bounds. Look at him, you.
Who is it. What shall we do?'
And they saw the griffons flying
Back and forth at the edge of the Field of the Dead, Puto's Sukuni.
And in the branches, among the leaves of a plane tree,
Puto himself, stiff as if frozen, the mighty man, who was known to them.
And they saw the chain that ran from rigid Puto's upper arm
From the tree down across the slope,
As tenuous as air, it stretched like rubber and did not break,
Ran to the arm of the human on the slope.
'Ah wretch,' screamed Chanda, 'hey, Puto, call yourself a priest of Shiva?
What are you up to? Think we cannot see you
Sat there in your tree and feigning sleep.
And full of perfidy you sneak a human here, wretch, onto Shiva's Field.'
Through the branches Puto came alert, fixed them with a hard eye.
They slid away to the side.
'Why don't you speak. Why stare at us with your

goggle eyes.
You think you'll scare us with your goggle eyes, Puto, wretch,
Cunning scoundrel, you hypocrite.
Ha, what are you up to in that tree? And your griffons, hey?'
Now his hands touched the ring about his arm,
And even before he moved they quivered, hid behind a stand of bamboo.
'He's renounced Shiva's service. He's fighting Shiva.'
And with a twitch of the foot they pushed off from the ground,
Like panthers leaping, whirred elongated aloft.
Puto's voice a blow behind them:
'Don't run away. Have a care, you dogs, jackals.
No doubt the God bade you guard his land, you, Munda, Chanda, Nishumbha.
The man down there is my child. Have a care. It is as if I go there.
He's Manas, prince's son from Udaipur in the land of Rajputana that is my home.
When the cotton tree flaunted its red flowers,
When he had had enough of victories, he fled his palace.
I shall protect him.
He seeks sorrow. Wants to feel horror, and suffer.
You imprisoned monsters, have a care.'
First they flew around Manas in wide arcs, fearful, curious,
They surrounded him like children a giant elephant newly fettered,
And watched every move he made.
By now the demons were huge, and Manas thought them clouds.

Then they burst out laughing. They pushed off pell-mell, stretched long,
Soared shimmering, bleated yak-yacking.
'A human. Wants to feel horror and suffer, hey.
So he shall, the dwarf, the little toad.'
Darted past crags, through the ravines:
'Spirits, oh lovely spirits. Hey, we have a visitor,
A newcomer, with a body! A human with a body!
Just look at him. Wants to feel horror and suffer.
A human. Just look at him. Has a body. Hey lovely spirits.'
Such a stirring over the ravines, stirring in the ravines.

+++

All three had humanlike form.
Small, humped, head on his chest, the one with long ice-grey hair was Chanda.
Fangs grew from his mouth down to his chin.
Munda was blind. Shiva had cast a glance his way in the heat of battle,
It put out his lights.
A jackal squatted behind him on his hump, and steered him with its paws.
Nishumbha was almost ball-shaped, like a hedgehog, cactus,
Set all over with prickles.
Sometimes he stretched his tiny white head, gave his surly bearded face an airing.
They passed uneasily over Manas this way and that.
'He still has the chain. Puto's holding on to him.
What do you think, what shall we do. Puto is far away.'
'Take him.' – 'That won't work. He has the chain.'
'See how he breathes. Already gone but still breathing.'
'He's dreaming. He must be taken.' – 'But how?'
Nishumbha's head poked out through prickles:

'I have an idea. Come here quietly. Chase away the Shades.
We shall take him. Puto is far away.
He's still breathing, but hears nothing, sees nothing.
He's as good as dead, defenceless.
We'll creep in. We shall creep into him.'
'And Puto?' – 'And go back to Puto. He sent him here.
We'll go to him. We'll outwit Puto.'
The demons soared skywards. 'What shall we do?'
'It's a gift from Puto, to us. We accept it. We'll take that thing and go,
Go into the world. Down to the Earth.'
Whoops and whistles. 'What can Shiva do to stop us.
Puto shall lead us out. This is our lucky day.
We'll go down to the Earth, look around the Ganges, in the temples!
Shiva can't stop us. Puto will protect us.
Careful now. First the Shades! Is all quiet?'
And as Manas lay there wrecked, on his face,
The three demons came down to the ground,
The ghastly spirits Chanda, Munda and Nishumbha,
The hunchback, the blind one, and the one all prickles,
Three ancients.
Munda lifted the head. He climbed in through Manas' eyes
And invaded the brain.
Nishumbha entered over the tongue and into the chest.
With each breath he rose and fell,
He sat in there quite still.
The breathing was lovely, he bobbed like a butterfly.
Chanda snuffled at Manas' body.
He went into the guts, bumped around in there.
The others signalled to him to be quiet, afraid that

Manas would wake up.
But he slept on. His soul held the veil tight over him,
Helpless, trackless.
Like a board held at both ends, his soul creaked,
awaited nothing.

★★★

The Spider's Web

The prosperous high plateau of the Muiscas has been plundered by European invaders. The Zipa makes a ceremonial progress to a sacred site to seek the meaning of this disaster.

THE SACRED way began at Chalcha. The lake of Guatavita is called "Fire of the mountains". It lies on a height, surrounded by thick forests. The summit of the mountain flattens itself to a little plain, and a cone rises from it, its base a circle, the summit encloses the clear lake, which is as round as the mountain that embraces it. The wife of a great king threw herself into this lake, the spirit of the lake took her to wife, in times of need they call to her as well. Extensive temples, dwellings for priests and laity sprawled around the foot of the tree-covered holy mountain. To the east, the sunrise, the plain had been cleared, and a broad avenue lined left and right with stones led to the sacrificial circle.

Sugamuxi, high priest, cacique of Irica province, received the guest in his dwelling.

Sugamuxi, black markings on his face, in a loose black cloak, grey hair over his ears and down to his shoulders, a low golden mitre on his head, as old as the Zipa but lean and sharp, with black expressive eyes, sat across from the Zipa. The bamboo screen at the window was hitched up, a cool mountain breeze wafted in. The Zipa sat with heavy rugs across his knees. No one else was there.

The Zipa glanced at his host. "Sugamuxi, I have no gifts to bring for your temple."

"Thysquesuska, you are welcome here."

Zipa: "Whiteskinned bearded men have fallen upon Cundinamarca. They have fire tubes and strange beasts. Funza, the town, is destroyed. Many people are dead."

Sugamuxi kept silent. Zipa: "You advised me, Sugamuxi, to make peace with the king of Tunja. Peace came. I meant to thank you at the festival of Huan."

Stern Sugamuxi closed his bright eyes for a moment. "It is a good day for the Zipa to journey here, at Huan, the festival of kings. In ancient times Ramiriki rose to Heaven at Huan and entered the Sun."

"The bearded white men are criminals. Their king is a creature of no understanding. He makes a gift of Cundinamarca, which does not belong to him and which he has never seen."

Sugamuxi fixed the Zipa with his big eyes. "We learned of a bearded man from long ago, who taught the people of our country many good things. They called him 'the Man who Disappears'. He wandered through the mountains and his cloak hung from one shoulder, his beard reached to his waist, an animal with two humps went with him. He died in Boza. Do the bearded white men look like the Man who Disappears? What do they teach?"

"They kill and take gold from all the houses. They have beards. There is a black man with them, he carries a black box with a cross and says this is their highest spirit."

"Have you spoken with this man, Thysquesuska?"

The old man shook his head: "I spoke with the leader of the criminals, to find out what they are. They forced their way in to me."

Sugamuxi: "Cundinamarca is well appointed with priests, warriors, craftsmen, peasants. Priests perform their office, craftsmen toil in the settlements, peasants in the fields. What do the warriors do?"

"My general Zaquezazipa advised me not to go into battle. When the fire tube bangs, people fall down with holes in their bodies."

"Does blood flow?"

"Yes."

They were silent. Garish painted vases stood along the walls of the low square room. The Zipa leaned forward: "Sugamuxi, has Bochica abandoned us? Has the pillar of the people left us? The white criminals make slaves of his children. Many die and can't be buried."

"Thysquesuska, I shall enquire."

Two days later, early in the morning, a ceremony of supplication took place.

Once the world was shrouded in darkness. Bochica contained light in himself, he created great birds, black, he tasked them to fly through the universe and carry light everywhere, the birds were filled with light. And every place they pecked at with their beaks became light. People appeared on Earth, from a mother who came out of the sea.

Next day the Zipa allowed himself to be massaged with the juice of a plant called trejelon. They puffed gold dust all over his body. The procession wound from the little plain up the flank of the sacred cone, along a narrow path. At its head were priests in black, they blew on conches and trumpets. The mountains responded with tremendous echoes. Behind them leapt figures in pelts of jaguar, lion, bear, conveying the homage of powerful beasts. Behind these a crowd of people who wept and cried and filled the air with their laments, sought to move Heaven. Behind them others who rejoiced, laughed, danced, wanted to thank Heaven.

And then the Zipa's entourage. With sumptuous fabrics they swept the path clear for the Zipa's chair. It was carried by six noblemen.

They arrived at the summit, before them the dark blue lake Guatavita, above and around it and them the dome of great purple-flaming Heaven, light, emptiness, cool wind.

The lake was ringed by people. Their blowing, wailing, singing, crying, laughing, the echoes from the mountains, rose up to Heaven.

Two naked crones squatted at the entrance. They wore nothing, for Death robs a person of everything. One, eyes downcast, blew gently on a flute. The other held some webbing. A person goes into Death on threads as slender as spider's silk.

A wide raft was moored to the lakeshore. The priests and the Zipa, that ponderous gold-glittering man, together with his entourage climbed onto it. The raft floated to the middle of the lake. Endless wailing, trumpet sounds, rumbling echoes.

In the middle of the lake, nobles poured water over the Zipa, the gold washed off. Priests, prostrate on the ground, eyes closed, packed shoulder to shoulder, sang to Bochica who climbs with his rays into the depths of the lake and rejoices in the gifts. Robes were draped around the Zipa, he dropped his golden discs and vessels into the water.

Sugamuxi, high priest, lay for hours alone in the temple on the black prayer mat. Above him stood the huge Sun-disc, image of Bochica. Sacred pottery vessels, painted, of many different shapes, stood along the walls, in them sacrificial offerings, golden supplicants with rays around the head and a staff in each hand on which a little bird perched, worshippers and supplicants from the animal kingdom, insects, lizards, snakes. This was the priests' chamber.

The high priest's soul left his body. It came out of his mouth and wandered to the middle of the earth.

It came to a river. There were spiders. They span him a web and led him across.

The priest's soul saw some who had just recently arrived, they still looked proud, they wore ragged clothes, and many were naked. The priest questioned them. They said: We died at our own hand, there is no one to care for us and clothe us.

"And why did you lay hands on yourself?" – "White demons came."

The high priest asked, asked ten, asked ten, asked ten. The same reply. He pretended not to understand. He was seized with great fear. I want to go back, I must leave, too many have come. The flood of souls continued unabated. A swarming heaving tumult surrounded him. He asked: "Are many more coming?"

"Many more, so many, look around you, oh look around you."

The throng was endless. And there came a long line, with men in the lead wailing and women behind weeping. It was the litter of Thysquesuska the Zipa.

The soul returned to its body, felt its way over the chest and into the mouth. When Sugamuxi opened his eyes it was night. He was lying on the black prayer-mat, priests crowded around.

In the morning the Zipa spoke to him: "Sugamuxi, did you enquire?"

Sugamuxi: "I passed through the spider's web into the Underworld. Many spoke of the white-skinned men. A litter was borne along, surrounded by wailing men and weeping women. Wailing men and weeping women followed it. The odour of Mocoba was around the litter. He had emeralds in his eyes, emeralds in his ears, nostrils, navel."

The Zipa was frightened: "Where did this dream find you?"

Sugamuxi: "In front of Bochica's image."

After a long silence the Zipa looked across at the implacable priest: "Summon your assistants. Let me prepare."

For five days they prepared the Zipa in the temple. He prayed, fasted, and did not sleep. The people learned that he would go personally to Bochica.

Before sunrise priests led the Zipa along the dark stone-edged path to the sacrificial circle. The dense forest was black, the sky blue-grey, the air was icy.

The priests, faces to the east, knelt. The old Zipa, painted black and red, in the regalia of a king, stood on the stones at the foot of the huge column of Bochica.

As the vault of Heaven began to lighten and the first weak rays of sun struck the column, Sugamuxi plunged the sacrificial spear into the Zipa. The priests laid him on the stones, opened his breast, cut out the bleeding heart. The high priest showed it to the Sun. Flutes and conches sounded, the priests sang.

★★★

Tauler

BECKER slept.

From an expanse of meadow, or was it a water-mirror, a figure emerged and spoke to him: "You're going away."

"We're going home."

"Why are you going home? Day after day your trains grind along."

"We've been defeated. We must evacuate from this country. Come closer, I can't hear you properly."

"Stay! Stay! Why would you leave?"

"With reluctance I leave this land where I lay for so long."

"Oh, stay here, do. I have no business with warriors. We are peaceable. Look around you."

"I saw."

"Look harder. You are devout and good. Stay."

"Who are you? Who's speaking to me?"

"You can see me."

"Your name."

"I am an old man, a blessing to his country. I am called Johannes Tauler."

"Johannes Tauler! You!"

"I once lived here. In times gone by. Oh you dear Christian, listen to me."

"I'm but a poor Christian."

"You *are* one. To the extent that you can lead people to God's truth. You can turn to the miraculous workings of God and reflect on the inexpressible gifts he has revealed to us, that flow out from him."

"You think so …?"

"Yes, good man. Why do I pursue you out of the darkness, like a mother who hears her child call? You have rejoiced and expressed delight at Peace, the sweet face of Peace, which is one of the countless blessings revealed to us, and to all creatures."

Becker murmured in his sleep: "How can I stay."

"Stay, so that you can know more. God stirs you and draws you to him. He wishes to sink his love into you."

"Come closer. Be clearer."

"Lift yourself to me so I can see into your eyes. Ah, such a sad look."

"I've been ill a long while."

"So speak new words to your sickness. Say: God greets you, oh you most bitter of bitternesses, you shall be my dear sister, you are full of grace."

"I shall."

"You have not done so yet. You are hard and proud, a great soul, a high mountain. Do not shut your eyes, my child. You must pray for patience and a merciful outcome. The Lord comes with a silent gentle rustling."

The carriages trundled. Becker lay there.

"You persist in your own comfort zone, my child. That will be no way out. You must turn. Repeat after me: Oh most bitter of bitternesses, you shall be my dear sister."

He murmured, murmured it again. He heard the voice:

"Oh you good Christian. Your wretched forsaken soul, in

what distress is it caught up. It cannot even lament properly. Come. Do not forsake me. Do not forget my country. One day I shall send you a sign, a helpful sign."

Becker's lips parted, he raised himself, questioning.

But he found nothing, and went back to sleep.

★★★

THEME 3. NATURE

Mosquitoes (from *Wallenstein*)
Desert (from *Mountains Oceans Giants*)
The Mountains Boomed (from *Manas*)
Turtles (from *The Land without Death*)
Hops (from *Citizens & Soldiers*)

★★★

Mosquitoes

FAR afield from his fortress – nearer to base he was considerate in his ravening – the army of the Bastard von Mansfeld went foraging. The pestilential stink that streamed to him revealed its location. A fever had broken out in the camp near Beidhaus; spread like wildfire by billet-finders foragers rangers freebooters across woods and hills, rippled through peasants and cavalrymen, armoured cuirassiers, musketeers. Midges and mosquitoes swarmed up from ponds. Just beneath the reed-choked mirror-surface of the water hung millions of larvae, ownerless litter discarded by Nature, calmly sucking air through the little breathing-tube. Heads swelled, lifted above the mirror, carapaces shivered, cracked, stretched, tore sideways from the head down; slowly the long juvenile thrust its way out, antennae limbs wings tight against the torso, rested spreading itself on a leaf of duckweed, hung wing-stretching long-legged on a reedy scabbard. They rose humming into the twilight, veined the air with chirping, their thin high song. Jostling humming flies with ringed darting bodies, long proboscis projecting between whisper-thin antennae stiff as a spear from the little head in front of the clunky thorax. Bore itself a thousandfold, tenthousandfold, millionfold through the evening air on little glassy wings. Lighted on a mouth, a forehead, a hand breaking bread, on a throat, between the trim beard of cornet or captain and his Venetian collar.

If a man jumping from his horse in a sweat tore off his jacket to allow cool air on his damp chest, the little flying creature clung unseen to hot skin, sucked its little drop of blood, injected its little drop of poison. Now the soldier can go hunting, hang people from door-beams and wells, drive away livestock, lead a high old life – and all the while fever courses through his body, night after night, turns his blood to tropical swamp. Let the cornet roar, gulp this year's sour wine from a jug, sail menacing on his steed at the head of a hundred men through silent chimney-smoking villages, papers tucked around the throat for protection, plump-cheeked and hot on an overfed mount: in his knees is a vibration, the collar must be loosened, no strength in the calves, rainbows shimmer before the eyes; the freezing and teeth-chattering begin, at night the man lies in hay, in a bed, swears hoarsely as if it's nothing, and day by day grows weaker, more spectral from one excursion to the next. Not many died of the fever. Those attacked became weak, raved worse than before. Those who died rotted where they fell. Men moved among each other jaundiced, smiled feebly in the heat.

Until the stink spread: first in the camp near Beidhaus, then in Weiden, in Kohlberg Market, people appeared with a new kind of ailment. Distraught plague-barbers told of peasants who had a new sickness in their beds. Lice assailed the army. They multiplied on the mercenaries in their pillaged jackets linens palliasses pelts saddlecloths, dropped them dead in muddy woods and lanes, made welts in the skin, dry or weeping; in many the beastly venom sank deep into the veins. They babbled feverish nonsense, some raved, lumps as big as peas erupted on the bitten skin, blood-flecks spurted horribly; sleepy and numb they dropped where they had fled, shunned, quarantined, starved. Learned pupils of Paracelsus spoke of the mercurial-sulphurous signal of the disease, or of mercurial-saline, of the fever-hunger, disorders of the urine, watery oedemas in the legs, spitting of blood, turgescence of the chest, melancholy.

★★★

Desert

THE DESERT, mighty being, extended over fifteen degrees of latitude hidden behind mountain chains from Morocco to Tunis, from Mauretania and the trade routes of brown Tuareg to the ancient Berber grazing grounds of Aulad, Soliman. It stretched grey and white, rose from coastal terraces as plains high plateaus dunes beneath a sun that lay on it almost touching. It elided from gravel plain to stony desert. Winds tore at naked glowing hills, abraded crags with flying sand, crags splintered worn down by the heat. Whirlwinds worked like whetstones. Slowly the age-old mountains of the Earth decayed. Black hills and cliffs rose out of sand flying yellow white. Skirting the stony plateaus of Hamada al-Hamra lay the rubble fields, crumbling sintering, of Sarir all gnawed away. Chalk became exposed, on its back black scoured sandstone; everything ground down to sand for dunes. Tibesti, wild mountains, covering two degrees of latitude in the south; dark-coloured massifs piled massively on one another, bald and naked. Blue green white chalk trickled puffed from vertical rockwalls under the sucking fire-breath. Huge slabs sheered slid slowly down from skeletal mountains, hills were levelled, slumped to a stony plain with tottering pillars and columns. Six hundred kilometres of nothing east to west, the stony land Hamada al-Hamra; the ground gave itself to wind and sun alone, fine sand blew over it. The land rippled south for two hundred dead kilometres. Waterless plains away to the southeast: this was Fezzan. In the bare limestone plain amid the black peaks of Tibesti dwelt the Teda. Lived with the furious wind that spun in whorls over the stony pavement of their land, grey-yellow sand-devils that swept across the plain. Thorny tamarisk bushes grew from the desiccated ground, sayal-acacias with broad crowns.

Rarely did turbid water ooze to the surface, to thistles thorn-bushes esparto-grass. Date palms in scattered sparse groves; the slender graceful plant-creature hung its thirsty roots deep in the damp layers of the ground, flourished its bushy crown atop the tall trunk.

The desert-dwelling Teda had slim dainty bodies, their skin dark yellow, flat drooping nose, thick lips, false furtive gaze not steady like the gaze of forest pygmies. In their dark tunics, dark veil over mouth and nose, little leather charm-pouches on turban throat arms, they trekked with their camels from waterhole to waterhole. Their diet camel-milk and dates, which wore their teeth to brown stumps. The soles of their feet so horny they could run over gravel and hot schist. Bleached camel-bones they found they pulverised, mixed the powder with blood from one of their beasts to make a paste; filled their bellies with it. Leather rings on their knives they macerated with stones, boiled them sliced them, filled their bellies. At night the sand-wind fell silent. When glittering lights came on in the clear deep dark sky, great moon-globe swinging high in the silvery ether, they rose mutely out of the rock-shadows murmuring a fatifa, wandered mutely on, unveiled. Tuareg in the expanses of the western desert lived like them, thin suspicious people with short two-pronged javelins and spears.

Above the waves and mountain ranges of the desert, restless white aviators appeared. They abducted frightened youngsters from nomad campsites, deposited them hours later near the panicked tribe. The Teda let them spend the night with them. But when the moon flooded the landscape with its white light, bronze-skinned men crept in shadows to the tents of the strangers, silently lifted the flaps, hurled spears. These flew barely a hand's breadth into the darkness. To the dismay of the cowering Teda the iron points seemed to hit a wall; the long quivering shafts fell back. When nothing stirred within where the men were sleeping, stealthy crouching nomads crept from all around to the strangers' tents, in their hands the revolvers they had been given in exchange for a red tarboush, indigo Sudanese tunic and leggings, indigo veil for mouth and nose. The closer they came to the strangers, the heavier the guns felt in their fingers. They had to urge the revolvers on, they seemed afraid to approach their former owners. But when the cocked hammer snapped and powder cracked, the exploding gases made it only a little way down the barrel, the bullet was forced back, the barrel burst with a roar and shattered the attacker's hands. The strangers rose calmly from their cots. They adjusted more tightly around their chests the little leather pouches containing the metal-repellent charge, bandaged the wounded, spoke to the attackers now grovelling in the sand at their feet, and to those lying motionless in ambush in the black shadows of tamarisks.

★★★

The Mountains Boomed

In Manas *the landscape itself is sentient. In the first of two excerpts, Savitri makes her arduous way up to the Field of the Dead. In the second, Manas is carried back to Earth, re-embodied following the coupling of his Soul with Savitri.*

Mountains had closed in about her.
The flowery meadows were far behind already,
The southern slopes, bedlam of beasts and trees,

Euphorbia acacia stands of bamboo,
Behind and below her the rivers in their deep
valleys,
Thundering Alaknanda, Kosi, Yamuna,
Ravines meadows rockwalls.
The mountains gathered round her. The mountains
boomed:
'Here we have stood since Time began,
We enclose the Field of the Dead.
Rivers stream out from us, little clouds fly over us,
Stones splinter and slide down from us,
Nanda Kot, Trisul, Yamunotri, Badrinath.
We buttress Kailash, Nanda Devi,
Our ravines are filled with ice, our summits are ice-
bound.
Shiva's breath is on us,
Shiva enthroned in the sea of mist.
Here is night, and storms and snow,
Leopards, ibex, blackhaired dogs.
Take care, stars, to shine the whole night through,
Take care, take care, vagrant mists,
When we tremble, when Shiva's tread is on us,
Boisterous giant dancer, his heels upon us.
Take care, take care!'

+++

AND there was no more rain.
Storms shredded the blue-black ragged clouds hither
and down,
Hurled them with thunderclaps over glaciers
snowfields ravines.

Through the thunderclaps the Rudras flew, eleven of
them,

Shiva's curly-head companions, moonhorns at their brow,
Bearing the man on their backs.
Over sombre Nanda Devi they flew.
Its double summit flashed blue in the storm's flickering.
The mountains, unsettled by Shiva's dance,
Now started their booming.
Gori brook surged white from Milam glacier,
Tumbled southward.
Rushing Pindar cascaded down from Nanda Kot.
To the west, Ganges had set out on its course,
Foaming through the mountains.

Such crepitating across the night.
Moon and stars hid from the boisterous Rudras.
Forests on the southern slopes awoke,
Euphorbia acacia stands of bamboo,
Howled along like dogs in the night,
One dog here, another there, responding with a long-drawn howl.

Eleven Rudras, on their backs the sleeping man,
Headlong through the dripping night, southward,
Swooping to flick snowcaps from the rocky ridges,
Shake them from their arms down into valleys.
They spat sprayed hail as they hurtled on.
By morning they were roaring over mountain jungle,
The flame-headed ones. Their eyes flashed green.
Here was the boundary of the Field of the Dead.
They snuggled wearily into snow that steamed.
They laid the man down.
Fell asleep beside him, until the sun flashed.

Then they let winds whirl them aloft
Light as air, stretched flat, they rode high, flickering
Whenever a ridge, as they passed over,
Brushed a back or a drooping arm, and grazed them.
Were giddy, called to one another, sang out over
distances.

★★★

Turtles

THE brown people show the Whites their enemies – but they do not call them enemies, they speak carefully, respectfully: termites that live in field and forest in little mounds that look like clumps of soil, they keep guests in their cells, beetles and spiders. They are so numerous, explain the brown people in wonder, that no human tribe can compare with termites. They themselves have taken to the river to avoid them, their houses stand on piles in the water and so are safe.

But termites are strong beings, even though small and blind. The natives point to old huts they have preserved, they knock on a plank, a finger goes right through, it is like sponge, the tiny termites have devoured everything.

Now they are surrounded by jaguars. The big cats slink around the band. No one knows what they want. They come in packs, never attack anyone. But the band of Whites attracts and unsettles them for some reason. As always the darkskins say nothing.

But one night the Whites are awakened by their sentries. They seize weapons, wonder why no alarm is sounding, but the darkskins make signs to keep quiet and follow, weapon or no weapon.

The broad rushing Apure lies below in the gentle light of the moon. Nothing breaks its rippling surface. Reflecting stars and moonlight, the river runs swift, the Apure, heading for the Orinoco. A cool breeze blows from the forested banks. No birds call. But as they step cautiously down from the forest to the river they hear a strange persistent noise, a rubbing, scraping, scrabbling. Sometimes a clacking and creaking. Sometimes a dull heavy crash, followed by the same general scrabbling. They realise it is not in the water but on the bank. A broad smooth high beach of white sand and mud extends along the southern bank to the east. In the moonlight a low dark mass is moving and shoving, it is many yards long, sometimes it seems to rest, but keeps coming at a steady slow pace. It is a huge dark blanket being drawn across the beach. They whisper to one another and marvel: these are turtles. They come to a halt. It's a whole army. Hiding by day, at night they go wandering, and now you can pick out individuals on the edge, brown-black chequerboard shells, a little sharp point like a sign, the triangular head stretched upward, hemmed in. They proceed, shell hard against shell, a huge movement of giant dark moonlit shells marching in their myriads. They halt in a clump, some are forced over the backs of others, the ones on top keep moving, the double-decker keeps on until a gap opens and those on top clunk down again. And behind them slink big wild cats, jaguars that encircle the moving mass, lunge at the scrabbling edges and try to pick something off. The turtles toil in the moonlight, the whole mass stops, loses itself in sand and mud, they bury themselves, this is their breeding season.

★★★

Hops

The hops that grew here were a tall vine. The ground was tilled and manured for them. Frames eleven meters high were planted in the soil, fastened with strong cables from which slender wires hung down to meet the climbing plants that twined about them. In rows two meters apart the plants climbed on tall grey stems from which floppy leaves hung. These were creatures that favoured a temperate climate, damp and mist caused them to shrivel, their roots needed deep soil containing humus, chalk and potassium.

When they bloomed in summer they were a total gynocracy: only female plants were allowed to grow tall, because they bore little fruit spigots that formed yellow glands with a bitter substance that made the beer that humans liked so much taste so pleasant. In summer the plants needed lots of water, in May, June, July they formed umbels and were ripe for picking. One hectare of land could produce ten hundredweight of umbels, but the yield varied, and on average in any decade there were two good years, three average and five with a poor yield.

Now it was winter and everything had been harvested, dried and stored in big cool cellars behind Station Square, sulphurated in metal boxes. The time for manuring and cutting the stalks was not yet. On some days men came to hoe weeds.

The plants bided their time quietly in the soil. Day followed day, it was as if they were filled with explosives, a detonation and a wildfire raged.

Red and yellow spider mites waited near the plants. They sat in linden trees, on the underside of leaves, and covered them in fine threads. Tiny as they were, these mites were armed with a sucking proboscis and puncturing bristles. They'll use these to tap into the young plants. They'll turn the leaves brown and withered. The farmer will complain of "copper blight".

When it's about to come into flower and the people are preparing for the harvest, aphids come across from sloe bushes. They are green. Wherever they settle, leaves will curl up and die, and shoots will wither from the top.

And sooty mould, a fungal blight, lurks in last season's hop stalks. It waits for the hour to come, at the moment it's all in gestation. There's a black powder on the old stalks. When summer comes with its warmth, the spores will bestir themselves and drill long thin wells into the young plants and suck them dry.

★★★

THEME 4. MAJESTIES

Tortoise (from *Wang Lun*)
Beer King of Merseburg (from *Wallenstein*)
Mansu (from *Mountains Oceans Giants*)
I the King (from *The Land without Death*)

★★★

Tortoise

CH'IEN-LUNG, the great Emperor, who had received the empire of the world from Heaven and ever-changing nature, emerged from his hunts and his musings on the northern steppes, made his way back to Mukden.

He had seen again the enormous landscapes of Tartary. Few days in their profound silence had been disturbed by tribute bearers. Tigers loped out of the woods. Week by week letters of fealty arrived from the Imperial princes and high nobility, enquiring after his health.

No great train accompanied the aging Emperor: two hundred men of his lifeguard, one pure Manchu company, a small number of favourites, friends, slaves, lastly the exquisite orchestra. … He made camp in the trough-shaped valley near Hsuanhua-fu. Houses were dug into the loess, with rooms, vaults, passages. Nomad families camped in big round tents of felt. Brown flatfaced Mongols prostrated themselves.

They crossed the outliers of the great Hsingan range, descended towards Mukden.

The Emperor's gaze was remote, his expression fearsomely bleak. Cannon boomed from the eight towers on the walls of Mukden. For five days Ch'ien-lung remained in his palace.

In the autumnal park by a pond the Emperor sat alone, his lap filled with green lettuce leaves. In front of him a giant tortoise slept.

The carapace was black with yellow flutings. The broad central plate was edged in yellow, with deep indentations. The clumsy forefeet extended sideways like flippers, toes like pegs driven into the feet. Hind legs drawn into the armour. The Emperor, dressed in black silk with a plain silk cap, rapped on the shell with a stout branch from which fircones dangled.

And then out of its lair the grey horny head emerged, that wonderfully passionless head on a wrinkled neck that sparkled like dried fish skin. The triangular skull turning in contemptuous unconcern. Jaws clamped, the severe work of plane and straightedge. Nostrils sunk with an augur. To the sides, lidless, immobile, clever wise eyes, windows of a gelid brain.

Slowly the shell lifts itself on one side, sinks back, pushes forward. It is the painful gait of a nimble but gouty and ancient man. The foreflippers swim, right, left, scrape. The armour sinks back, the hind legs stretch and follow. A highpitched wheezing, a gentle hiss comes from the punched-out nostrils. Again the rump heaves, the front flippers slide forward. It is a climbing over level ground.

The Emperor sat on his stool with his fir branch. He tried to keep pace with the tortoise, to imitate it, and pondered. As it heaved forward it seemed to turn its eyes on him. He slid slowly after his branch to the ground, knelt behind the creature as it moved away towards the pond. For some reason he bowed down behind it.

Very slowly, as Ch'ien-lung wished, the procession continued on its way. Wide sandy spaces alternated with fields of watermelon. …

★★★

Beer King of Merseburg

IN BOTH of the Protestant Electoral lands – in Saxony's Dresden, and the Brandenburg capital Berlin – they split their sides laughing at Vienna's latest proposal to resolve the Palatine question once and for all by means of a decree of the entire Electoral College. Johann Georg, the Prince-elector, was as pleased by the news as the president of his council, Kaspar von Schönberg; for several days he neglected his chief care: the supervision and regulation of the beer industry, and sniffing around for obscure brews. As other sovereigns have envoys in foreign lands, so he had reliable expert tasters across most of his realm, and some too in the famous Hansa towns, who spied for him and made reports, and had the finest little kegs, the most lovingly crafted beers, sealed and leaded with secret ciphers and delivered to him by courier. If the brew was selected – its secret truly remarkable – then the clever discoverer would soon want for nothing; he had his access card to the Electoral Saxon court; the Beer King of Merseburg (a nickname Johann Georg relished, even if students in Leipzig thought to mock him by it) would receive him with gratitude and honour, as befitted one who contributed to the welfare of the Saxon body politic.

Johann Georg was easygoing and somewhat weak in the head; he had never lost his eye for the important things in life, and had an unerring kindly understanding of human frailties. For the details of existence, and also for official business, he had engaged Kaspar von Schönberg; but to prevent the man growing too high and mighty he had placed some of his trusted nobles around the man's neck like a millstone. In this way, with God's help, he steered the coach of state, relying on the anti-clerical religion he had inherited. He observed the career of the Palatine Frederick with much head-shaking; the man had the right faith, the right wife, a lovely plump Englishwoman after whom any poor German would lick his finger. But where would it lead, asked Johann Georg in moments of depression, when he brings this woman up the Rhine and the Neckar to Heidelberg in a barge fitted with plate-lockers, bedrooms, refectories, bathrooms. Let them enjoy such fineries, worthy of a born prince-elector, or king, and such a delicious wife; but where did the money come from, insofar as it was not he but the King of England, James the Curmudgeon, who was the dupe? But what of it; all good fortune and hopes are built on sand. A German prince – yes, it was so, and it happened, and it had to happen, with all the consequences for him, for Emperor Ferdinand, the Holy Roman Emperor, the Protestant faith; and one could only wait for all the rest. Such was his directive to the "Actuary and Harvest-mouse of the Realm", as he smilingly referred to Schönberg, even in the matter of this new decision to resolve the Palatine question by Collegial decree.

It was late autumn; Johann Georg sat by his cabinet of curiosities in a wheelchair, his nose blue, freezing in padded jacket, wolfskin cloak, fur cap down over his ears and a thick bonnet; chamois-leather mittens over which he had pulled huge wolfskin gloves; legs wrapped in lambskin. A broad grey beard flowed in waves over the jacket, the stubble around his mouth was green. He curtly dismissed wool-gathering Kaspar von Schönberg, arrogant cringing skeleton. Then he cast a benevolent eye on his asthmatic valet, Lebzelter, who stood at a lectern perusing the beautifully illustrated Eichstätt volume with the tulip pictures, taking notes. For two decades Lebzelter had made notes of everything he saw happening around him, for the sake of order, tidiness, so that one did not scamper mindlessly about like an animal.

"What do you think of the business, Lebzelter?"

He at once hastened across, defensively raised both hands, opened his eyes wide in respect, until from under the curly grey wig: "Your Highness: don't touch it! Privy Counsellor Kaspar thinks in a rush, in a tizzy; Lebzelter – your Highness knows it."

"What's it about, Lebzelter, what shall we do?"

"Don't touch it, your Electoral Grace. Not today, not tomorrow. Nature must take its course. I shall make notes."

"Day after tomorrow, Lebzelter. And keep Kaspar away from me."

Two days later the valet carefully dressed his master up, and when he had stood him directly before the cabinets, beer-stein placed to one side with a little basket of pretzels, he quickly made a note, brushed himself down and bowed, ready to begin his lecture. But Johann Georg remarked after the first deep draught that first it should be ascertained whether they were in accord on the main point.

The main point – Lebzelter took up the thread – was that the two Protestant Electors and the Estates represented in the College were to have the wool pulled over their eyes by the Emperor's own hands. Johann Georg with some emotion extended an arm to him: "Lebzelter, wet your whistle." Whereat the gratified valet pronounced: with Electoral Saxony consenting, we return to the starting point: everyone will laugh. For the stupidity of the appointed imperial counsellors in this business is too much; every Saxon, Brandenburger, every child can see it: the Electoral College is to ratify and pay for whatever the Emperor eats. Those little lords in Vienna, most honourable, upright and noble one and all, have found it ever harder to shoulder the responsibility and the cost; so let the prince-elector with his broad back do so.

"But I would suggest," remarked his master thoughtfully, pulling at the wolfskin gloves, "that it's all decent and above-board, what His Roman Majesty has undertaken and embarked on with imperial authority at his back. Now now, don't laugh so hard. It does no good and looks bad, it's disrespectful. Well, what should I, who am after all your prince-elector, your gracious lord, what should I say when you laugh as the Empire totters?"

Again Lebzelter raised his hands – a grave imperious gesture: "Won't! Won't happen! That, by your Grace's leave, is why I laugh: because they are all mistaken. What sort of laughter is it? A laugh of mockery, a contented, very earnest, rebuffing laughter."

"Well then, I'd better enjoy it. We shall rebuff them."

"We rebuff, your Grace. Same will happen as with Count Palatine Frederick and the barge."

"Why, my son?"

"In that case the Englishman had the money, so the Palatine could not stay too long in the barge. Now the Bavarian and His Majesty mean to sail along …"

"Good. But I too have no money. Good, Lebzelter. Every man must bear his joys and sorrows, for that is how the Lord God created us. The Emperor is an honourable earnest man and so too, more so, the Bavarian Maximilian. Truly devoted to 'em both, loyal supporter. But they go against God's law; they must run on their own two legs."

"If your Grace commands, I shall convey this to Kaspar Schönberg as your strict unalterable opinion."

"I command Kaspar to – . No, I don't command him. He should not stick his mousey nose into this. He has laughed too much at me over this business, he lacks respect and gravity."

"What does your Grace command?"

The prince tugged testily at the wolfskins. "We won't involve ourselves in politics, Lebzelter. The two of you buzz around too freely in the world. It's hot in here. Drink up, run along and see if my mother is feeling better."

★★★

Mansu

As the dire effects of Synthetic Food plunge people into despair, strolling players from Africa stage parables that clarify their predicament.

THEY performed the fate of a great king. He imposed himself on all neighbouring kings and drove their ponderous bodies, victory fanfares blaring, in chains to his house. He could tame rivers. They had to flow where he wanted, had to water his dry fields so that palms and breadfruit would grow, had to flow against cliffs to undermine and wash them away. When he commanded, they had to flow into his house, creep through narrow pipes, creep into every room, those wild waters from the cataracts. Soon he had piled up so much gold and jewellery from his victories and looting expeditions, bracelets rings carts, that his sheds and barns could not hold it all. The delicate Fula, these brown men and maidens with their crinkly hair, showed what happened next.

How the great ruler sat in the hall of his palace, and all the stuff closed in around him because he would not let it from his sight, it reflected his glory. They showed the paradise of Mbutiland in the interior of Africa, its gently rolling valleys, slopes covered in banana trees and oil palms, groves, innumerable springs. Sugarcane grew thickly along riverbanks, sweet potato on the sunsoaked hills, big fields of peanuts sesame tobacco. But the king, bloated blackbearded face, big earlobes pierced with thick smooth copper rods, on his head a huge hat with swaying feathers of peacock and parrot, flabby womanly breasts uncovered, and then the hundredweight of gold and silver chains, copper rings, carved amulets, heavy copper plates on the fat resting arms, around veined swelling calves. In the dangling right hand his sickle-shaped chiselled sabre with pearl inlay. Mansu the King behind his stockade now never left the palace. He grew fatter and fatter on his splendid throne. His wives massaged him. Every day another one must come. It amused him to have movement around him, to behead them when they were done and he was feeling comfortable on his throne. More and more stuff was heaped around him: lion's fangs, great piles of civet skins, giraffe tails. Beside his hall were storehuts and granaries, directly in his line of sight the armoury along the passage to the door, with spearpoints daggers shields sabres machetes.

He swelled and swelled, Mansu. Became immobile, stuck in the woven seat that had become his bed and table too. More and more adornments were strung around his neck. From every one of his teeth a copper ring hung on a hempen thread. Under his hat his hair was twisted in little braids, on every braid an amulet to ward off sickness. The skin of upper arms and thighs was pierced, strings passed through for the heads of neighbouring kings conquered by his warriors. His narrow throne room of solid timber, with only one door and one window, grew dark with the riches that filled it. Only one narrow passage was kept clear. Then one morning King Mansu, yawning awake and slurping palm wine, swung his sickle-shaped sword and called for his women. Dawn was about to break. Behind the hills of skins and lion's fangs he heard horns and flutes and his wives singing: "Ei, ei, Munsa chupi, chupi ei." He called and waited, slurped some more, became apoplectic, blue in the face, tossed about, called again. Swaying in front of him the big fly-whisks, bunches of red parrot feathers. Beyond the skins the tooting and singing continued.

But suddenly something was moving in the passage. A delicate little man came slowly down the narrow space, pulling a cart behind him. Bowed: he brings gifts from the Babuker, who are his loyal servants, as the great king knows. He lifted great round lumps from the little cart, wrapped in leaves, laid them beside the king. The king sat straight, stared at him, roared: "I want my women," thrust with his sword at the little man, who stepped smartly aside, calmly unloaded more lumps.

"Cheese. They're cheeses," he whispered. "We're poor people, goatherds. The Masana have more, the Mongo; we're just goatherds. It's goat's cheese, you'll like it."

Mansu, half out of his seat, snapped at air, tugged at his amulets. The women nearby behind the civet skins kept shrilling their "Ei, ei, Munsa chupi, chupi ei." And as the sweating king, half-dazed with foreboding, pressed an amulet to his brow, the little man disappeared, bleating: "They're very tasty, you must try them. The Babuker are your loyal subjects."

The fly-whisks stirred. He opened his eyes wide, called out. Beyond the feathers an old man was rocking himself left and right in the passage, the big straw cloak on his head and body leaving only eyes and nose free. He had the appearance the gait the voice of the king's witch-doctor. Would not approach, ignored Mansu's command. "You are sick, Mansu," he whispered, prostrated himself.

"Bring me something to drink to make me better, or I'll beat you to death."

The witch-doctor whispered to the ground: "I have the drink. I knew you were sick. I brought it with me. It's here, under my cloak. I mixed it an hour ago in the temple."

"Give." – "I cannot."

"Give. Give it me. I'll cut off your head."

"You must take it with water, at sunrise, out there in the temple."

"Give it here. I'm not going outside."

"Come," the witch-doctor cajoled; he retreated a little, "or it won't work."

The king rose snorting, called help to his women. "You must come," whispered the straw-cloak man on the ground. "The sun will be up soon, the drink will spoil, you might die."

"Wait, wait," Mansu threatened as he stood, fumbled on the throne for his sickle-sword, fell back. The witch-doctor cajoled: "Come, come. I'll put the drink here, by the door. Here, you can see it."

Mansu stumbled down from the dais, picked himself up. He tried to undo the strings holding the heavy hangings round his neck, could not. His hand snagged on the jumble of rings and chains.

"Here's the drink. By the door. Hurry. The sun will soon be up."

The king groaned, the passage was too narrow. Lion's teeth tipped his tall hat down, it flapped against his mouth. He turned sideways, he was too fat, couldn't come through. He roared to the witch-doctor, to his wives: "I can't come through." The witch-doctor had vanished. The songs behind the hill of skins hummed soft and jaunty; clappers clapped, the king in his half-daze liked this. He wrestled with the pile of animal skins and tails sliding down onto him. He assailed them with his sickle-sword. He fought with them. More and more slid down. He shoved at them.

The drink was there, not far to the door. He dropped the sword. His hand caught in the chains at his throat, he couldn't extricate it. Screaming in fury he stomped forward; he tried to push through the skin-mountain with his head. He turned and turned about. A heavy pile of giraffe tails slid clattered over him. He freed himself, tottered into a heap of dried bananas.

As he threshed around he pulled strings of lion's fangs and a big tusk down from the ceiling. They knocked heavily onto him. His head was squashed down. Bananas squeezed his throat, his screaming face. Soft thick pulp rose to his ears, blocked his snorting nostrils, filled his gaping mouth. He gulped at it, spat, spat, wanted to scoop it out with his hands; they were jammed fast against his knees, he couldn't feel them. His head jerked this way and that like a fish out of water. Then the sweet pulp engulfed him entirely. His jaws ceased working, the panic in his eyes faded. He suffocated in the pulpy fruit, his legs sinking as into a bog. Hours later, when his wives arrived to the sound of flutes, they found him completely buried in the soft churned mess. The women, the sons praised his death; they wept: such a kingly death.

And the dusky players hauled the dead man from his yellow coffin, sponged him down, set him on his feet. He pulled on his big tall hat. They danced together around the stage, blew away the pulp. The king danced in a puddle on his fat legs.

★★★

I the King

IN SPAIN, in Buen Retiro, when I the King read what the Jesuit Fathers planned he was certainly not pleased, for sourness was his nature, but when he stood up from the desk he could move his knee more easily. He was concerned with all that happened around him in the palace, for he felt duty bound to keep it under control, but what happened outside in his realm also concerned him, for the same reason. I the King was like a scullery maid in a hostelry, to whom at every hour from morn till midnight they bring dirty dishes, for the eating never stops, but all she ever sees of it is dirty plates.

The Fathers of the Society of Jesus out there in the New Indies were a ray of hope. There was no more pleasant reading for Philip than their letters, they were better, braver than those of old Las Casas. The scrolls found a place on his enormous desk, which was a kind of operations centre, close to the spot reserved for his right elbow, in a region he secretly called the 'consolations of his heart'. Here were gathered a prayer book, his rosary, a locked box containing the daily report from his secret police about goings-on in the palace, especially among his family, for he almost never spoke to his family, preferred to be informed of their activities and opinions by spies. Beside this box a basket with food for his two massive hounds, trained man-hunters. And here the scrolls from the Jesuit Fathers in the New Indies ended up.

I the King, the dumb man – he had forgotten how to open his mouth to speak, speaking seemed such a servile activity, he would have preferred even to confess in writing, and his Father Confessor would not have minded, but there are rules – I the King had cares. He made no progress in the world. You could spy, decree, set up a ubiquitous network of police, troops, priests. Always something fell through the net. On some days I the King collapsed in his chancery under the burden of painful purgatives, reports of failings, complaints, and thought: it would take ten kings to put all this right. Then he had himself carried in his litter, sour and careworn, into the fresh air, and gazed through the curtains of the litter at figures who loomed close and vanished into the distance; meadows, woods, people, all looked so harmless, disgracefully harmless. But how they plague one with worries. However much one writes, decrees, punishes, orders, it all happens over again.

He and his Council of the Indies had issued particular instructions concerning the New Indies. But governors, generals, captains, eager adventurers brought it all to naught. It made one weep to compare the magnificent intentions formulated in the King's cabinet with the fate they suffered. For example, a certain governor Don Diego de Centeno died before he could take up office. Another was called Don Juan de Sanabrar. He was very rich, which was good, and taken into account. He was tasked to gather two hundred soldiers and a number of white families to accompany him. They considered in detail the country over there, which consisted only of forest and grassy savannah, inhabited by idolaters; in Buen Retiro they wanted only the best even for Indian forests, and instructed the governor to load his ship with wheat, barley, rye and seeds of other useful cereals and plants, and in addition to take ample supplies of iron, steel, provisions, they prescribed what kinds of artisans he should procure, and named him captain-general, governor, alguazil mayor of the province of Rio de la Plata, with extensive rights and authorities. These things the royal chancery most meticulously heaped upon Don Juan de Sanabrar. Who at once set off for Seville, and there at the last moment received a royal edict, forbidding him under any circumstances to engage in trade with the Portuguese. And Sanabrar, armed with these most sagacious instructions, stood there gazing at his ships. And then died before they could sail.

They reported this to I the King at Buen Retiro. They wrote that there was a son who mourned the hidalgo. The King decreed: offer the same commission to the son. He was just as wealthy, and still young. The son agreed. Ships, crew, cargo of passengers and merchandise were all in place, he climbed aboard, climbing aboard was all he had to do. For a long time no news came of the son and his squadron. At last he sailed into the great bay of the Rio de la Plata and gazed upon his province. Then he suffered shipwreck and was drowned. Some sailors saved themselves with planks, and in the town of Assomption told what had happened.

Hot on the heels of this, from the same troublesome region came a report of a remarkable novelty. Juan Romero, a brave captain of troops, had gone about the country with a hundred soldiers to pacify it, and in order to bring even the Indians of the riverlands to heel he made use of two brigantines. He travelled with these up a small river that flowed into La Plata. One noontime he went ashore with his soldiers and set up a tent on the riverbank for their dinner. And as they sat there eating, the whole broad bank suddenly collapsed and took them on an excursion downriver. When the people in the tent noticed that the bank was moving, and the ground under their feet loosened and gaped, they tried to swim to the brigantines still anchored nearby. Despite the strong swirling current they reached the ships. And as they stood dripping and breathless on deck, gazing at the suddenly swollen waters, the bank collapsed again, the ships themselves were overturned, and this time swimming was no use, it was as if a jaguar had been hunting a deer and now went for the kill. All the people and the brigantines sank and drowned in mud and debris.

Such incidents were reported all the time from the New Indies. And as for the authorities, all selected and instructed with such care, their fascinating antics left nothing to be desired. Some behaved like madmen, some scooped up gold with no attempt at concealment as if the world were blind, and you had to arrest them, confiscate their gold and throw them in gaol. In one corner of this vast empire a man, an ordinary man holding no office, even declared war on the King of Spain himself! The king is long past astonishment, he would like to hear what his faithful secretary, who stands at his side reading and listening to everything, really thinks about it, about this madness, this chaos that ever and again trickles through one's fingers like sand, but his mouth is frozen, he cannot speak.

That distant land is truly a chamber of horrors. Once I the King managed a smile as his secretary read out among other curiosities: In the town of Assomption, on the Paraná, the royal lieutenant-general attends the cathedral to hear Mass, and the bishop has him arrested. "This can't be true, the bishop, and my lieutenant-general?"

"The bishop holds the royal lieutenant-general prisoner in a dungeon. This is what the governor-general writes." All they can do is recall both men to Spain and never let them return.

In the place on his desk reserved for consolations of the

heart lie letters from the Jesuit Fathers. The king has arranged it so that his right elbow nudges them as he writes. He immerses his thoughts in the Jesuits. They have had their fill of aggravations with stupid and useless events and people, and can no longer be bothered with them. They want to bring Christianity, people try to stop them, they leave San Paolo to its devices and go into the wilderness. If only he could do likewise. A clear plan, a settled system, every point thoroughly considered and put into effect without opposition, and in the face of all ridiculous events and people. Enviable men. They deserve every protection. The secretary takes notes, he inscribes marks that attest to the king's pleasure in this matter. The marks are meant for various officials spiritual and temporal, who for their part keep a close eye on the king and his family.

Having settled this account, I the King is better placed to turn his attention to matters closer to home. The stagnating morass in the Netherlands can be set in motion, a duke is dispatched to the region with plenipotentiary powers and an army; the fools there want to become Protestants even though they are Spaniards, they are hanged and beheaded and then everything goes swimmingly. The same method works also in Our own household in the case of Our son Don Carlos, against whom secret agents lay unfavourable reports.

Now, says I the King, lying abed one evening looking at his very pale thin arms and legs: this meagre flesh suffices to steer the affairs of the world. People have fat and heat. They are an utterly deranged, stupid and helpless breed. I believe that if they were not led, they would never take even one straight step. They would be at each other's throats out of sheer cluelessness, of course also out of caprice, lust for power. They have drives, and that is everything to the little creatures. I thank God that he made me. And placed me in this position, rather than one of those many princes who prance about the world.

They make their nations unhappy. Perceptive people know to thank me. The masses of course do not. They scream because they cannot go where they want. I shall continue to shepherd them strictly and well. Thank you, Lord, for my office, for my wisdom. Finally thank you, great Creator, for me.

And he thanked his mother for being Isabella of Portugal, and not from the house of a mere marquis, hidalgo or, perish the thought, peasant. It was a major act of Providence that preserved me from such a fate and gave me this woman as my mother. And then he thanked Emperor Charles V for being Emperor of Rome, King of Spain, and his father. And thanked all their parents, grandparents and great-grandparents, lay on his bed and, after gazing once more at his yellow bony hands, fell asleep.

A remarkable scene filled his dreams. He's strolling with his two hounds through the gardens of Buen Retiro. A sentry stands at every crossing in the path, and as he approaches they thumb their noses. It's astonishing. He goes up to a sentry, tries to pull down his arm. But it's impossible. He goes to the next. Same thing. He goes along the whole line, without success. Troubled, he seeks out a grove where he cannot see the sentries. He thinks he should ask the sentries what they have against him. Then he sleeps. In the morning he had no memory of it.

***

THEME 5. SERMONS

Recruiting Sermon (from *Wallenstein*)
Court Sermon (from *Wallenstein*)
Priest of Shiva (from *Manas*)
Sermon in the Forest (from *The Land without Death*)

★★★

Recruiting Sermon

PRIESTS began to recruit for Wallenstein. They railed at the Protestant Pelasgians, Epicureans, herders of swine, Calvinists, bloodsuckers, devourers of the Lord God.

"What do they do with the gospels of Mark Luke Matthew John? They pick away at the very foundations of the Saviour and His works, split hairs, distil, these quacksalvers in the body of our holy Church. The Gospel is tough, raw, leathery, teeth must be especially sharp and pointed; the Church hangs it well for you, makes it tender, stacks it in the smokehouse, sets about it like a good butcher-woman, cuts for you the best most nourishing morsels; we never stop making a nice little soup for you, stewing, roasting, a joy for your belly.

"Now see those Lutherans and Calvinists; they go about with sour bitter faces, their vitals are overloaded, they cannot digest but will not let it be. I shall purge you, dear souls, so that none of you suffer such shameful distress. Who on this Earth has the best Heaven: the heretic Lutheran, or the Catholic? Now, it is not credible that heretics should enjoy a better Heaven than pious Catholics. And indeed, who can say that heretics may enter Heaven, when Hell lies there better suited to them? But what if we assume, suppose we can, that they are Christian folk who sin all unawares? They have not yet licked at our sugar-cakes, it has not yet run into their mouths, the manna that daily consoles us so heartily through every season and weather. As soon as we open our eyes the manna begins to flow, in indescribable astonishing excess – only not to those wretches who are too idle, who toss and turn abed and find the early morning bells that so delight the Lord a disturbance to their blasphemous repose.

"And so, I say, for these unwitting sinners there is made ready either a purgatorial fire, or at best an antechamber to Paradise. They will be tolerated, perhaps not tormented too greatly; comfort, a somewhat sluggish pleasure is all that blooms for them betimes, and on Sundays. And this would be the case, if it were, as it should be and they sin unwittingly. But care is taken not to allow too great a thronging in the antechamber. People of every estate are summoned by our Saviour and Lord in order to make room. They do not shy, the pious people and true Papists, the banner-wavers and cross-bearers, from belabouring the sinners and their dirty unkempt hides. These the ones who sin knowingly. A jubilation goes now through the world, an end to half-hearted prodding and tapping, now from behind they feel a hard blow on the backside that says: watch out! It is their mercy and mildness that leads true Papists to act thus, so that a trembling and gnashing of teeth overcome the damnable Luther-boobies until repentance squeezes them and drives them like wretched ridiculous clots to the seat of judgement and the confession-stool, begging to be lifted up and received into Paradise. And truly, lifting them requires feats enough.

"There is no time now to speak of a Protestant Heaven. Satan has been informed; he has the grim task of gathering supplies of helpers knives tubs barrels kindling bellows, not forgetting slack jaws, strong fists; he will belabour the sinners, drag them hither and thither, iron and hooks to stoke the fire.

"Goats run around, not those that Satan and the witches ride upon, but others, wholesome, they assail sinners with their horns, spear them, throw them through the air and amuse themselves as in a ball game. And as for the proud and the haughty, scrawny monkeys jump around them, clamber up their skirts and doublets from behind, clutch them under the armpits with both hands, legs in front about the belly, and they tickle, tickle to make them laugh. Yes, now they can laugh, roar, fling themselves about until they turn blue, and burst. And a devil stands before them, punches them in the mouth, screams Silence! and holds out a jug to the monkey so he does not go thirsty. What laughter is this in the bowels of Hell! Verily, not like the soft melodious laughter of our Heavenly kingdom.

"A beast is there that creeps about, its belly measures a hundred miles square. It has the snout of a dog, its body white and plump like a pig, its feet green with knobbly lumpy toes like a frog. There it sits, the monster, in a corner, and always when the Hell before it is packed right full, it bends down, its tongue cracks like a whip, and slurps up a hundred of the damned, tumbles them in its gorge and belly where they seethe in a muck and a jumble of lye, then it sicks them back out, slurps them up again and another ten and twenty times until it has had enough, and spews them out in a lump. And the beast rinses its mouth, and for the rest snaps with its warty lolling tongue at the hundred lying at its feet, and slides them into a circle until they dry out, and then it lets them go.

"Shall I tell you of the Devil's locksmiths, who hammer people as if they were red-hot iron, of the carpenters who saw at living people and make chairs and stools from them so they can sit as they go about their evil business. Any Christian would be a fool to endure such torments out of sheer obstinacy. But my Lutherans are not fools, they have been washed by many waters, and those among them who are washed the most are those who proclaim themselves learned men, preachers, who tempt pious souls. For these an especial punishment is created, so that those who in their earthly life were a special thing may preen themselves even here. For delicate little threads hang down from the ceiling of Hell, you must picture it exactly, little threads, not many, for just so many is not too bad. The threads are not easily seen, for a fog, a mist, a steam as from a cooking pot rises constantly from below. And when the devils have caught good hold of such a decrepit old abortion of a preacher, who thought to slip just like that and all at once into Heaven's antechamber, they lift him gently onto a nice comfy little chair, tie it to two of the threads, pull him aloft, and now let loose with the steam and daub him all over up to the ears in pitch. And every day at the same hour a devil comes, scrapes the pitch from his ears and begins to dispute with him, so that his superior wit may not grow dull.

"This seems nothing to you? Oh, oh! to live, yet eyes see not, ears hear not. They shrivel like apples in the steam, they sit all day like washerwomen in sultry dampness, dripping, cannot draw one breath of good air, and are never dry. If they could look around, if they could snap at the smoky air to see if there is anything to see – there is nothing. They drip, and shrivel, rot away over a long while. But a nail sticks out of the back of the chair, digs them in the back when they want to sleep. If great numbers of these were to come, the busy devils would be happy enough, and have their delight. How they twist and turn on the chairs, would you not like to see how they rage, never become dry, try to blow the damp away and always they are boiled from below, how they foam like the enraged boar, how they assail one another in their isolation up there swinging from the two little threads below the ceiling of Hell, how they bite their knuckles, would gladly kill themselves if only they could. There is nothing in them but foaming and vengeance, screams, weeping, until they grow weary, and when they feel fresh again, again they see nothing but their own self, and it is nothing."

★★★

Court Sermon

THROUGH the pair of crystal windows in the ornate pretty chapel of the Residence in Munich shone a red wintry sun. The narrow vaults, white polished plaster, took on purplish flecks and lines, as if breathed upon. Floor of jasper and agate; above it the Bavarian court on kneeling-stools; Spanish costumes, lowered shoulders, bowed heads, grey hair, white wigs, dark tamed locks. On the pulpit to the left of the big silver altar with the relics and St George on his charger – in gold, three plumes on the helmet set with diamonds, rubies, emeralds – a tall priest with glowing eyes, dressed in a tight-clasped black Jesuit robe, was speaking; in his intimidating zeal he waved his arms over them, though they did not see:

"It is permitted sooner to hate God than to love him. For God is too far from us, too lofty; it is a sin to approach too close to him, even in our thoughts. To dare to love him like this or that everyday person, drape ornaments jewels and gold on him in order to demonstrate tender feelings: this serves only to demean him. It constitutes an insult to his divinity. Crawl before him, shrink from him, resent him even: this well befits a person. In that moment when you no longer fear God, you have already denied him. He has not suffered you to be his friend, is not your father, mother, your paramour, your bosom brother. He is not even your king and prince; he declines to be your judge, his judgement is not accessible to you, he pronounces judgement when he chooses and against whomever he chooses. He does not permit us to comprehend him, or investigate his being, and so in his presence the only proper feeling is one of Awe – and with this you have fulfilled your duty as human beings.

"Woe to those who believe that God is our Father; almost no further step is needed to embrace heresy. So Sunday should be held holy, for the sake of God; yet you do not hold God holy? Forget not who you are, whence you have come. Do you know how the original sin of your life came about? Are you conscious of all the sins you drag around ever since that day – auspicious day, or inauspicious? See the baseness of humanity, its pitiful desires – and you the children of God! Look at your day, filled with toil, the satisfaction of bodily needs, a hundred vexations, a hundred joys, all blown away, of no more weight than a lightning flash. Lawsuits – envy – the urge for riches, for status – rebellious underlings: this is your life once you are fully grown or old. Now more fun, now less, games, men, women, wine, beer, tourneys, deer, boar, music, pictures, sleep, languor, comfort, bitterness – all for nothing and a bit. Gloom and groaning when you grow gouty and bent, crouched behind the stove, your empty jaws sup only broth, pain in the kidneys, constipation, incontinence, stomach cramps, and then sleep and sleeplessness. Such is the life of the child of God. You feel ashamed, I feel it with you all; you need but grasp this, remember it, keep it always in view. Yes, reflect, remember! Calm the soul, quench all desire! Know him alone, God alone; you have the right to know his name, hear of his existence: it is enough and enough for us. Have the right to fear God: see, I have said it.

"And you feel that I speak the truth. We do not cradle ourselves in the sentiments and dreams of a maidservant. For us, life is too serious; it is ever present to us, we have endured it, know what awaits us today, tomorrow. There will be no angel to greet us, no promise will be made to us. Let us leave aside the games of children, dear things, and of fools, dear things.

"Tomorrow bells will ring out and there will be early Mass. Menials will clomp in the courtyards, the steward will sit high on horseback with his whip and plumed hat. Tomorrow early the bells will ring out: we shall lie half asleep on our backs, then sit up, say our prayers; and the cries of infants for milk and attention resound in our ears. We drink our morning broth, it may be thin and cold, we must inspect our cellars where we keep our treasure and our goods, fasten the chests, for soon carts will rattle across the bridge; they must all be loaded and sealed; we shall exchange curses with the labourers who will try to cheat us about their wages, we shall be on guard; peasants shuffle past.

"When the bells ring out tomorrow, a mother will have given birth, she will rejoice, her husband will rejoice, and the siblings gaze on the poor little worm. And in many places during this night a change has occurred, one has died of hunger, or of cold by a well, at a stable door, one has been struck down by robbers, one swept away by fever, someone old, sick, who welcomes death, snuffed out in the bedroom. Our life, our life! How can anyone be proud! How can anyone dare be proud, and claim the title Human in a boastful tone – unless he has formed an image based on the strength of his muscles, the cunning of his thoughts, the immoderation of his desires! And what dumb beast is not, in this respect, his superior.

"Our life, our life! We have died a thousand times, out of pride, when we have seen what we are; and it is not by the emperor's crown, the prince elector's crown resting on our head, nor by the bishop's mitre, the tons of gold, that we are lifted up, but rather by Awe, and horror.

"Our only comfort is our inability to reflect. Forgetfulness, intoxication only pretend to carry us across the abyss. As far as we can see, the only salvation against death and nothingness is Awe.

"Break, o my knees! O my heart, let your pillars fall! Roof above, crush me! Let a hundred cannon, a hundred siege guns be aimed at me: here are my heart, my eyes. I am frozen. Yet I still can laugh at you. You turn your iron and marble to dust in the air. I can pray, can tremble!"

Ailing elderly Duke William had fallen forward from his stool, his white face slumped, the stool scraped sideways. His son the Prince Elector, hard-faced, grabbed at him.

★★★

Priest of Shiva

Manas, re-embodied, has returned to the land of humans with three (now tamed) demons. In Amber he is confronted by a priest.

Now the priest stood up.
He was naked, the triple mark of Shiva on his forehead,
His body ash-smeared.
He saw giant naked Manas, rat-tail around his hips, at his back a nervous crowd.
Recognised who it was,
Rumours of this one – his marauding like a pack of tigers –
Had raced across radiant Punjab.
This was the one. Standing right in front of him.
This one.
He laid the book aside, made an averting gesture, was unafraid.
    'Begone from here. You! Begone from here.
    Do not stand there, you. You cannot stay here.'
'What's that you're whispering, priest?'
    'You hear me. Be on your way.
    Dog, the sight of you is loathsome, loathsome!
    You – who could say your name.'
Manas dreamy, looking at him: 'Yes.'
    'Shiva sent you back here, to our shame.
    Now you are among us.

It has come to us. We are to suffer like all the others.
Let me look at you. What did Shiva have in mind for you, you scourge.
We are meant to see: that we are you,
As wicked as you are, a horror just like you!
Shiva now does so, and then does so.
Now he sends us spirits that should save us,
And then sends beasts, evildoers, mirrors.'

'Go on.'

'Go on! Still you stand there in my sight, you sinful creature.
I already know myself. Have long known it.
That's why I sit here.
I know your father, Jayanta of Udaipur, and your mother.
You were on the Field of the Dead,
You for sure are not the same one who went away,
Our jewel who kept us safe from slaughter by the enemy.
Then your eyes were not so big and wild.
Who now would want to gaze into them.
Those lips: how you thrust them out, how you smack them.
This moist entry to your mouth: worse than the Field of the Dead.'

'Go on.'

'It is enough already.
I can keep watching you, watch how you bloom,
You sleek monster, standing there.
I must look at you, for I am pious, and the Gods sent you here.
You don't know, d'you hear, what I have long

known,
You do not know extinction.
Do you know, you, you, what it is to be extinguished?
And what it is, the sea of birth and death?'
The holy man, the priest, coughed, had swallowed the wrong way,
Stood up.
Ash-smeared, he stepped down close to Manas,
Leaving the ancient book behind him on the stair.
'Revulsion and delusion, you hear me, revulsion and delusion, nothing else!
Repeat it after me! Wash your mouth out as you say it!
Extinction, you,' he pressed close to Manas,
'The world must be extinguished, we with it, you with it!
All must be extinguished, so that calm may come!
You do not know this, you with your beast-face.'
'No.'
'No. You rampage, and you know nothing.
You run around like a Shade, and do not know whose Shade you are.
And turn up here, you,
You feel your fat thighs, your beast-face,
Squeeze your plump cheeks, twirl your moustache.
Now it is thick and black.
Once you had none, and soon it will be grey, grey and bristly like a cat's.
Why do you stare at me? I am telling you the truth.
Clutch your loins, your genitals that give you so much pleasure.

Some time something else will spurt from them:
Bitterness revulsion misery,
Just what I feel when I see you.
Then everything turns bad. Then you gasp and groan.
But your belly brings you no more pleasure.
You are withering, Manas, as everything must wither,
People, animals, plants, all of it, all the stars and suns.
Better to be extinguished, to make an end.
For there must come an end, d'you see, Manas?
Perhaps you are human enough still to see it.
There comes a time to spit out this life of ours,
Like a rotten fruit, a mushroom that is poison to us.
A slug lies at our feet, decaying. We must kick it aside.
The decay is in your belly,
You understand me, hey? You understand?'

★★★

Sermon in the Forest

THREE times Las Casas sent envoys to the Motilones with presents. The envoys brought them back. Las Casas wept. He tipped the last of the envoys and shut himself away. But this envoy went back to the Motilones to report what he had seen. They debated a long while. The priest's distress unsettled them. They arranged a meeting.

Near Mahates, Las Casas climbed from the boat and up towards a plane tree where he could see a cluster of dark people wearing festive plumes, one group was armed. As he approached across the grass the spear-bearers made a sign.

Those escorting Las Casas explained: he is to take himself to the spot assigned him, within earshot of the group. When the priest heard this and saw the spearmen, he stood still. He sent one of his escort ahead to announce: he comes as a friend, unarmed, they can search the boat. They answered at once that he was welcome, it was their custom to arrange things so.

Slowly and sorrowfully, almost fifty paces from the natives, Las Casas lowered himself onto the grass at the spot they had marked with a broken branch. He prayed and asked help from God. Then he began to speak boldly. He asked if they were his enemies, had he harmed them or any of their tribe. – They denied this. – Then he asked why they had abandoned their old villages. – Because of the animals they hunt, they have moved away from the old places. – And why they no longer come to the lovely little church and let themselves and their children receive instruction. They are baptised, after all. – They replied: also because of the animals. When they and their children go to church, the hunting is poor.

Las Casas was hurt to hear this, he knew their dreadful superstitions. His eyesight was no longer keen, he strove to make out their faces. He recognised the two chiefs and their eldest sons, named them: "Have you been busy again with reeds and leaves, making mask costumes? Have you built another hut for your masks?"

They shook their heads, but he could not see their faces at that distance. He turned to one of his dark escorts and whispered: "What are they doing? Are they signing to one another?"

The man said: "They look calmly across to us, Father."

"They do not wrinkle their brows?" – "No, Father."

Las Casas tried again: "You know I am well disposed towards you. You have guided me for great distances, have spoken for me to your friends. I've often sat by your fires."

"You are still our friend. So we have come to greet you

and sit across from you. We rely on your friendship."

"Tell me in accordance with the truth, why you who have been baptised avoid my instruction and keep your children away."

"It is hard for us, Father Las Casas. We are poor people and have much to do, and we cannot send our children by themselves. It is our poverty, Father Casas."

"You were not nearly so poor before. Now you live in a bad area."

"We are not as clever as white people. We like to sit with you when you talk to us. We are not clever. Do not scold us for that."

"You have made no masks?" – "No, Father Las Casas."

He prayed quietly that it might be true. "Listen to me, my friends. You are Christians like me. There is no barrier between you and me. We are brothers. I beseech you, do not go into the forest. The Devil dwells there. You are my brothers, but your faith is a tender plant, and weak. You risk its destruction. You must strengthen it. I will keep you from temptation. Here I have several rosaries for you, they bestow great strength when you take them in your hand and speak the words I have taught you."

Las Casas stretched the hand with the bundle of rosaries out towards them. They whispered, then two young people came slowly over with spears, stopped a good way from him and one of them held out a spear: "Give." Las Casas, red with anger, berated them: "What? Are you not ashamed?" They stood there uncertain, glanced back at their people. The elder of the chiefs said: "We have experienced many bad things from the Whites, and we are afraid."

In anger Las Casas flourished the bundle: "These are holy chains."

"We know them, Father Las Casas. Be our friend still. Several of us and our children have them. When the rains come we'll sit in our huts and carve some more."

"You will carve idols."

"Father Las Casas, do not be angry. Be our friend still. Accept presents from us."

The two young warriors ran back and fetched a live graceful deer, a dwarf deer, pulled it along by a string, and one held a pretty parrot. The young men at once ran back to their people.

Las Casas stroked the creatures, his escorts held them: "I am greatly pleased. I see you love me still. But will you accord me one more gladness? Will you listen to me?"

"What would our friend Father Las Casas say to us?"

"Oh, but see how I must talk to you, you placed leaves here where I must sit and you sit over there, this is my misfortune. But I will admonish you and beseech you to the best of my ability. My dear friends, for whose salvation I would give my life, do not forget what you have learned from us."

"The white man should not weep. He knows we have learned much from him."

"When tribes first meet, they are ignorant of the other's language and their customs, and if they come from different parts of the world, discord easily arises. But the hour also comes when they understand one another. For we are of different skin colour but are all the same humanity, created by the one and only God, and the one and only Saviour appeared to us all."

"You speak clearly, Father Las Casas, and your words are honey to our ears. But why do you speak to us and not to your own people? We never encountered your people because we never sought them. Our ancestors and fathers lived here in peace."

"In Heaven dwells eternal God, who created Earth and Heaven and everything above and below, in six days. He has ordained all that shall pass. He separated light and darkness, set sun and moon in their place. He formed the grasses and herbs, trees and plants that bring nourishment, and fishes in the waters, and everything that creeps upon the earth, and the fowl of the air. He ordained that the sun shall revolve and there shall be day and then night when stars and moon shall shine. He directed rivers to rise and fall, drought and rain to follow one another so that every plant and animal finds sustenance. On the last day He delved in the earth and from the clay in His hand fashioned the figure of Man, in the likeness of Himself the great Creator, and when He saw the likeness He blew His own breath into him. Then He placed the man among the trees and plants, birds and creeping things, and gave to humans dominion over all that lives, even all plants and herbs. And this was the creation of the world.

"Then men grew wicked and heedless of His word. And then – He sent a great flood over the whole Earth, and all seas and rivers rose and the floodgates of Heaven opened....

[Las Casas relates the story of Noah.]

... Las Casas paused. He stroked the delicate deer, which nuzzled against him. Las Casas thought of the unfathomable ineradicable depravity of humankind and how he was now sitting among his friends.

The chief praised the white priest: "Truly you are a man of great knowledge. We rejoice that you remain our friend, for we would learn from you more that we do not yet understand."

The other chief: "All people are descended from the great father Noah, who travelled in a ship over the mountains?" – "Yes."

"Do the white people know this? Have you told this to them?"

"You ask something, but leave something unsaid."

"They do bad things to us, and you say to them that great father Noah is the common father of them and of us."

"I have not told you the end of my story, what happened

on the earth after they rode on the waters that drowned the wicked people. Once the waters receded people spread again across the earth, and many tribes and peoples arose. They dwelt under other skies, they were of different colours, they began to speak different tongues. They forgot their common father and almighty God, the one and only, who created them out of clay according to His own image and blew His breath into their nostrils. They no longer knew one another. And afflictions again grew great."

The chief: "You will tell us of this also." The little deer had settled calmly at Las Casas' feet, the brown people were pleased.

Las Casas raised his arms in their flowing Dominican sleeves: "I have still not reached the end. If this were the end, I would have to sit here before you and lament: see, my friends, it has come to this, the great destruction of the earth was to no avail, humanity failed the test, it again fell into iniquity. War, murder and hatred ruled. I would have to sit here before you, embrace this placid creature and beseech great God in Heaven: Lord, do with us as Thou wilt, we deserve nothing else! But it is not so. Now I shall bring my report to a conclusion. Great God in Heaven saw what we see. His ears were assailed by lamenting over the crimes of humanity, over their iniquity and wickedness. The poor also gained a voice from Him, He hears poor and rich, ruler and servant. And as the lamenting grew beyond all bounds, this time He did not send a punishment upon man. For it was He Himself who created him from clay. Instead, in His goodness He sent succour. He came down to a human virgin, whose name was Mary, and she conceived a son by Him. The son of God was called Jesus. He appeared on the Earth. God sent him to humans because He pitied them. Jesus lived among people in a distant land, long ago, in the form of a man. We know the words he spoke. He became the saviour and redeemer of people, of all people, of every tongue and every colour. The Whites and many dark peoples know of him. They rejoice in him. Now all can attain in Heaven the state of happiness and peace that they cannot attain on Earth. God has opened His own Heaven to those who believe in Him and his son."

For a long time no one spoke. Then the chiefs whispered among themselves, the elder thanked Las Casas for his report: "You are our friend, and we shall ask you later about those things we do not understand. But tell us, Father Las Casas, if it is no trouble to you: we would like to go to this heaven where peace and happiness are. Our old men speak of this place but do not agree on where it is. Tell us, where is this heaven of peace and happiness, and what paths must we follow or cut to reach there. Some of our tribes have sought in vain."

"Heaven lies above the clouds, beyond the sun, moon and stars. There sits the Creator of us all, the one mighty God. His son sits at His right hand, Mary and many angels are with Him. No road leads from Earth to there. God alone calls those to Him who die believing in Him, loving His son and obedient to His commandments. To these He shows the way, these only."

This seemed not to satisfy the dark men. The chief asked: "What are the commandments?"

"Not to kill, to be peaceable, to worship God, Jesus and the saints. Come to me as you were before. I shall tell you everything again."

But the dissatisfied expression on the faces of the people did not change. The chief sat up straight, his voice was very firm: "With these words, Father Las Casas, you yourself betray that God wants to know nothing of the Whites. We have discussed your words that you have repeated to us and came a long way to say to us. If you had travelled alone across the wide ocean, Father Las Casas, we would have welcomed you as a friend. You would have become our brother. We would have made you our leader and teacher. But you came with warriors. You know the bad things they do to us. They chase us from our huts and drive us into the mines. Preach to them, hinder their actions. But we have seen that you are powerless among them. They just take you along when they attack us. Father Las Casa, either you are playing a false game, or you are seeking help from us."

Las Casas pushed aside the little deer, which at once stood and ran around him. He was shocked: "You are my enemies?"

"We know you are honest. What help do you seek from us?"

"I want to advise you to be peaceable, leave the forest, attend the church and school that you built."

"They'll force us to do work we do not want to do. Will they release our brothers from the mines?"

"Everyone must work, and obey their superiors." – "We are not prisoners."

Las Casas sat slumped, he held a hand over his eyes and they saw that he was weeping. The elder chief spoke more gently: "Tell your Whites that they must release our people from the mines. Then come back." Las Casas nodded and remained sitting. The chief screwed up his eyes and spoke more softly, as if he were alone with Las Casas: "Perhaps our friend does not dare to speak out in front of these men. Perhaps he fears betrayal. None of our people will betray him. If you are afraid of your escorts, who are known to us, we shall seize them."

***

THEME 6. TRICKSTERS

The Music God's Temple (from *Wang Lun*)
The Decoy (from *Manas*)
Nadji the Tippler (from *The Babylonian Exile*)
Sao Paolo (from *The Land Without Death*)

★★★

The Music God's temple

HE recognized it by the thick sweet smell as a temple hall. In the round carved doorway an old sturdy man sat in a bright green robe with wide sleeves, queue tied neatly on his crown. He sat in front of a little table with incense sticks, paper figures, made an unctuous face by pushing his lips down to form a snout, placed his hands before him with fingers twisted in a peculiar way. The women had bought six sticks of incense from him, and set them up in front of a brightly coloured wooden statue, a seated god. Beside him on the bare wall stood drums, mandolins and panpipes.

Wang walked past the women's basket, saw from the corner of his eye as the bonze counted his few cash and made them vanish into a box on the wall by the door. This was a temple of Han Hsiang-tzu, patron of musicians.

As Wang turned to leave the bonze stood up, bowed, praised his exalted visitor's piety in a well sifted rhythmical flood of words. Wang too bowed politely. At last the bonze enquired whether the subscription list for a water Mass had yet found favour of admittance at the palace of his patron; five poor blind musicians had drowned as they returned from a village on the other side. Wang gave a false name and residence, offered to enter his name there and then on the list affixed to the wall.

Then in the dark he broke without effort into the temple,

got away with 700 cash.

He lived contentedly at the inn for more than a week, then chance brought him face to face with the bonze in bustling White Tombs Street. To his astonishment the bonze passed him by, grinning, with a wave of a hand.

That same night he broke again into the bonze's place. The money box was locked but empty. Wang felt his way to the offering table; under the ashes too there was nothing. Only when he pulled aside the soft cloth on the Eight Immortals table did something clink: under the cloth was a handful of copper coins.

When that money was spent he worked for a few days as coal hauler, yamen runner, but the paltry wages stung him to fury, and he could get along with no one; his swaggering nature, hot temper allied with a giant's strength impelled him everywhere to deeds of violence. So he broke again into the Music God's temple. He pondered where the bonze might have hidden the day's takings. Not in his bed or sleeping room, for sure he suspected Wang and would certainly fear for his life.

For an hour Wang felt about, tapped walls and floor. He set the bonze's stool on the altar table, tapped the mute statue. The god's throat rang hollow; he clambered onto the wooden thigh, reached for the moneybox. Three handfuls of cash slid into the pouch at his belt. But when he tried to climb down he felt something pulling at his queue. It was stuck to the ceiling and back wall. With a free hand he fumbled above and behind him. A thick tarry mass was daubed there. He freed his hand with difficulty, fearing he and the heavy statue would topple together. Painfully and with the loss of much hair he extracted his queue from the sticky ooze. Softly cursing the bonze he slipped away into the street.

The stuff stuck like resin to the shaven part of his head; his hand clung to whatever it touched. His friends at Unicorn

Street next morning scraped him painfully clean with sharp little sticks. He bled. No one laughed; they feared and loved him, wondered at his daring. Also, he had divided the spoils with them.

Now he had only one wish: to avenge himself on the bonze. The fellow seemed to know where he lodged: a few days later the grey robe strolled slowly down the street. The wrinkled face assumed an expression of pained sympathy for Wang's bandaged skull. The bonze kept turning to look at Wang, who made faces behind his back.

One afternoon, head still bandaged, he went to see the bonze, who was sitting solemnly as strangers viewed the temple. Recognising Wang as he swaggered in, he hurried across to thank Wang for his handsome donation, and enquired after his health. Frowning, he reported on the troubles afflicting the temple. Some cunning rogue was plundering the poor musician god and his humble servant T'o Chin – that was his name. After a pause Wang asked what precautions had the wise bonze taken against this criminal. The bonze then took him on a guided tour, pointing to man traps, and the smear of tar on the wall.

That night Wang paced outside the temple, afraid of exposing himself to the old joker's ridicule but unable to allow him a triumph. He considered waking the wily trickster, thrashing him, and giving himself up to the police. The he felt his way across the pitch black yard. He stopped by the outhouse in one corner, and there spotted a long ladder lying on the ground.

He pondered. One of T'o Chin's little games. There couldn't be any more hiding places in the temple itself. He tried jumping onto the outhouse roof, but couldn't reach and made too much noise. He hauled himself up by a damp post beside the outhouse, swung onto the roof. Fearing to stand, he crawled along and at every door slam and watchman's drum fell flat, at risk of sliding down the steep tiles. Roof rib after roof rib negotiated; then Wang let himself down to the warrior figure on the eaves, which held a shiny shield. Behind the shield something dangled: the purse. It took a tricky half hour to regain the street. He growled in anger at the old man's guile.

Just after lunch, as Wang was chewing tobacco on the terrace, the landlord hurried up to hand him a visiting card. T'o Chin enquired after his benefactor's health, evinced pleasure that his scabs were healing - life in Chinan-fu is so hard! When they had drunk their tea, Wang paid openly from the bonze's purse, and then accompanied him back to the temple to find out what the ladder business was all about. T'o leaned the ladder against the temple roof, climbed a few rungs. Wang, puzzled, climbed after him.

Wang knew: this game which he always won and lost would be resolved today.

At nightfall he crept angry and nervous into the yard, placed the ladder against the roof. A purse hung there again on the warrior's arm. He lay prone on the roof, uneasy; something seemed to be moving in the yard; once the ladder jogged. He climbed quickly down, without incident. But - he stood rooted at the foot of the ladder. He couldn't move. His felt shoes were embedded in thick slime that rose over his ankles. He worked his foot free by pulling himself up the ladder. Anger made him almost senseless. When he stood barefoot with gummy trousers in the yard, he hurled the purse at the door of the bonze's room. He yelled: "There's your money, you son of a turtle!" A soft voice came from within: "What do you want, my dear? What presents have you brought this son of a turtle in the middle of the night?"

"You'll pay for my shoes and trousers!"

"But the dear tempestuous man has already had the price of his shoes and trousers."

"You prattler, you swindler, I'll show you what I mean by

pay!" As Wang shivered in the yard, T'o Chin put a kettle on to boil. The cup of hot tea the host proffered with both hands Wang drank in two gulps, while T'o poured a strong smelling liquid onto a cloth and rubbed the pitch from Wang's legs.

In his conversations T'o Chin proved to be as good a reader of men's souls as he was a rogue. His defeated opponent waggled his head in wonder at such artfulness. T'o had caught himself a trusty collaborator.

★★★

The Decoy

IT was in a sweltering thicket, she lay wilting, not asleep, not awake.
Something grabbed her from behind, pulled her by the throat,
A human hand turned her to face the sun.
She stammered: 'Oh, I want nothing here,
I mean no harm. I'll be on my way.'
  'I believe it. But stay put.'
It was a blackbrown man, a steppeland man, his body naked.
He pulled her by the hands:
  'What are you looking for?'
'I am Savitri.'
  'And what are you up to here?'
'I'm not up to anything.'
    'Lazing about, not up to anything, and lurking around.'
'No, good man.'
    'Stand up now. Why won't you stand, are you so weak,
    Why don't you come to our huts?'

'I didn't see them.'
There in the scrub, huts of branches and brushwood,
Very low, some dug into the ground,
They were creeper-covered, all overgrown,
You really could not see them.
The man laughed: 'Oh, it's you,
The one they tell of, running about,
Looking for her sweetheart.'
'My husband.'
'Yes, I know, you idle loitering creature.
He should have beaten you more often,
Then you would have stayed at home.'
He grasped Savitri by the shoulder:
'Come off the path. You'll give us away,'
And pushed her on ahead, gagged her mouth when she tried to scream,
Pushed her into a dark hut.
'I shan't hurt you. So slim and fine. You'll help us.
We're poor people, we have no time for sweethearts.
We must look to it that us and the kids don't starve.
You'll stay and help us. Will you?'
'I don't know you. I've never seen you.
Why did you drag me in here?'
'Such burrows are all we have. Will you?'
'Don't be so rough with me, good man.'
'We are not good people.'
Urchins playing in the scrub around the huts
Fled when they saw Savitri,
Head over heels into the scrub, into burrows, disappeared.
The man's face did not change.

'Why are they hiding?'
    'They're afraid.'
'Not of me…?' – 'Of everyone.'
She lowered her head. She took the man's hand.
She did not look at him. 'I – shall stay.'
Sat in the scrub with men and women.
Her breathing calmed. She slept long and soundly.
They sent her to caravans, herdsmen, who had lost
  their way.
She had to behave like a native woman.
And when the slender lady came by singing, with
  her high-born grace,
They followed her gladly along paths through
  untamed scrub,
To where robbers lay in wait with slings and bows
To plunder them.
Savitri stood, went somewhat to the side when the
  screaming started,
Stood, one hand at her hip, the other slack,
Looked this way that way, felt no emotion,
Hauled spoils.
She had to go with other women around the villages
And sell the goods discreetly,
And look lively in darkness and by day, and never
  rest.

★★★

Nadji the Tippler

Conrad and his two companions, dismayed that Babylon is now a field of rubble and they've forgotten how to speak Ancient Babylonian, seek a language teacher. Defrauded once, they have high hopes of a new tutor …

THE new teacher, pointed out to George in his caravanserai, was a decayed drunken person of middle years and Turkish origin. He had no fixed abode, turned up every day to make himself useful to someone or other. He generally met with great distrust, but not to the extent of being thrown out. Such creatures were as much at home in the caravanserai as cockroaches. He wore a pair of coarse once-white wide trousers, and possessed a broom, a candlestick and two lengths of rope, occasionally also an axe with which he could help chop wood.

This man, Nadji by name, was to be Conrad's second Babylonian teacher. Certain confidants in the caravanserai assured George: Nadji's a failed teacher, at one time he taught in far-off Constantinople. His lamentable taste for drink and indifference to all external events has brought him, they said, to this rickety pass. George should lose no time engaging him. And he's stashed a pile of books from better times with his cousin Himmatyil, a tavern-keeper.

Conrad and George soon found themselves at Himmatyil's, along with their mute Syrian guide and Waldemar and the old grey nag. Never expecting to see such noble visitors in his dive, the host fussed about them all evening, cleared half the barroom of its crowd of rogues and layabouts, and they had to sample many varieties of his wines. He presented these remarkably cloudy concoctions, now yellow, now red, now hyacinth-blue, as wines from "Aleman", i.e. Germany, "Ingiliz", meaning English, "Moré", Greece. "Bozdja Ada" he praised a supposed Muscat, "Kata Khoriya" a marvel from Constantinople. The crowd around him, unemployed artisans, habitual topers, fishermen with willow baskets, contented itself with a specially cheap liquor, analogous to the meat left clinging to tendons in that it was made from grape residues and was called *bir shisha düz*. A big lamp hung from the ceiling, a Negro, a waiter and a candle-pourer sat at a side table where a feeble light burned, each had a glass in front of him, and because they weren't allowed to bellow just now were playing an exciting game with an apple. Each held a short knife, one threw the apple with his left hand, and each tried to catch it on his knife and in one stroke split it in two.

Out on the stone terrace, the greater part of the clientele had piled around the trio trying to find out who they were, and because these bravos could make no headway with the dumb Syrian they attached themselves to Waldemar and his nag. First they tried to extract money from Waldemar. Then they set about ascertaining his disposition, or at least that of his nag. "What do they call you," one asked the nag. It kept silent. "You see, she doesn't answer," said another, "she doesn't know your language. Come, horsey, tell us your name. Tupsus? No. Hedy Agam? No. She's not called Tupsus or Hedy Agam. So what might our little nag be called? Has she confided her name to you, stranger?"

Waldemar explained that he had named her Elsa. They all burst out laughing, and offered the old man ironic congratulations. They made circuitous friendly overtures. Waldemar, they all agreed, had taken the easy way out: see a horse and give it a name. "But where did you get the name from? Every animal wants its proper name. Or we could call you Knapsack, or Piglet!" So they continued to examine the nag, and it came to an end only when one stepped up to her and asked: "Is your name Okkalyk?" meaning Litre-guzzler, and breathed up at her from liquor-smelling jaws. Whereupon the nag threw her head high, they took this for a yes, and amid general enthusiasm christened her Okkalyk with the dregs from their cups of wine and liquor. The owner protested, for his little nag couldn't stand even a dram of liquor. They laughed: "She says otherwise. She should know."

And then, knowing now who they were dealing with, they went into a huddle to discuss how to separate the little nag from her owner. For they reasoned that he didn't feed her properly, and maltreated her.

Inside the barroom, meanwhile, the poor devil had turned up, the Turkish sage, who wrapped his baldness in a huge turban and hobbled in on bandy legs. The legs, he explained, had gone crooked while he was still a youth, a schoolboy in Stamboul, for he'd had an insatiable appetite to devour the wisdom of the Koran, to become a *hafiz*, guardian of the doctrine, and his tender legs weren't up to the task. The hairs on his head had fallen out early, deprived of the nutrition sucked away by his brain. But then sorrow for a lost love brought liquor into his life. For while love is an elegant little plant, love denied is a knotty oak tree. Grief for a lost love suppressed all the knowledge in him. Then came wine and liquor, and proof of the proverb: wine turns a man into a flea-market, and whatever a man has in him he lets out into the daylight.

The host did not lead Nadji at once to the parlour where he had accommodated the honoured guests, but first sat with him at the counter and did what he could to make him aware of the situation. "They want you to instruct them, Nadji." – "I know."

"You will take no more drink, Nadji." – "I know."

"I shall give you these anchovies, to sober you up." Nadji eyed them with a worried look, swallowed some down.

"Now stay by my side, Nadji. I've cleared out my room so you can teach in it. You will show me, honestly, what knowledge you have in you to impart, and we shall make an honest division, for you still owe me lots and will still owe a lot."

"As God wills."

"They can drink as they learn, as much as they want, for it eases the uptake of wisdom, but you must remain sober, Nadji. Do you understand?" – "Yes."

"Otherwise they will soon stay away and I shan't let you

in here any more." The host now tried to nudge Nadji into the room, but still he sat miserably and was an obstinate mule. The host could say what he liked, he always answered, "Yes, for sure," and just sat there. At last he lifted up his tearstained face: "How am I to speak and instruct such critical noble persons, when my old grief has returned and a band of iron has wrapped itself around my breast? I won't be able to say a word."

"You will. Pull yourself together."

"Do you know what *halym* is, host? The illumination of the heart. We have a human heart. And when we grow old it beats sluggishly. It is no longer wood, but stone. My heart doesn't want to burn. I am without illumination."

"Then you are no sage, Nadji. Then you are a fraud and know nothing."

"I know everything, more than anyone here and in all Baghdad. But the well is plugged. Take tongs, remove the plug, and the well shall flow again. Give me *halym*, host, and I shall speak." So there was nothing left but to dress the anchovies with a little light wine, which dried Nadji's tears. Nadji smiled again, and stood on bandy legs.

"Oh God," said the host as he led him along, "into what puddles does your light fall." In they went.

★★★

Sao Paolo

THE captain declared that this was the smoothest, most pleasant passage he had ever experienced. And the crew, after loading the copious baggage of the clerical gentlemen into boats, was of one mind: it's a shame such people have to take themselves off into the wilderness, they must have got wind of something there for the taking, such people don't cross the seas for nothing and again nothing.

First of all there was a bay, lovely and wide, a good anchorage, and favourable for the pursuit of every peaceful trade. Then they traversed a hot, wide sandy beach; to the left was evidently a swamp, they could see a patch of water, the whole place smelled bad, and to the right another broad arm of water stretched away, doubtless an indentation of the sea. Beyond stood a few huts, called Santos after Santo Andres de Pira, but it was no great hamlet. They eyed the huts gloomily, and learned that some people fished from there.

When they had trudged across the sand for a considerable time they came towards hills, and on these, overlooking the sea, Piratininga was said to lie. The pious Fathers had been ferried from the ship in boats, bombarded along the way with lively chatter in Spanish and Portuguese about the beauties of the landscape and the splendid opportunities for trade, as the locals tried to find out who they were and what they intended. The padres were pleased to find such helpful people, and confessed that so tumultuous a welcome was quite unexpected. The huge quantities of baggage, all carefully packed, were shifted cheerfully. The settlers, as chatty and curious as children, wanted to know what was in it all. The Fathers smiled: "Playthings, and food." They would overcome the world through play. This made the settlers even more lively. They strode ahead of the patriarchs. The Jesuit invasion rolled along in a great column from the ship across the beach to the hills rising on the right. Others too had come from the ship, they peered around inquisitively and were regarded less amiably by the settlers. No one carried *their* luggage. The settlers, clearly a most pious community, all gathered about the gentle Fathers.

And now, after much wiping of brows, here is Piratininga, consisting of a great many miserable huts, little houses and lanes, as well as hints of a church on a wide empty area that might one day grow to a plaza. The sturdy ragged crew guiding the Fathers smile: "We've left space for everything." They won't take them right away around the whole settlement, it's very extensive and there are many branchings and buddings, it stretches a long way, it'll be a new Cadiz. This the Fathers were able to confirm that day and the next.

Despite all the jollity, the walk had been strenuous. They rested and enjoyed the rather damp floor underfoot and the hut roof that leaked rain.

The first notable news that reached them during these days concerned their baggage. It was, quite understandably given their goal, very considerable and had made up almost the entire contents of the ship's hold. Some part of the baggage had, regrettably, disappeared. Two Fathers had been entrusted with supervision of the transport, its unloading, loading and storage. The Fathers reported anxiously: according to their inventory, more than half the cargo was missing. Half must still be on the ship. At this the Fathers rushed down the sweat-inducing path, threw themselves, accompanied by several settlers, into boats and rowed across to the ship still anchored there. The captain, along with the entire crew, welcomed them with reverence and joy, the wonderful voyage still in their thoughts. He was not a little astonished to learn the reason for the unexpected visit. The ship had been emptied completely, the captain declared, like a cork it floated a yard higher in the water after the unloading, and to convince the gentlemen he led them down into the hold, where it was very dark and many tarpaulins and sails and spare masts lay. Lights were shone here, shone there, showed up this corner, that corner, there were rats, but the Fathers had no use for these.

Back on deck they discussed what could have happened. The captain said: the first thing that comes to mind is that the inventory is wrong. Who drew up the inventory? But it was made by the two Fathers in person. Had they seen everything themselves, marked it all with a cross, been on the spot when it was loaded aboard ship? He showed them in his ledger how he did it. The padres said yes, they did it just the same way, but more legibly. The captain treated the matter from a humorous angle: he placed the entire ship at their disposal for another search, they can turn it upside down if they have levers and winches with them, and knock on the bottom to see if anything falls out. Well, what was going on? It was one of those mysteries of the sea, the padres were men of the world, but clearly not so much so as they ought to be in a seaport, dealing with sailors and stevedores. At this the padres looked sulkily down at their black robes. The captain advised them to take refuge in prayer. They thanked the pious man. There was nothing they could do but leave this ship that had grown so dear to them, this witness to so many pleasures, and erase the bad impression their enquiries must have made.

Outside they noticed that the ship was even now being reloaded, numerous boats were moving between ship and shore, the Fathers now realized what other purpose was served by the supposed fishing place of Santos: big canvas marquees had been erected and a kind of giant shack improvised, they looked across with interest, the rowers said this always happened when a ship was about to depart, people even stored goods here pending the arrival of a ship. Despite the Fathers' great interest in this mighty commerce, they rowed vigorously around to the other side of the ship, for they mustn't become entangled with all the boats, also a man stood on the beach openly signalling with a white cloth, pointing to the west.

Empty-handed, their prayers unanswered, the Fathers climbed back up. They rode on mules. Along the way they passed an unending stream of merchandise heading down. A merry life. What a shame, thought the Fathers, that such an aggravating circumstance prevents us from joining in the general merriment. Suddenly they noticed that several chests closely resembled those that had gone missing. They commented to one another, pointed, one of the mule-drivers let fly a contemptuous remark: "There's lots of stealing here! You can nail something down and it'll be stolen away, nails and all!" Another driver shouted: "Don't tell tales! That stuff going down comes from the big storesheds, it belongs to Senhor Johann Conquisto, a very rich man." The padres repeated uneasily that the chests did indeed greatly resemble theirs, they really should stop. The mule-drivers all laughed: "Chests are chests." The padres wanted to dismount but were embarrassed, you had to be careful among new people. Before they could come to a decision, thanks to the fleet-footed beasts and the unusually energetic yelling of the two drivers they were already at the top. And at once they took their dark suspicions to the Superior. They debated back and forth. The Superior praised them for guarding their thoughts and not making the terrain, already tricky on its own account, even more dangerous for them. During this conversation one of the two Fathers was seized by an unruly notion, he excused himself and slipped away without explanation. After a considerable time he came back, red in the face, inventory in hand, under the Superior's gaze he compared the list of goods still there with the earlier list. More chests were missing.

"What a climate," smiled the imperturbable Superior, "disappearances on a tropical scale." Without betraying any hint to those around them, they quickly checked all the items. It was indisputable that other goods than those of the Fathers had been stored in the sheds, it was not entirely to be ruled out that theirs might have been carried away in error. The Superior voiced this conjecture, with all circumspection, to the chief supervisor of the storeshed, whose presence they requested. He declared himself ready to check the whole of the consignment for the ship. Father Emanuel sighed with relief and thanked him. He asked that this be effected without delay, for clearly mistakes had already been made, and since huge quantities were involved, more than half a ship's hold, it should not be too difficult to ascertain the truth.

The chief supervisor hoped they would not form a bad impression of Piratininga right away. That lot down in Santos are a useless bunch, but Piratininga is a real place, here you must dare to tackle things head on, he'd already had a dagger at his throat. And he would have regaled them at greater length with cases older and more recent, but Father Emanuel assured him that they believed him, that it was precisely Piratininga's reality that had led the pious troop of Jesuits to this place, and once again would he go with them down to the shore and check the loading of the ship. But as was inevitable with such a phlegmatic temperament as the chief supervisor's, upon hearing these words from the padres he burst out at once in a stream of delighted exclamations touching on their trust in him, and could not praise enough the Fathers' understanding of people and the world, so different from those other men of the Church he had encountered along the coast.

Father Emanuel grew insistent, his two companions exchanged anxious glances. And then at last the inspector, a very slow comfortable man, immersed deep in his memories, gathered himself to leave the storeshed and go to his room nearby to fetch a leather jerkin and leather boots for the journey. He had so much in his heart, the Jesuits had such an effect on him, they deserved such trust, he was so happy to have someone in whom he could confide his view that the only thing lacking in Piratininga up to now was the Fathers, the Jesuit Fathers, only them.

And while the Fathers listened to all this, looking now towards the sea and now back into the room, they noticed that their ship, their dear ship, was moving. Their dear ship had hoisted all sail and was leaving harbour under a stiff breeze!

Now the chief supervisor appeared, booted and spurred,

came over to the visitors and bellowed a frightful roar: "The robbers, they're evading our inspection! They seek the open sea. Hah, just let them come back." Gazing blankly ahead he sat on a basket, sucked at his pipe, seemed to become annoyed with his heavy boots, flung them aside, took off his jerkin. The clerics were frightened, his anger seemed directed at them, they were happy to make it with skin intact past the fellow sitting there with a huge straw hat jammed on his head, feet bare, swinging a stick. Slowly, as Indian children ran around whooping and the wind sang, they made their way to the little house.

As they sat together that evening, the Superior moved hesitantly from one to the other, gazed at them, his brethren, gave each his hand: "I am glad that you at least are still here. It's possible one of us might disappear in just such a puzzling fashion."

Once when a couple of Fathers went down to the beach at Santos, they fell into conversation with some Piratiningans loitering there by their sailing boats. "They treated you badly up there when you arrived," said one, tipping his hat. The others showed interest. "That was a scandal. Weren't you furious?" It seemed they were on well-tilled soil. "The way those people behaved makes a man ashamed of his town. The governor knew what was going on, but he didn't interfere because they bribed him."

One of the Paolistas, a silent man who played with his big black beard and had a way of letting flies settle peacefully on his arm or hand and then squashing them, this man said: "That wasn't the worst. The worst would have been something else. But it never came to that." Asked by the Fathers what he meant by this enigmatic remark, he looked around the circle of his people, and once he had their general assent he sighed. "If I hadn't been there, the dear Fathers would not be standing chatting with us today." "What, what?" exclaimed the dear startled Fathers. A snigger ran along the line, the sun climbed higher, the terrible swampy stench grew stronger, they retreated under a sail awning. Blackbeard spoke in a penitent tone:

"From the very start you were to have gone back on board, all and sundry, where you'd had such a good time anyway. And then," Blackbeard laughed, the others knew already, they all laughed, even the discomfited Fathers laughed, they knew not why, "and then, it would be a case of 'whatever the case may be'. That was the word we were supposed to bring to the captain. Either he should take you back to Spain, Cadiz or Malaga, wherever you came from, or he should set you down in some harbour or on some island along the coast. You were supposed to find out what it's like for thirty men to sit somewhere in the jungle, if you just pray all the time like you do here. Some told the captain he should just sell you."

"Not possible," countered the horrified Fathers.

"No, not possible," said Blackbeard with a friendly nod, "for who'd he sell you to? Whites? What good are priests to them? Who'd buy a priest? To savages? Maybe. Wouldn't have been a bad idea. But how to round up any who have gold to give."

The three priests stood there in shock. One of the group added: "The captain was taking a consignment for Coro, he had no stomach for mixing up Whites and Indians."

"It'd be too hard here," confirmed a third. "In the Mediterranean, from Genoa across to Africa, it might be done. You can mix Whites and Blacks together there."

Blackbeard nodded sagely: "Yes, over there. But you have to be in the Med first." In the grave silence that this wise commercial consideration demanded, the priests turned to go. The mariners one by one extended an honest hand to them: "Don't worry. We'd never meddle with clever people like you."

One of the Fathers was able to pull himself together enough to ask Blackbeard, who was seated again on a barrel squashing flies in his malicious way: "Tell me, are we really making your lives difficult?"

This was acknowledged with not so much as a look.

★★★

THEME 7. AILMENTS

Shaman (from *Wang Lun)*
In the Grotto (from *Wallenstein*)
Degenerating (from *Mountains Oceans Giants*)
Oyampi Cure (from *The Land without Death*)
Chief Medical Officer (from *Citizens & Soldiers*)

***

Shaman

THE greatest event in the life of Wang Lun's father was the journey he made to his brother's house three hundred li from Hunkangts'un. For three weeks he didn't see the beach or the scrubby beanfields. A barber who was also a sorcerer on the side lived in his brother's house. Wang Shen sat with him in the evenings.

And the morning after his return he walked with slow steps to a man who knew something of woodworking, and promised him a quantity of dried sandworms worth 450 cash if he would carve a tall red plaque with the inscription:

WANG SHEN
PUPIL OF THE RENOWNED SORCERER
KWAI TAI OF LIU CHIA TS'UN
MASTER OF WIND AND WATER

At nightfall, six days later, he fetched the gleaming plaque – black characters on a raspberry-red ground, blue-edged – with his eldest son, climbed onto the roof of the house, with two ropes taken from his boat attached it to the projecting ridge beam while his wife slept, so that the plaque hung down over the doorway.

Next morning his wife, seeing the splendid plaque, suffered the first recurrence for years of her nervous attack. Back then, when one of the bandits had demanded through the window if others were in the house, in her terror she had concealed her two little boys in the folds of her wide trousers, and as she replied "No" had jerked her head sharply to the right. Now something green surged through her head, the ropes holding the plaque grew broad as leaves, sawed between her eyes; a blue unjointed arm reached out intermittently, a hand sent fingers streaming towards her. Rhythmically the woman threw her head left right, right left, her legs knocked together, she danced like a figure in a puppet show; the children hid from her on the brick bed. And they screamed out loud and ran into the village street among yapping little dogs when Wang, the great elephant-legged clod, burst into the smoky room from the yard, stomped up and down with a tiger mask on, sang wheezily over his prostrate wife, stroked, whispered. In half an hour the woman was asleep. A crowd of children and women stood silently at the door, in the yard, scattered gabbling when the tiger mask came near.

★★★

In the Grotto

ONE afternoon the dwarf was escorted to the Grotto Courtyard of the Residence. The old longbearded ivory carver Angermaier was just leaving, his face gloomy; behind him two assistants carried out a whole ivory-inlaid table. Among opened boxes and tapestries in the middle of the flower-bright yard was extravagant blackhaired Hans van der Biest, painter, to whom Maximilian was not listening. Beside the Prince-elector, seated by the rim of the fountain dressed in tight Spanish clothes, young counsellor Küttner stood leaning face-twitching on his silver cavalryman's sword.

"I must find something to disgust me," Maximilian played with his knife; at a gesture of Küttner's hand the painter stepped back with a stiff bow. "Küttner, the doctor told me I must feel revulsion. That would be of the speediest benefit to me."

"I know, Serenity. The Fool is here."

"Begin," Maximilian hissed.

"What am I s'posed to do?" the dwarf cried as he was pushed forward. He was pale.

"Begin, varlet." – "And do what?"

"Will you begin, rascal!"

"Why the curses, rascal, rogue, varlet? Open your own mouth, say what you want."

Maximilian wearily turned his head, softly: "Talk to him, Küttner, keep it short."

Küttner, a young man of Gallic elegance, proud, went blade in hand right up to the nostril-flaring dwarf, whispered: "Perform your tricks, dog. You know why you're here."

"Dog? And why it's here? For the food, you dolled-up Frenchie."

"You, you're the Fool, don't you know what you're supposed to do." Küttner brandished his blade in anger, he came from Paris, had spent little time at court, had no idea what tricks the Fool played.

The Prince fixed both with an embittered stare, so apathetic he was in no condition to speak. "Begin, get on with it!"

With stately gait on tall red stilts, a tame stork approached from the terrace, now and then stabbed its beak into the boggy ground. It followed the watercourse leading back to the spring. In impotent rage Küttner began to assail the dwarf with the flat of his sword. Maximilian observed the scene, fists clenched. The outraged dwarf leaped about under the rain of blows. "Eat. He must guzzle," cried Maximilian.

The dwarf ran free, howling. "What must I eat? What

must I eat? Stop killing me!" Before Maximilian's hard gaze, amid spraying grit from Küttner's ill-aimed blows, he flung himself howling, arms outstretched in despair, onto the sandy bank by the spring. And now with ponderous grave steps the long-legged big-beaked bird approached.

When the dwarf heard it he pulled himself together. In deathly fear he rose to his feet, and now flung himself at the stork. He was no taller than the bird's legs. He fumbled with his arms towards the creature's breast, it retreated cawing and flapping its wings, shook itself, and flew at the little man. Again and again the beak flailed down on the dwarf; defenceless, he took a direct hit just under the chin. His cap was torn, his knees bent, otherwise he seemed not to notice. His gaze was fixed on the great bird's feathered breast, he was already hanging by both arms around the long neck that twisted and turned, tried to shake him off. His feet scrabbled, the strong creature stood a moment cawing cawing, and then fell forward. The Fool coiled about the stork in the sand. His face was buried in the screeching creature's breast, its cries were almost human. He spat feathers, chewed gnawed at the tough skin, the convulsively twitching flesh; his own blood flowed; he licked and slurped at the bird's blood. And now, wits still addled from the sword-blows, he forgot who it was behind him, who it was leaning forward in his chair watching him with a long startled face. He began to work his jaws, and at first reluctantly, then with a wild abandon began to eat, to annihilate, destroy the frantic screeching creature. The stork, lying on its side, stretching its neck and kicking out like a fallen horse, tried to stand. The munching dwarf's heavy weight held it down.

As the bird emitted a shrill penetrating trumpet-cry, the Prince desired Küttner, who was squinting on at the side playing with his sword, to pull the dwarf away. Küttner bent, grabbed the dwarf's back. The dwarf clung doggedly on. As Küttner dragged at the bird, the dwarf loosened his arms from the bird's neck, but in a ghastly manner his face hung like a growth in the sticky red mess that was the bird's breast. Blood dripped and spattered bright red all around on the ground. With an oath the cavalier clamped the sword between his knees; the dwarf's passionate chewing grunting slurping gulping could clearly be heard as his arms sought again to dangle from the bird's neck. The stork held its neck upright over him, dreadful blows with the beak rained down lightning-fast on the murderer's calves and back, mingled with horrible piercing screams. Küttner set to, grabbed the man's legs, a tug, he swung the dwarf around, dumped him heavily among flowers. The bird staggered, cawed, stood a moment, blood dripping, then flapped its wings, turned, stumbled quickly away. The dwarf's horribly smeared head emerged from the flowerbed; howls of rage, tears.

The Prince lunged past, took up Küttner's sword, turned vomiting back to the flowerbed, plunged the blade straight down through the struggling dwarf's right thigh, fixing him to the ground.

In the art gallery in front of a sumptuous carved chest – club-swinging centaurs in relief vainly assailing a gentle group of humans, Righteousness Wisdom Strength Moderation – the Prince and Küttner stood half-shadowed by a pillar. Maximilian told him to retrieve his sword; the dwarf was still loudly complaining. When Küttner returned with the bloody blade, the Prince was sitting by a window. They listened as the laments faded into the distance. In the silence Maximilian, on the chest, shook himself: "My doctor should howl like that."

★★★

Degenerating

"WHAT are these spirits? Neither living nor dead! Ghosts of beings like us, were born but never flourished." And they pointed to the lanky wasted arms of their believers, their weak muscles. How hair fell out a few years after puberty, a time of violent overheated lust when they were on fire; and after a few years they could no longer reproduce. How women melt into their fat and can hardly give birth. People flicker for thirty years, then die. These are their spirits, the ghosts of parents grandparents siblings, pressing and thronging and filling the cities, they can't come free from the walls towers streets, just as they couldn't come free while they lived. They fly to trees, to ponds and lakes. But always the towns bring forth more.

Such words shook the towns. Fed the fears of everyone who lived languished sickened in the towns. People wept. Decades earlier some individuals had wept, now whole towns whimpered laments. They saw themselves dying, rotting away. Their lives shortened, bodies decaying. At the age of twenty, teeth could be pulled painlessly from the jaws between two fingers. People never grew as big as their ancestors. Only the head everywhere was a great swelling; the brows of later generations were prominent, deepset eyes below. In some regions people grew unnaturally tall, their bones two yards long, thin smooth muscles pasted onto them. They walked slowly, the heart was too small; these types fell apart at an early age.

People who survived to twenty stored up inordinate amounts of fat. In the western townzones there were people with big bony heads, throat wobbling between plump jowls, but on their arms and legs fat hung literally in blobs and bags that swelled over fingers and toes, made walking grasping laborious. The fat grew over some like a malignant parasite, grew from top to toe: neck and chest remained narrow, the head above gazed out amiable and helpless. From the chest down they began to swell, rolls of fat thickening; the body expanded to three times the width of the chest, not swaying when it moved, the mass solid and steady. Legs and feet were wrapped like bulging parcels. People stomped about in them, groaned stared like pyramids of flesh. Depending on the race they filled out or stayed thin, grew tall; descendants of Negroes fattened quickest. In some regions a few grew up with knobby swellings and knots at their joints, like plants. Slender delicate limbs flexed from huge round hinges, trembled. Thick knobby elbows, tiny finger-joints knees bones of feet and hands. These could move fast, had the strongest muscles, but they quickly faltered weakened ossified. Everyone felt it must come from the sweet peculiarly rich food that they were given, that their parents and grandparents had demanded; from inactivity, lounging in weatherproof houses, covered plazas and streets. But it was like a runaway horse, no one could stop it.

The sorcerers were besieged by weeping people, victims of paralysing ailments that no one could name or cure. The lame were legion. Arms and legs grew limp, eyelids couldn't open, in the end they gurgled, had to be fed by others. They couldn't feel the food in their mouth, swallowed, choked. There were no doctors for these people. Doctors belonged to senatorial circles, kept silent. The sick the wretched listened entranced to the mysteries of the shamans. Long queues flew or drove to the hills where the little temples stood. They gathered like winter birds around a feeder. Showed their arms and legs. Their bodies and expressions were horrible under the harsh light of day. Many died at these gatherings. Many refused to be carried back. The sorcerers had to summon nearby Settlers to build huts for the desperate people. Some recovered. When people from the heated artificial towns climbed here and looked around at fields and little hills, their misery was great. Angry soft fist-shaking complaints were uttered hissed swallowed back.

***

Oyampi Cure

AS they linger a long while near a plantation that they assume belongs to bush Negroes, they are observed by Indians. They had come already to the Tumuc-Humac hills, the high peak they could see was Timotaken. The Oyampi wanted first of all to know what kind of people these were, and if others were following. So for several days they allowed Largi to gather maize from a field without interfering. But when the convicts started pulling themselves together for a march into the hills, where the village of Hocco lay, the Pirai people sent word to the people of Hocco. Largi's loud singing seemed threatening. People from Hocco blocked the forest path up into the hills, people from Pirai surrounded the climbers. Poor Largi tried to shoot, he took aim, his precious rifle must do its job now, the others flourished their bows and arrows that were good only for shooting fish and birds. But the powder was damp. Largi was hit by a spear, lay there, blood streaming from his mouth. Since he couldn't speak he encouraged them by hand movements to defend themselves, shook an angry fist at the assailants, and died.

The other five were taken to Pirai: the mad Chaplain who walked bent like an old man and talked to the ground; the blind Annamite, hands tied behind his back – now the strongest of them, he'd defended himself; the stocky Negro Mustafa who wept and whimpered, not for himself but because his friend Largi had been left behind, he was towed by a rope around his waist because he kept trying to pull away; the two white men, Vivien with his swollen forehead and nose, seeming blind, and the young soldier Perros, shrivelled to a skeleton, stumbling behind Vivien, clinging tight around his neck. All five wore ragged breechcloths, the Chaplain still had a torn shirt, howling Mustafa still displayed the blue-red officer's tattoos on his scrawny black body, scratched and bleeding. On one arm the mad Chaplain had 'Fear not the judgment seat' and on the other, 'Sorry Cecilia, amen' with a snake underneath.

The path led down for a stretch. They went very slowly, Vivien and Perros often had to lie down, the warriors dared not grab at them. At last they were in the valley, a little shining river meandered through it. They went through tilled fields, the convicts looked around, they were among people. They weren't taken into the village. The sorcerer appeared at the old shacks outside the village, looked at the men, a chief and several warriors kept their distance. Mustafa and the blind Annamite sat bound in one shack, the three Whites in another. They were given manioc mash, bananas, and a great deal of thin beer. The young soldier died the first night. Dark men came in the morning, drawn by the Chaplain's loud prayers and singing, peered into the shack. Soon others appeared, dug a hole behind the shacks, laid the dead young soldier in and filled it. Vivien and the Chaplain sat through the afternoon in the shade near the grave, the Chaplain grew calmer.

That night, when the light of the fire between the shacks and the village died down, Mustafa and the Annamite broke free. They didn't go far. They were confronted on Tacapatere hill by one of the Cussari tribes. Although both were unarmed and the Cussari were merely checking them out, they barricaded themselves in a thicket. When the Indians signalled to them to come out they refused. Mustafa fell after the Annamite.

In the first days the Chaplain became very quiet and lucid. When not sitting silently by Perros' grave, he occupied himself with Vivien, who squatted moaning in the rear of the shack. Both sported wild beards. The dark people had sent out into neighbouring villages to find someone who knew the language of the Whites. Every two days the sorcerer grabbed Vivien by the hand and pulled him out of the shack, clappered around him and blew smoke. It was no use. Vivien pointed to his head. His face was now so swollen he was unable to open his eyes.

Then several people appeared with the witch doctor, and the Chaplain grew fearful when he saw their preparations. Vivien lay quite passive. When all the procedures had been completed, the sorcerer lit the kindling that had been piled outside the shacks, kicked aside a few embers and threw down a handful of leaves from a sack carried by a child. Then he made a sign, and forced Vivien to lie on a plank that had been placed over the embers. He was reluctant. And the Chaplain said he shouldn't. Finally the sorcerer, a strong man, seized him, flung him onto the plank and held him down. Vivien had to breathe acrid smoke. He lost consciousness, but did not die.

He awoke with a terrible cough. He was still stretched over the fire, the dark man's fist pressing on his neck. Fly larvae were swarming from his nose. He spat more out. His head rang. He could see better. He turned his head to the side. When the sorcerer felt the movement he let go, helped him sit up. He pointed at the larvae. The dark people went away. Vivien stumbled by himself into the shack. The Chaplain sat outside, face hidden in his hands.

By evening Vivien felt better. He ate and drank. The Indians didn't bother them.

★★★

Chief Medical Officer

Shortly before the evacuation from Alsace, the CMO of the military hospital has a painful corn removed. A few days into their long train journey back into Germany, fatal sequelae appear.

THE Chief Medical Officer's condition pursued its course. The red flush in the left leg had spread above the knee, poultices were applied every day, salves were tried one day but they couldn't identify the right one. They painted iodine along the edges and placed a thin adhesive bandage over it, this was meant to hold back the redness, it seemed to work, but suddenly it sent feelers out under the dressing, and advanced. "We'll soon be on top of it," the doctor in charge said soothingly, "we'll isolate the breakaways," and again he set to with his magical iodine painting and with the help of the Chief's wife wound a pink adhesive bandage around the whole thing. His temperature went up and down. When it went up they said scientifically: "Just as we expected;" when it went down they were pleased: "You see?" And the good Chief, whose body was now so much under their administration, beamed contentedly from on high at both the ups and the downs.

He was always in good spirits. He said his heart had never been so robust. He enjoyed lying down, having a thorough rest, you can only do so when you're ill. In the afternoons (but he never mentioned this) the dreams were wonderful; he soon realised they were linked to the fever. He strongly resisted attempts by the doctor in charge to give him an antipyretic: "It weakens the body, it weakens one's resistance," he declared; "I want to know my body. You surgeons don't pay attention to that. Keep your poisons away from me." They were able to agree on one point raised by the patient: "The antipyretic messes up the chart." That made sense to the doctor, and the Chief could resume his rest and his extraordinary dreams.

Already more than eight days had passed since the revolution broke out. On the very same day something disquieting happened in the Chief's compartment. As lunch things were being collected at a little station where once again they had come to a stop, and everything that could walk was promenading alongside the train, asking for news, besieging the station master to know how they would be proceeding, how long it would still last. At this stop even the Chief's wife had left the compartment and was chatting farther back with Lieutenant Maus, who had stuck his head out of the window. As she stood there several people came running, calling for her. She ran back in shock, Maus too climbed down. Up ahead a little disturbance had developed. The sick Chief was trying to descend the steps from his compartment in his nightshirt, people had noticed him at once, he chatted with the soldiers amiably but incoherently, they took hold of him and manoeuvred him back with little difficulty. He was already smiling again at his wife from his bed; his bandages lay on the floor. The doctor in charge soon came along. The patient was cold, shivering. Towards evening his face was grey-white, there was an obvious change, the eyes looked out as calm as ever, but they were sunken, the skin around them yellow.

The Chief lay now in the corridor car, where special cases were being looked after. The doctor in charge drew the Chief's wife into the corridor. They looked at one another under the light bulb, the doctor rubbed the leather lining of his cap: "We shall be in Würzburg in an hour. I can no longer take responsibility. There must be blood tests, doses of serum, we have nothing here."

"You want to unload him in Würzburg," she said, her eyes indignant. "I don't know a single soul there."

"It's Germany, dear lady. The doctors are the same, Würzburg is a big city." She was almost in a rage. "Why didn't you bring any serum along. You told us you had everything you need."

He calmly placed the cap back on his head, his hand on the door handle. "I don't know what kind of serum, it can only be ascertained after a blood test."

She at his side, anxious, imploring: "So … it's blood poisoning?" He, shrugging: "That cannot be excluded."

"From corns, from a corn?" She pouted, wept bitterly

protesting like a child, both hands clung to the window frame; the train was travelling unusually fast, and swaying.

In Würzburg at the goods yard there was enormous activity. Already on the way in they could see red flags in the city. All the doors of the train opened, it was late afternoon, the conductor announced that they would be here for the night and maybe tomorrow morning too; in fifteen minutes they'd be shunted to another track, so no one should leave the train. They peered out of the windows. Ambulance men with a stretcher went along the train, looking for something. Jeers from some windows: "Not us, we're off to see mummy!" But towards the rear they saw the men stop, another one's croaked, they jumped down to see who it was. A lady alighted, it was the Chief Medical Officer's wife, yes, the old man, he must live in the area, then the ambulance men carefully lifted the stretcher off the train, they've covered his face, he's dead already, the doctor in charge followed slowly behind the stretcher as it was carried all the way down the platform and across the tracks. The old Chief! He lives here, no, they say he was poorly, his heart. They all felt sorry for him, then the shunting took all their attention, and they made ready as far as they could to march into town, and adorned themselves with red armbands.

At the hospital they kept the wife waiting outside for two hours. When she went in – he had a bare private room, a single electric bulb glowing – he at once stretched out his hand towards her in his old loving way, he rubbed her cold hands between his and thanked her for overcoming her objections and bringing him off the train to lie here. "I sometimes thought of it, Antonia, the train rattled so, but I didn't want to suggest it." He was visibly improved, but he soon grew quieter, graver and curiously mysterious in his tall nest of cushions.

"Do you want anything, Otto?" – "No."

"Did you nod off?"

"What? I … was just thinking about the eastern front.

Their journey is much longer than ours. Hm." He'd had a blood sample and a serum injection, he said.

"Thank God, that's why I had to take you off, the doctor couldn't do it on the train."

"No, we had no supplies of serum." Strange, he never asked why he needed serum, was just glad to have it. "Tomorrow you can bring me the plant catalogue from my briefcase," he said, half asleep.

Next morning around six, when she turned up at the hospital all smiles – she was happy, for the first time in days she'd had a good night's sleep in a hotel – the night nurse was coming out of his room holding a bottle of champagne and one of cognac.

"How is he, nurse?"

The nurse didn't immediately recognise her. "The night was all right at first. Then the fever rose, I gave him champagne, the pulse was irregular."

The wife wanted to go in. The nurse blocked the doorway. "We must wait for the doctor, I've sent to wake him up." They stood mutely outside the door, the nurse with her hands full. The wife begged: "But let me see him, won't you." She could hear a curious sound from the room, regular, and became agitated. "He's asleep. I suppose? But I can just sit with him."

Now along came the doctor, unkempt, collarless, in a white medical gown, a pale long-legged fellow with a cold face, without greeting her he opened the door, the nurse followed. They closed the door behind them. After several long minutes they came out, the doctor peered down at her, tugged at the narrow collar of his gown, and cleared his throat: "You wish to visit the Chief Medical Officer?" At her frightened stare he asked hesitantly: "Did the nurse not put you in the picture? So. Yes. It's not going well. We gave him another injection. How did it all begin? How many days now?"

"Since Tuesday, doctor."

"Not so long then. Yes. So. The heart." He gazed at her a while without seeing her, seemed sleepy, gave a nod, went off.

In the room she at once took everything in. It stank of alcohol and camphor. The sister was cleaning needles in bowls at the little white table. He lay with his upper body raised, arms on top of the blankets. He was snoring noisily. His eyes were closed. His red sunken face twitched and flamed without pause. Chills ran down her spine as she cautiously touched his hand. He didn't react.

He was enormously hard at work, clearly. He snored lustily, like a saw, dreadfully deep and loud, regular, as if at an important task. Often he puffed out his cheeks, and the breath escaped through his mouth, pushing the lips out and forming bubbles of spittle that dribbled down the white stubble on his chin. She saw this, observed with emotions she did not trust herself to acknowledge in front of the nurse: anguish, fear, embarrassment. This regular snoring and sawing and inflated cheeks. She turned to the nurse, who was wiping a long syringe with her back turned, asked: "Has he … been like this for long?"

"Oh. He grew restless after four. Then it all kicked off. I've just given him caffeine."

The wife stood there uncertain, look back and forth between the nurse and the bed: "Why … is he doing this? Is it the lungs? Can't he get enough air?"

The nurse, surprised: "Aren't you a doctor's wife? Haven't you seen sick people?"

"My husband's a medical officer in the service."

"Ah. The snoring always happens. They do it when … well, you can see."

The wife took a chair and sat for an hour, two hours at the bedside. The sick man continued to labour. "You can see": clearly she meant when someone's dying. She wiped his sweat with a handkerchief, then a face cloth. As she wiped, the expression death-sweat came to her, and she paused paralysed with horror and dropped the cloth. It was terrifying. She opened the door, and was glad when the day nurse came in. The day nurse, a strapping elderly person with metal-rimmed glasses, studied the patient carefully. The wife held her hands to her eyes: "How long will it last, nurse?"

"A few hours, maybe the whole day, we've had some who lasted two days like this."

"Is he in much pain?"

"He? He's not aware of anything."

She bent over him, touched his shoulder, spoke to him: "Chief Medical Officer! Sir! See, he hears nothing." She gave his face a quick wipe, straightened the pillows and his head which had drooped sideways, and said: "So, you just sit there quietly. If anything happens, come out into the corridor."

★★★

THEME 8. LOVERS

Eleonore (from *Wallenstein*)
Servadak (from *Mountains Oceans Giants*)
How Savitri found Manas (from *Manas*)
Sweetshop Mamselle (from *The Babylonian Exile*)
Deserter meets Housemaid (from *Citizens & Soldiers)*

***

Eleonore

NOT long after, even before winter set in, the city experienced within its walls the greatest festivities in living memory: the wedding of the imperial widower to the young beauty Princess Eleonora of Mantua. Counsellors and Lamormaini had pressed forcefully for this; the Emperor, at first angry, then fearful he might be ousted, offered no resistance. With the greatest tact and reverence, sad and humble, old Eggenberg pleaded with his sovereign for the role of matchmaker. On a pilgrimage to Loreto, in sight of the miraculous tumbledown hut carried by angels from Bethlehem to Upper Italy out of the Turkish lands into blessed Christendom, Eggenberg first encountered graceful tender Eleonora, and broached to her father and herself the desire of the Imperator of the Holy Roman Empire. The Duke of Mantua had hardly to speak to his daughter; knowing his wishes she curtseyed low, placed acquiescent hands into the open hand of the fine old courtier, who spoke so lovingly of his mighty sovereign back home in the barbarian north; and betrothed herself through his representative.

The bishop of Mantua, who had baptised her, gave the blessing at the exchange of rings. In Vienna that same day the

Emperor elevated his matchmaker to Duke of Krumau.

They met at the Court Church in Innsbruck, each escorted by priests. Before the altar they saw one another for the first time. The princess looked away, shaken by the sorrow-ravaged, half-entreating half-impassive face that moved above the huge ornate cloak, above the priceless chains clasps points edgings and rings; the puffy elderly greybearded creature tucked away in his shell, mistrustful and grieving. She was unaware how she shrank back, turned her eyes to the chinking golden monstrance – it showed the Tree of Life, its foliage winding high, amid the leaves sat a wonderfully concealed Mary listening to the songs of angels – so that he too was afraid of her and drew back with a slight dislike. She was richly dressed, wore a deep red costume, the crown of pearls on her brown coiffed hair had no more colour than her small well-chiselled face with its dark thick eyebrows and undeveloped mouth, which suddenly felt dry. Her overgown and undergown were both ornamented in gold; the arms of Austria were embroidered on her left lower sleeve, the sash at her hips bore Ferdinand's signature. Her own ancient white ruff collar languished against the cold throat and jaunty chin ...

As they approached Vienna, the train grew so large that a part of the citizenry had to vacate their homes and move into barracks. Four companies of heavy cavalry came out to meet the imperial couple. They had still to pass through the Stubengate, where the mayor of the city, Daniel Moser, waited on a grey horse with the keys to Vienna, behind him the municipal judge Paul Wiedemann, his assessor. On horseback holding silver staves were the city councillors; hordes of city clerks city chamberlains under-chamberlains asylum-keepers bridge-keepers toll-keepers church-wardens taxmen beadles, dusty and glowing in the warm breeze. Under the baldachin, borne by six city councillors, amid the joyful pealing of bells, the procession moved forward, crowds of youths in the lead brandishing tall stalks of mullein, to St Stephan's-gate where ambassadors and the University delivered speeches; Te Deum in the cathedral, blessing by Verospi, the Nuncio.

And in the corridors, through the halls and courtyards of the proud Castle, there soon moved a bewildered bleak-eyed empress at the side of the mute bleary Emperor.

★★★

Servadak

Unwilling to join the Townzones underground,
survivors of the monstrous onslaught that followed
the Iceland-Greenland venture are settling in benign
southern France, and trying to restore their humanity.

SERVADAK sat alone beneath a cherry laurel in full leaf, a young blond person still very pale; called across to Light-For-Me, the woman who had settled near him on the banks of the Dordogne. Oh she should come to him. She had already gone many times with him to the thicket where a holy cabin stood, had embarked with him on the sweet voyage. He always called as if for the first time, Light-For-Me liked this. He sat under the knotty laurel with its untidy tangle of branches. She laughed through pea-stalks: "Servadak, you're just like a root the way you sit there. Look up: it grows so green out of you."

"Light-For-Me, you've toiled enough."

"See my arms, Servadak, how thick they are. They grow thicker every day. I expect they'll burst. I'm so happy."

"Who are you working for so hard?"

"And if I have children, Servadak, who will provide their food."

"I'll feed them. And the others."

"I have arms, Servadak, they're my children. I don't just sit under a tree. Look at my peas."

"Come here, Light-For-Me."

"That's what the peas say: come. And my hens. And the truffles."

"Come, Light-For-Me. Light of my eyes. My willow. I sit here just for you, to look on your garden, I'm happy when you walk by. Look at my peas. Are they nothing?"

She laughed. "Such a mess. All those weeds! I won't help you, come picking time."

"Come closer." – "You want to go to the cabin? But I don't want to."

"I just want you closer." – "What for, Servadak."

"It helps me. It helps me if you come just one step closer."

"Ah my friend, it makes me sad to see you so pale. How long since we left Bedford."

"I'd been away a hundred years already. When I saw you by the chalk cliffs on that coast, the hundred years were up. That was yesterday. Or today. Today I saw you for the first time. Just now I saw you for the first time. Come, Light-for-me."

"Same old song, Servadak. Whenever I come to my peas there you are, like the thrush."

"But the other thrush responds."

"I'm responding."

"You're not a thrush. You don't respond to me." He stretched an arm out to her. She lowered her head to the stalks, wept, fiddled with pea-sticks, came slowly then faster towards him, as he knelt before her let him kiss her, kissed him gently on the mouth, eyes. Next day he called to her again, and the next. She was always there, tender, brown-black curly hair, slim figure, always lively, a little tired, her attention lighting always first on trees earth people, more radiant and open every day than any fine lady. She wore the drab work-clothes of a British Settler, long grey-brown jacket, black trousers loose, tied at knee and ankle. As she tucked the bright headscarf behind her ears, he stood up beneath the laurel tree.

"Servadak, I brought you this. A nice jacket. Look, they all wear such bright jackets."

"Who wears bright jackets?" – "Snakes. Men. Lots of them."

"Light-For-Me, I am not a Snake."

She was shocked, came closer. "Don't say that. All of us are."

"You know I'm not."

"No, don't say it. I won't listen. Don't frighten me."

"A jacket? If you want, if it's from your hand, I'll wear it."

"Thank Heavens! Oh Servadak, stand up from under that tree. You won't get better sitting there. So pale, you look as if you only just left London."

"I left London a hundred years ago. I'm not pale. I work, see the vines, my Light."

"I came to give you this pretty jacket." – "Come here then!"

She was at his side. "Stop hugging me, Servadak. Take off your smock. Look, it's green wool. Do you like it? It's pretty. You'll look good in it."

"I'll look good? Let's see. How do I look?"

"Good, good, wonderful. You can see for yourself."

"I'll wear it always."

"No, you are not to grab at me all the time. Let me look at you. Aren't you fine. Would you like to come singing with me tomorrow?" And she led him gaily across his field, called to the rows of beans, showed him to the laurel tree. "Servadak's betrayed you, laurel tree. He won't sit under you now. He needs light. He wants to keep moving. He must strut around."

She led him to her garden. "This is Servadak. How do you like his bright jacket. Isn't it pretty, like my headscarf. Come, I'll put a fresh garland of peashoots around your neck. Well, peashoots, what do you say to Servadak's jacket?"

"Give me the garland." – "No, let me put it around your neck."

"I want to hold it. It's from you. You cared for it. And when it wilts I'll squeeze it between my palms and its life, no, your life, will flow up to my shoulders."

She turned aside, sighing.

"What's up, my Light?" – "Call me something else."

"But you are my Light."

"Call me something else. I want to be called Crocus or Little Breeze or – I am Mayelle, as I always was."

"You're sad."

"Yes. You don't want my garland, Servadak, you don't want anything. I'll take it off."

"My Light."

"Say Mayelle to me.You don't even like the light." – "Oh!"

"Oh.Yes, oh, Servadak, my night-moth. Oh you are sick from London."

"I've lost so many people, Mayelle. Now I have you. Don't be cross."

Tanned Mayelle kept herself to herself, said not a word at the great gathering in front of Diuva, the woman who led this group of Snakes. Servadak came often, invited her to the cabin; she embarked on the voyage with him in both joy and sadness. Waited to see if he would change. But after every voyage he came back to her still more wildly yearning. Her garden lay alongside Servadak's; his eyes spent half the day gazing at her trees her ground her peapods artichokes herbs. Always she was waiting for him to see her herbs her fruit trees, whether he would delight in her hens. He did delight, but as his smile showed, only in her. Close by their gardens was a placid lake. She swam blissfully in the limpid water. Servadak whooped beside her; she let him kiss her embrace her in the water, saw his face contort with ardour.

She ran to her hut, threw herself down: "Oh what what

should I do! What should I do! He is not sick. I want to be good for him, he's dreadful. He suffers. He's devouring me. What to do."

+++

Thrushes sang, as they had so often heard. Doves fluttered. Agents of the Snakes appeared at Servadak's hut; he was waiting for them. "Don't take off my ring," he groaned, as they went for the Snake-symbol at his foot. They took him west to another settlement. He burned like a fire lit in a windy chimney. Spicy dark red Medoc flowed into him. Servadak leapt, his body stretched. Mayelle was far away, stayed far away.

★★★

How Savitri found Manas

SILENCE in the streets.
Women peeped out from latticed windows.
And hundreds thought, as they turned their heads
To the latticed windows where the womenfolk
  moved,
Of Savitri.
What must she be feeling, Manas' beloved wife,
Manas' calm centre, behind that latticed window?
Tomorrow she would cling to him one last time,
And be burned at his side.
Savitri moved behind the latticed windows,
Stood and looked, as much as weeping eyes allowed,
At the procession trailing behind Manas,
The soul-bereft.
And hundreds thought of how Savitri had found
  Manas.
She did not seek the one who drew the strongest
  bow,

Who won all the competitions, came first in every race, game, hunt.
'Now, father, grant me this.
If I am to choose a consort – You want me to, and that is good –
Let me seek him in my own way.'
And for three days long she prayed to Shiva,
And went calm and delicate, weak from fasting, to make her choice.
The seven royal scions in the great hall formed a semicircle,
In the hall consecrated to the Soul-bestower, Shiva.
And all seven youths were veiled down to their feet.
And Savitri, who came in alone, knew none of them.
Not her father, not her mother, nor her women were allowed to be with her.
Towards the motionless young men in their heavy drapes,
Silent pillar beside silent pillar, this one as nameless as the next,
Savitri tripped light-footed from the door,
Did not even turn her head, stood a moment silently among them.
And then she raised her arms, pirouetted up to one,
Laid her arms, her smooth ring-decked arms about his shoulders,
Lifted his veil.
And Savitri smiled at Manas for the first time,
Smiled at him as if this were nothing special.
They smiled at one another like old acquaintances.
This was the first time Manas lost the ground beneath his feet,
And yet did not plunge into the depths, but only swayed.

When he realised a man cannot only walk and stand
robustly,
But can also sway.
She walked with him shoulder by shoulder to the
door,
Asked his name, gave hers: Savitri, as if they were old
acquaintances.
And the other princely sons, veils removed,
Felt this, were secretly embarrassed, and made way.
Through the door Savitri led Manas to her father.
And everyone, even the young loiterers by the
fountain in the now silent courtyard,
Praised the Soul-bestower, blue-throated Shiva, who
is everywhere.

★★★

Sweetshop Mamselle

AND because fog lay now so thick over the city and Conrad had no idea which direction he should go in, suddenly he found himself –

– outside a sweet shop. The street was an abyss, the building with the sweet shop an attempt to throw a bridge across the abyss. Conrad noticed that his feet down below were wet, and up above water was trickling around his mouth. He opened the door, the floor was dry, he and the counter were all alone in the shop. But from the next room came an uproar of women and children.

And now, one after the other, there appeared through a curtain a very small boy with a paper helmet on his head, at the sight of Conrad he jumped back, whereat the din grew louder, out through the curtain along with the boy came a bigger girl with tangled hair and a very red tearstained face, they stared at Conrad through great big dark eyes, whereat the girl pulled the boy back in again with considerable energy, for a few seconds the din abated, then the small boy appeared again for the third time, now in the hand of a particularly ancient and very fat woman who couldn't see well, for she stood at the curtain turning her white-haired head this way and that, scanning the room and seeming not to notice Conrad. She vanished, and the din next door rose to a hellish level, and flushed with anger a youngish female person came from the next room, was not quite dressed but held a big blanket firmly in both fists across her breast, shouted back over her shoulder to keep the children out of the shop. She gave Conrad an evil look, and when he said nothing grabbed one of the little bags near at hand and held it out to him. Whereat Conrad smiled and had a look around on the counter.

All sorts of things were laid out there in little boxes, he pointed and asked: "What's that, what's that, what does it taste like?" The woman put down the bag, shouted over her shoulder, and all three persons listed above appeared, assembled behind the sweet counter, and provided explanations in numerous foreign languages all talking over one another, apparently of the sunrise, the sunset, Mohammed's ascension to Heaven, of houses, rents, real estate agents, of bad and good weather, of rainbows, of cats, dogs and mice, of voyages by sea, of life on the land and in high mountains, of Lottie's canary, and the treatment for mites.

All this and more, apparently, was conveyed by the four persons behind the counter. Conrad understood none of it, whereat the four persons directed their narratives with gusto against each other at even greater speed and with the strongest expenditure of vocal capabilities, accompanied by many gestures. Now it seemed to be about Kemal Pasha's martial undertakings, differing opinions on the Sèvres Treaty, of which Conrad had no memory …

For whole long minutes, perplexity reigned in the little

sweet shop. Had Conrad been just any old body, the scene would have come to a rapid end with the help of neighbours who would have thrown him into the street. There our hero would have been consigned to his wet feet and dribbling mouth, and we would have had to begin our love story from a different starting point. He and we alike were spared this by the initiative of the children, that pair of grubby inquisitive creatures. Since the stranger seemed not ill-disposed and had a refined and mysterious appearance, they stepped out from behind the counter, inspected Conrad fore and aft, and commenced a new barrage of questions. In the utterances of the girl, who kept scratching her head and knees, the word "pana" sounded often, Conrad racked his brains. What could they mean by *pana*? The Indian unit of weight in which the Maurya king Chandragupta around 321 B.C. produced his silver coins? Out of the question. A word that seemed to be "hind" could be made out. "Hind" could mean many things: a female deer, fishes of the genus *Epinephelus* found in the warmer waters of the western Atlantic Ocean, or it could mean "back" as in "behind" or "hindquarters" ...Maybe, maybe.

By this point Conrad was growing annoyed, shook himself and posed a counter-question: "What is infinity? What is the origin of the spectral lines?" And answers had they none. They were overawed by his coarse tone, and stuttered excuses. If the two children had not been there, it would have ended badly. They fingered Conrad's spattered boots, his lovely coat, felt without embarrassment in his pockets, and as they did so recited the nursery rhyme: "Goosey goosey gander, what did you lose? Seven dear goslings, they all had no shoes. The cobbler had no leather, and he had no last, so seven shoeless goslings now come past."

An old bald-headed neighbour, alerted by the din, entered the shop, removed the pipe from his mouth, and thundered at Conrad: "$x_i^3 x_p + x^3 x_i + x_p^3 x_i = 0$." Quick as a flash he retorted:

"$x^2y^2 = 2a^3(y - a)$." At which the other scratched his head, laid down his arms, and resumed smoking. Now peace descended, the storm was over. Conrad now at last without hindrance picked up a bag, popped a sweet in his mouth, and felt he was at the goal of his desires.

And with that our sweetie episode in a typical sweet shop would have come to an end, the sweet shop owner would have flung open the door for him, bowed, jabbered, clapped her hands together, clutched her brow, would have run to the neighbours, told them all about it, it would have blazed like wildfire through every alleyway, and a few days later the legend would have faded. But this was a predetermined, predestined sweet shop. For, as you have already correctly surmised, Conrad had made his greatest impression on the youngish person with the blanket around her. It was the value of the cockade Conrad had unthinkingly attached to her nephew's paper helmet that unleashed in her an indescribable sensation.

Could it be, she asked herself, and with lightning speed the answer clearly came, that a man, so refined, so respectable and rich, would step into this shop only because of sweets? No. He means me. She looked at the banknote in the boy's helmet, and knew: "He loves me very much."

This girl will play only a small role in Conrad's story. But she initiates a whole sequence. And Conrad, when he stood on the bridge and felt that this was the city of his destiny, had felt correctly. The young woman now disappeared. In the next room she completed her toilet. On the open stage Conrad engaged happily with the youngsters, sat on a cane stool, the children counted the buttons on his coat, inspected the lining, and chattered away.

***

Deserter meets Housemaid

AROUND two in the afternoon, the deserter and malingerer Walter Ziweck from Kaiserslautern slipped out of the military hospital, where they were about to put him back in the cell on account of his erratic behaviour. He'd caught wind of it, and had also reconnoitred the location of the two rifles the hospital sentries kept tucked away in the building. When Ziweck appeared on the stairs in hospital gown but over it a soldier's greatcoat, cap and rifle, the porter, still ensconced in his room by the entrance because it was his post and he was paid to do so, was unwilling to open the door. Ziweck took underarm aim at him, and the porter cringed. He let Ziweck out, you never know who it is in front of you. The deserter ran, gripping the rifle butt-first, down the road to the town. It was noon, people ahead screamed, moved out of his way, no one stopped him. There were soldiers along the way, they signalled grinning to the shouters to keep calm, he's just letting himself go, people have to let it out after holding themselves in for so long.

Ziweck knew the town, he had been house servant, delivery man and carter for an iron-monger's, the owner had sacked him. That's where he was headed, he meant to settle accounts. He found the place easily, didn't enter the shop but at once climbed the stairs in the building and rang the bell. The owner was in the shop, the woman and her daughter in town, the housemaid opened up, he shoved her aside, she squealed, fell silent in terror when he raised the rifle butt, she didn't know him. She had to tell him where the master and mistress were, he searched all the rooms with her in tow to assure himself they weren't there. Then he declared that he was seizing the apartment and its contents, the master and mistress no longer had any claim on it. He locked and bolted the door, barricaded the kitchen exit with chairs. The rifle stayed with him all the while. In the kitchen she had to finish what she was cooking, with him beside her. He calmed her as she did so, handed her flour and salt, took a taste.

Within half an hour, Ziweck and the girl – he said he could see she was a sensible person – were engaged in friendly chat. She felt a certain attraction to him. He explained among other things that they'd locked him up and wouldn't let him out even with the revolution going on, the authorities still liked to act large. He told her of his service at the front, of torments and malingerers, and now he and the girl were of the same opinion regarding the boss class. It seemed only just to her that she'd once put one over madam and daughter during a big cleanup, they tyrannised and maltreated the staff; but Ziweck kept saying: "That's over and done with now."

After a while they sat down amicably in the dining room at the table they'd both helped lay. He invited her to sit, there's nothing to worry about. She laughed shyly, she'd no idea the revolution included domestics as well, and was so nice for the common people. "How's that," he said, stuffing bread into his mouth, "you think the oppressors will stay on top in the revolution? The military police are on the case."

Encouraged, she fetched the best wine from the storeroom, cognac, she knew where the mistress hid the good coffee and tinned milk. In this way the meal stretched over one and a half hours, then he lit the master's cigars, she smoked cigarettes. And then he wound up the gramophone and played popular tunes. They danced a bit, had a little kiss. They drifted to the master bedroom, she carefully drew back the bedding, he stood the rifle against the mirrored wardrobe and declared: "I'll shave after, then we'll go down to the shop and have it out with the boss." The housemaid was happy as she undressed, the revolution was just like a birthday: "What would madam say if she found us in her bed?" Ziweck, holding her in a wild embrace and groaning with excitement – how long since he'd felt a woman against his skin: "They'd all just better notice that there's revolution."

It was almost five when she woke him. He didn't want to wake up. The doorbell had rung. She crept in a shirt to the door and peeped through the spyhole, it was the postman, he rang again, then went slowly back downstairs. In the bedroom she found Ziweck silently pulling on socks and trousers, yawning and grumpy. When he had the heavy army boots on and was buttoning the braces, he stood up, and she looked at him. She had lain down again, wanted to go back to sleep, she was a silly happy creature from the countryside, thought what had happened here was the revolution, soldiers in the street had already told her so many wonderful things about it, and now it had come to her. But she was frightened by his silent demeanour and the innocuous facial tic that now reappeared; his mouth formed a pout, there was a snort, then the mouth went back to normal. She dressed uneasily, and suddenly had a dreadful fear. She said nothing, he said nothing. She said: "I'll be right back," and disappeared into the corridor. But he heard her working at the lock and asked: "What are you doing?" She whimpered: "I thought – I thought, because the doorbell rang."

"Come back," he ordered, and was quite composed, "we shan't be frightened of anyone." Then she flung her arms around his neck and gave him a big kiss, no, it was revolution. Then the bell really did ring. He said, "Come into the living room." And when she didn't move, he pulled her in.

The owner was standing outside. There now developed the scene that by evening became the talk of the town. The ironmonger banged on the door, Ziweck wouldn't stand for noise and warned he'd shoot through the door, there was nothing here for the owner. So the ironmonger withdrew and went to the police. The two policemen who were sent along negotiated with Ziweck through the door, he was rude to them, they'll be put up against a wall by his comrades if they don't skedaddle. They weren't sure what to do, it was a military matter, they'd rather not be involved. The shouts of the ironmonger attracted a small crowd in the street, which didn't take his side. A window opened, Ziweck yelled down threats, suddenly a shot rang out, at once the street cleared, no one was hit. Ten minutes later a truck pulled up with ten armed men. One, wearing a Soldiers' Council armband, called boldly from behind the truck: "Comrade!" Again, "Comrade!" Ziweck showed himself, rifle aimed: "What d'you want?"

"We're from the Soldiers' Council. Nothing will happen to you. Come down."

A curse was the answer. The man below tried again to negotiate, he thought Ziweck was drunk like everyone else. "Comrade, this won't do, come down now, what will the good citizens here think."

Another curse. Now the man below roared a warning. Ziweck spat down at him, and tapped his brow: "You're just horned cattle. Call yourselves revolutionaries? Rabble." And fired. It hit the truck, they flung themselves behind it for cover, and directed a regular fusillade at the building. Windowpanes shattered, women screamed from neighbouring houses.

The man upstairs gave no more thought to the girl. And gradually it dawned on her through the fear that he was no longer watching her. All he did was hurl insults. They had already brought him to a reprise of his cell situation, barricaded behind the bed. Bullets whizzed merrily through the gaping windows, into masonry. But Ziweck was back at the table, drinking master's cognac. Barbara from Ensisheim was for sure a blend of goose and calf, as the ironmonger's wife told herself daily. But beneath her peasant ineptness lay hidden instincts and knowledge, and just now she was governed by the well-known mix of curiosity, libidinousness and respect for a man that in so many females counts as attraction and gives them second sight. This was Barbara's first amorous adventure, at least since she'd left the village, she'd never come close to any man in town. But now she was frightened of Ziweck, who'd descended to her so suddenly from Heaven, still she liked him very much and didn't want to lose him at any price. She was obstinate, especially in matters of love. They'd made him ill in the war, now he was out of hospital and she had to stand by him. And she left him at it because he was the man after all, but for her part did what she thought would help.

First she sat on his knee at the table, a habit from her village days. Then, to the astonishment of the men below, she closed the green shutters, they stopped firing as she did so and for quite a while afterwards, believing the girl he was holding hostage to be their confederate who would deliver the man up to them. She left one shutter ajar for observation and considered what to do. She'd love to know from him why these other soldiers were bothering them, him being a soldier too, and making revolution. "That's what I'd like to know," Ziweck replied in between threats, and he wanted to stand at the window and hurl curses. But bullets ploughed into the ceiling, stucco fell, she pushed the armchair in which he was now fixed, and the table together with the bottle, up against the door. He tried to stand, eyes on the damaged ceiling. Swore some more, eyes bulging, damned traitors to the people, but he overdid the next swig. Barbara knew how men drank, she knew too it was dangerous to interfere. She stood there perplexed, determined to help but with no idea how.

Then it dawned on her: all I need do is tell the soldiers we're in the revolution too. Suddenly she was disgusted by the soldiers still firing away. They were screwy. Ziweck tried to stand, but as he swayed she pushed him gently back into the chair. Eyes glinting, he offered her a little glass of cognac, she took a sip, but had to empty the glass. And now, as he continued to pay close attention to the tracks of bullets in the ceiling, such a remarkable play of nature, she slipped away to the front door.

The assault squad beside and behind the truck saw her at the street door, two men ran across. So Barbara the presumed hostage had escaped. The man must be dead. That's what they thought. Instead the girl went for them, screamed and clawed like a maenad. Blonde hair hung loose over her shoulder, she wore no blouse, only a green dressing gown, shirt and socks just as she'd climbed out of bed. She went for the men spitting and shrieking: "What are you doing, what's all this shooting, he's a soldier like you, he's ill, he's come from the hospital, and you're shooting. But it's revolution."

They crept perplexed and embarrassed out from behind the truck, one by one each with his rifle. What had they landed themselves in. The girl screamed: "Why" and again "Why". They really didn't know why. One said: "The police raised the alarm, it's not his apartment." But it caused consternation that the girl had suddenly taken his side, and they listened to her. Actually she was quite right. What are the police to us? To crown it all the ironmonger now pushed forward to hear what was going on. But words stuck in his throat when he saw Barbara in his wife's green dressing gown, holding it closed in front of all these men. The soldiers angrily shoved the ironmonger back, they really shouldn't have got themselves stirred up for the likes of him. They said: "Now, gorgeous, what state is he in?"

"What are you going to do with him?"

"Is he wounded?"

"He's asleep. Why don't you leave." Now the men laughed at her, two grabbed her and held her tight, others stormed into the building and up the stairs, she screamed "Ziweck, they're coming, Ziweck, Ziweck!" But he didn't hear.

When the first man entered, rifle at the ready – the girl had left all the doors open, and they could see the man from the doorway – there was Ziweck in the armchair with its little wheels, struggling with what consciousness remained to steer the chair out of the living room into the corridor, no doubt intending to prolong the conflict.

And he did strike out at them as they entered and leaped on him, he yelled in fury. But he soon slid helpless to the floor. They dragged him out, legs flailing, they hauled him down the stairs, into the truck. Barbara tussled with the men. They didn't do anything to him, they recognised a hospital patient from the gown, off they drove. They made slow progress, Barracks Road was thronged with a dangerous crowd.

But Barbara was taken to the police. She was wearing the ironmonger's wife's dressing gown, and was complicit in Ziweck's spree.

★★★

THEME 9. METAMORPHOSES

Incident at Bodenstadt (from *Wallenstein*)
Tower Humans (from *Mountains Oceans Giants*)
Kalongs (from *Manas*)
Melusine (from *Babylonian Exile*)

★★★

Incident at Bodenstadt

BY the end of May it was only too well known in the whole region that they were absconded demons. They once spoke of it themselves: During a disturbance in Hell none could hold us back; the tumult in Hell increases day by day, everyone growing bolder, it will come to violence; we are merely the forerunners of whole hordes.

Thereafter the pair allowed nothing more to be seen of them; and one evening cowherds on the slopes by Bodenstadt observed two figures wrestling silently in the clover, apparently going at one another with spears. But they were demons, who had sworn either to kill themselves or be rid of the spears. In the heat of battle they flung themselves right left; the shafts waggled over them like erect tails; suddenly one lifted the other up, a loud crack!, a piercing scream, whimpering; one lay pale and motionless on his back, the splintered spear thirty yards away, the victor crawled towards it, snuffled at the end where green satanic blood dripped. He lifted up his unconscious companion, dragged him along in his jaws by an arm, pulled out the spearhead and pissed burning urine into him, whereupon the other gagged, stirred and came round. They plugged the oozing hole in his back with tree bark. Then they went at it again, yelping. The victor ran howling with envy around the straight slim other, who picked up the detached iron spearhead, tied the other to a tree and began banging lustily on his spear-shaft, spat at him, and heedless of his wails pulled on the shaft until he fell on his back spraying green ichor – he'd soon be done for. The other, grimly determined, sat on him back to back, pressed the wound closed, plugged it with pitch that oozed from between his teeth, and with the body of a little kitten that happened to be lying at his feet.

And once they both appeared one noontime at the crossroads outside Bodenstadt, as naked hairy demons with ungainly horse's hooves, red fur, staring goggle eyes, hanks of black hair combed backwards, hardly bigger than boys of ten; they jabbered coarsely together. Birds in the fields flew up at their approach. Suddenly the demons themselves flapped as ravens behind a young girl, dropped to her shoulders jabbing sharp beaks into her bare flesh. Blood-curdling yells from women and lads; horrible to hear, the bellowing of spooked oxen, hens flapping, pigs squealing. Peasants barricaded their cottages, bells pealed. A good hour later two fashionable gentlemen came along, mud on their silk-laced shoes, seemed exhausted. They gazed in surprise at the empty village street, called softly for people, a mug of wine, fingered their swords. Doors opened hesitantly, people enquired through windows whether they had not seen something. But they had noticed nothing, had only – they said this with a puzzled air – smelled a disgusting stink, but that might have come from a mouldering cow.

The peasants would have suspected deception, had not the dumb beasts still been kicking vigorously in their stalls; the barber was still treating the hole in the poor girl's shoulder. They came out, all smiles that two noble trustworthy gentlemen should come along just at this moment. One of the gentlemen, lips contorted in fierce glee, observed the girl's wound through his spyglass; she flinched back wailing, ran across the street, summat's not right with them, one of 'em's the demon that pecked me. General mockery of the wounded girl from the peasants thronging the street; they bowed to the visitors.

But the gentleman had been ready for the rabid girl, he made them show him the salved wound again, he would apply an Italian cure. The girl resisted, the man raged with a harsh laugh and threats. The shamed and offended peasants pushed the struggling maiden into a shed; haughtily he dismissed the mob. He sat alone facing the girl, gazed at her, feasted on her fear. And as he grinned and folded his arms behind his back, his nose grew long and suddenly it was a thick strong beak, his loose cloak was splayed and lifted by ruffling plumage, and a raven sat there on the bench, jabbed its beak into the wound, pecked, hacked, tore. It flapped around the girl as she jumped up beating about her and bleating horribly; forced her away from the wall, out from a corner, went for her forehead, the screaming mouth, clawed and cawed, had its fun. With one leg it held fast to the apron-string at her shoulder, then sank its head into the bloody wound, meanwhile felt with the other leg for her mouth, clawed streak after streak from her nose downwards. Its fat feathery body pressed against her pallid cheek, beak stabbing; it jumped onto her nose directing jabs left and right at her flailing hands, pulled her knotted hair into disarray, the powerful wings beat before her eyes, blinding her.

So engrossed was it in the frenzied struggle that it failed to notice the knocking. Only when the door burst open did it flap wildly up from her. All saw the mighty raven, feathers flying. At the very same moment there sat the sword-clinking gentleman, he lunged fuming, eyes flashing, right at them: What impertinence, he'd only been driving out the evil spirit that had entered her; see the feathers, now it's vanished, useless unruly fools and bumpkins that you are. His hands were behind his back; when he brought them forward they were bloodstained up to the knuckles. In their terror they kept silent, let him through, the girl threshed unconscious on the ground, foaming.

In the priest's parlour the two gentlemen calmed down over a glass of wine; they caroused noisily all afternoon, until towards evening the hapless cleric plucked up the courage to celebrate late Mass: he meant to question them, what had brought them to this village, such an honour, by what paths had they come, and …

★★★

Tower Humans

AS the wave of Greenland monsters abated during the summer, Delvil's helpers achieved their first success. New weapons were laid along the southern tip of Scandinavia, Jutland, over the North Sea, on Scottish peaks south of the Moray Firth. They were the strangest most terrible things the Earth had yet seen. On huge platforms in the sea, on Scottish hills – Cairn Gorm three thousand feet high, Sgorr Dhonuill, Creag Meagaidh – tall tower-like structures were erected. From a distance they were slender columns of rock with irregular protrusions. But anyone observing for a while noticed that they changed their outline, grew broader here than there, a protrusion now lay higher than before, or descended, stretched up high. Dark structures like flecked porphyry; some parts gleamed like wrinkled skin, others reflected light rays, shone like fur.

These monstrosities had been erected on the hulls of ships, the peaks of Scottish hills, with the aid of Tourmaline webs. Rocks and treetrunks were piled together and allowed to marry. When they began to grow under the fire of the rays and before they expired, layers of animal bodies plants grasses were strewn on the glimmering coals. Finally people were added to this base. Biologists and physicists of the Meki-factories were familiar with techniques to do with living organisms; they had quickly seen that radiation from the webs provided an unlimited and at first uncontrollable stimulus to living substances. The motive and growth force that lay confined in the animal-plant-rock body, that caused the animal body to mature and then age and die, streamed massively like a cataract from the vessels of Tourmaline crystal, endlessly. These primal beings that housed the fire of the Earth and the stars were now fully in human hands. They could dispense with the nutrient and stimulant solutions that Glossing and Marduk had used for their experiments on plants and trees. Experiments made clear the terrible destructiveness of this force: it exploded every relationship, boosted body parts at the expense of the organism. It was like a flame indiscriminately seeking whatever moves, is at rest, hard or soft. In experiments on plants and animals they succeeded in targeting the stream of stimulus onto the glands and fibre systems that the organism brings into growth from within. The youth of the organism was prolonged. The body was not destroyed. Then Settlers were seized and used for human experiments. The people who were now planted into the base layer of rock and timber were supporters of the Senate. Delvil had volunteered himself; they held him back. Enough came forward from the bands who had followed him in the extermination campaign against the Settlers in Britain.

Scaffolding was set up on the ships and peaks, towers built of living substance. For the first time people stood on scaffolding galleries platforms over the base layer, directing, dosing bits of web, steamed mixed coaxed animal and plant life out of the material. Such delight: engineers biologists physicists watched Delvil, who as always went about observing in high excitement. He had asked the Scandinavian survivor whether he would hold his tongue about the vaults on the Flanders coast. The man said no, and was taken to Sgorr Dhonuill in Scotland and baked into the lowest layer of rocks and timber.

"Not a problem for you," Delvil smiled at the man when they brought him to the scaffolding; "you've already lain under one of these reptiles. There'll be no surprises for you. It's only thanks to the webs that you are alive. You'll serve a useful purpose." The longhaired Scandinavian howled in horror as he gazed down on the heaving dough, into which moss soil logs were being thrown left and right.

"This is happening, my friend, so that the others higher up, our men and women, can devour you. Will you hold your tongue."

The man's features were twisted in torment, but still radiantly fresh: "When I see your tower, Delvil, I praise the power of the Earth. You will never conquer it. I praise the great power. I feel I am with her. There is no boundary between me and her. I am not afraid. You want to dissolve me. Hands off. I go willingly."

And as they seized him, naked, shoved the big crystal shard under his ribs, held him over the dough, he sang his trilling fading hymn to the Earth. Then his dangling hands and feet, caught by the upsurging motion, scrabbled clumsily in the dough. The shard withdrew. He stood, fell onto his hands. Crouched as if he would spring high, free of the Earth. But vertebral processes now jutted out of his back; his ribcage bulged like a barrel. His head sank into the mass; jostling timbers, branches incorporated him into their matrix.

The structure went up stage by stage. Then the tower was loaded with the chosen human, supporter of the Senate. The planting lasted weeks, weeks to embed a single human. They were dropped onto the deadly nutritive and support material, these little naked wretched male and female bodies, onto the eager popping stew. Projections and prongs of the lower tower sank slowly, continually moderated by the controllers, into the legs and arms of the human bodies. The more vines and shoots from the lower tower twined themselves against the body, the more feverishly the willing sacrifice was fed into the mix. There was communication with them: the speech of the sacrifices became thicker more babbling as the tongue swelled. It was necessary to wait until the body the skull the jaws caught up. Huge megaphones were tied to their mouths; soon it became clear these were not needed. The sacrifices, fearing that the megaphones would grow into them, tore them free. Their voices droned deep, sounded far away unclear distorted.

★★★

Kalongs

And the demons strained and tottered.
Suddenly he threw them like a flock of doves into the air,
They whirred, rushed back, rushed down again.
Nishumbha howled:
'You lord, great lord,
Set us free, we mustn't go beyond this point.
We must not go into the land of humans.'
'Must not?'
'We belong to Ganesha, lord with the elephant's head.
We are his servants.'
Manas dashed them onto stones, swung them high, dashed them down:
'Whose servants, Ganesha? Say again, who do you belong to?'
They howled.
'Say again, Ganesha.' – 'You, you.'
'What about me?' – 'We belong to you.'
He stumbled lurched behind them,
They fluttered whirred over the hot stony slope.

There was no end to the slope.
It led into a ravine. Manas would have to scale its walls.
And he stood sweating, stared at the massive mountainside.
'No more walking. You lot must carry me.'
He untied them, looped the leash around their necks.
And in a flash they transformed themselves
Into Kalongs, flying foxes,
With strong bodies, canine muzzles,
Pointed hairless ears.
Their cries as they flapped up from the ground were like cocks crowing.
Brownblack their thick fur,
Brownblack the mighty flight membranes enfolded in their arms.
They waggled yelped could barely leave the ground.
Manas threw himself on Nishumbha's soft back:
'Why do you shiver, Nishumbha?
Did I tie the leash too tight?'
'The leash is not too tight, lord.
We can't see by daylight.'
'Why not?' – 'We are blind by day.'
'Don't worry, Nishumbha, you Chanda, Munda.
I shall steer you.'
'We'll break our heads. You'll fall with us.'
'I shall steer you. Mush! On!
Out of the sun. Even I am burning.
Into the woods now, over snow.'
And the three flying foxes rose blind into the sky,
Nishumbha leading.
He carried Manas, who steered him,
Munda and Chanda following on the leash.
Over the ravine, high above the slope
Where Puto stood gazing after them.

***

Melusine

THE Duke of Poitiers once came upon Melusine, little mermaid lady. His heart pounded when he saw her on the beach, he'd never seen such a mouth and eyes. He said: "I lost my way in the forest. Tell me, what is your name and will you stay here?"

She went with him up to the castle. "Your castle, Raymond, is dark and grim, all the walls are so constricting, you must build me a new one."

In Lusignan he built a castle on the rock, full of halls and verandas, air and sun could get in everywhere, it was a veritable garden.

Melusine went every day down to the water, neither rain nor cold troubled her, she sat there for hours, the count heard her singing. He said: "Melusine, you are so lovely, you shouldn't go to the lake, I'll build a chamber just for you." But she had to go down.

One day he broke through the thicket, tormented, tormented by jealousy. There she was swimming with fins like a fish, a young fellow of similar kind held her by the waist, and now on the shore a third lay senseless: Count Raymond, dead to the world.

And when his eyes opened again she said: "Once you met me at the lake. Now I languish within your walls. I am still a merrmaid creature, you mustn't reproach me for it, Raymond. I kiss you one last time, my husband, adieu."

Ankara lies on a height. The Grey Wolf lodges in this city, the Turkish soldier Kemal Pasha, the Ghazi. Anadolu Ekspresi is the name of the train, Haidar Pasha the final Asiatic station. And over there –

Byzantium, city of seven hills, on a triangular tongue of

land between the Golden Horn and the Sea of Marmara: Constantinople. Istanbul, Hearth of Islam, Gate of Prosperity.

They drew near the city as if on clouds, gentle airy clouds over the city, little lamb-clouds floating white and lovely at great height.

The train hauled one sleeping Waldemar in the luggage van towards Haidar Pasha. The two up front sat alert, serious. It was early morning.

***

THEME 10. WORK

Mushrooms (from *Wang Lun*)
Coining (from *Wallenstein*)
Oil Clouds (from *Mountains Oceans Giants*)
In the South (from *Babylonian Exile*)
Cataldino (from *The Land without Death*)

★★★

Mushrooms

TWO apothecary's assistants laboured in the long courtyard of their house in a large village nearby. The elder shovelled charcoal into a little iron stove. On it steamed a broad deep-bellied porcelain basin. The thin white fumes of the charcoal escaped through a spout at the side. The medicine stove, smoking, looked like a giant teapot. The fellow was an adherent of Wang's, but unsuited to the wandering life. When he glanced up phlegmatically from his work, it was evident something stirred in him that gave him no peace.

Upwind from the smoke the younger assistant sat astride a stool by the wall of the house, trod the wheel of a treadmill to crush dried herbs to powder in a wooden tray.

The gate opened, a tall beggar stood beside the stove. The assistant said, Please to wait outside. Then, recognising Wang, he was about to prostrate himself, but Wang grasped his shoulder. An hour later the assistant walked with Wang on wild overgrown hills and valleys west of the village. Then Wang left him alone to search the swampy landscape. Broad peat bogs, yellowed kaoliang stalks, sprawling ferns. Evergreen oaks clustered on the higher hills. Close-meshed shrubbery obstructed progress. This was the domain of little bright boys, so called from the profusion of gaily coloured mushrooms.

Between massive trunks, on the ground, lurked the puffball with the greeny-white cap. Pretty white ruffs hung about its throat. So as not to touch the oozy damp soil it wore a delicate toecap, a shoe no thicker than skin. The apothecary, wide blue simple-pouch at his breast, scurried down a slope where red flashed and the fly agaric flaunted its purple pomp. Many caps were dotted with little warts, white dots exuding a viscous glassy substance. He broke off a large number, threw them into the pouch. Not far off grew saffron milk-caps, their heads covered with broad brick-red depressions. Brown-white veils fluttered from their caps, seemingly torn to shreds by the wind. When he snapped the stems a slimy latex oozed and stuck to his fingers. He stuffed the pouch full until juice trickled.

In the afternoon, back to the courtyard. He withdrew to his room. With the help of his companions he carried the little stove over the step and set to work with the door closed and the window opened just a little.

Into the seething water in the basin he threw a handful of mushrooms cut into little pieces; after a short time, indicated precisely by an hourglass, lifted the basin using wooden handles, poured the viscous brown brew with the mushrooms through a fine strainer into a wooden pail. He emptied the strainer into another pail. Again he brought water to the boil, poured off the broth, strained it. Once he had boiled all the mushrooms, he began to pound the retained pieces to a pulp with a wooden mortar, flushed them into the basin, boiled them for a long time and again filtered them. The residue in the strainer he packed into a thin pouch which he squeezed over the big pail containing the liquor. He flung the fibrous pulp in the pouch into a rubbish bin.

Now began weary work on the liquor. On the stove and on the hearth in a corner of the room, where a kettle hung from an iron hook, the brown liquid was slowly evaporated.

Holding his breath he tended the little fires in the stove and under the hearthplate. Then he opened the window wide, and returned to his duties in the pharmacy, mixing officinal pills. From time to time he sidled back to the room, poured more liquor into the basin and the kettle. Bustled all night between the pharmacy and his room. Towards morning, when the liquor had reduced to syrup, he emptied the contents of the kettle into the basin. The juice was now sticky, dark brown, formed threads on the stirring spoon.

The assistant spent a long time inspecting and sniffing the result. Then he fetched a sack of black powdered charcoal and some whitish earth, stirred them in, poured in a layer of hot water, and filled a tall glass jar with the black liquid. Barely an hour later a white layer and a brown had separated at the bottom of the jar, brown transparent water above them. Carefully, using a narrow wooden funnel, the assistant filled to the brim two gourd flasks, tall big-bellied vessels. After some thought he divided the contents among six little earthenware jars that he stopped tight, hung by cords over his shoulders. Day had not yet broken when the gate creaked and the assistant slipped out and away.

★★★

Coining

THE Imperial Prague Mint was theirs for a fee of six million for one year.

They could mint as much as they wanted. They picked up tricks of the trade from Jews and other counterfeiters: clipping, mixing in base metal even to the point where no noble metal remained. The four men, under Michna's direction, threw themselves into the business with the trampling fury of a stampeding herd. The Mint was secured by two platoons of fully battle-ready troops. Five neighbouring houses, half the street, were bought up; not a minute to lose given the short time and the risk of adverse events. While Bassevi and de Witte contributed nothing more than their money, two men drove the business on: Michna, and Wallenstein.

The Serb almost out of his mind, always ready to pounce on anyone, terribly afraid of losing his investment, being cheated. He skulked around the buildings; his wife, a shy pretty woman, had to patrol the streets while he slept.

The gaunt Bohemian nobleman imperious, incisively calm and unwavering. Once, outside the main gate of the Mint, he arrived splendidly in a coach and six, bowed to the exhausted muddy Serb: "It seems, sir, matters do not go well with you. Plan to stay alive. Else I shall be your heir." This stung the Serb, who went easier on himself, at the cost of some torment.

Ingots and coins piled up in the long low stable-like rooms; in stonewalled rooms the minters toiled at the muffle-kilns, stoked, glowed. Week by week the number of iron crucibles grew; men stood behind barred windows and stirred the molten masses with graphite rods, long thick staffs. No one had access here from the rest of the building other than the workmen and the masters; what they were to smelt and stir in the crucibles was passed to them in closed crates of zinc and copper. Choking fumes pervaded the houses; wooden pickle-barrels stood marshalled side by side like a regiment, full of boiling acid; the coins, heated, clipped, were rendered unrecognisable, masked against the eyes of the crowd. Workmen toiled in the rooms, their movements like those of a torture chamber; the victim for whom the torture was prepared was nowhere to be seen.

Silver began to flow less freely. A furious confrontation occurred in de Witte's study between the Bohemian colonel and Michna. First: "Either Herr Michna is not exerting himself, or he is holding silver back." Then: "You may do as you will, sir. But look to it that you obtain silver from the Jews. You stuffed their bellies full with stolen goods." When Michna, lips and cheeks a-tremble, strode up to the gaunt trim-bearded colonel, who towered over him, he raised his hands: I'll not duel with you, but will stop your mouth with my fist. At this, Wallenstein left the trembling man.

Silver became scarcer. The price rose. Michna, worried by the outcome of the affair, proposed seeking new partners. These grew gradually to fourteen; only a few of the names were familiar from the ranks of imperial figures. Old Prince Liechtenstein joined – the colonel arranged it – so he could have a hand in it on behalf of the Emperor. Then he was seized by a passion, and was unable to back out.

The pot-bellied hard-browed Master of the Mint, old Wresowicz, who was also president of the Chamber, was brought in; the machinations could not be kept secret from him. He had allowed his office to decay, he thrust himself forward greedily, the company was safe, he would soon be aboard the good ship *Fortune.*

The consortium became giddy; they were rolling towards an abyss.

Buyers of silver, hired and freelance, flitted about the country, burst into peasant cottages; several lost their life for ten ducats. Soldiers of fortune organised their own gangs, dressed in military garb; in such disguise they went about robbing. Imperial buglers proclaimed in town squares that all silver must be delivered to the Mint; whereat, amid heady rumours of the goings-on, it vanished completely from the market. Soon only four new guilders were offered for one imperial thaler. Angry mistrust grew rapidly among the people; in consternation representatives of the merchant guilds besieged any Bohemian official of their acquaintance. Received in reply laughs and sympathetic shrugs, no one was losing out from the debased coinage, things would stay the same. For ever? For ever! And some believed it, most could not let go their fear, they saw goods and chattels stolen away from their homes with no door opened. Terrible rumours persisted: behind the buying up of silver stood a company of usurers, to whom the Emperor in his need for funds had pawned hair and hide; Jesuit priests were behind it, to inflict vengeance on the Bohemian Brethren.

That they were in a sack tied tighter day by day became clearer to all each morning: hunger set in. The paupers of the town loitered defiantly in forbidden marketplaces, their captains declaring they had no authority over them; too many were dying, men and women no longer in control of their senses. Mobs of these ragged brutalised people made town gates and thoroughfares dangerous; peasants dared not enter with their carts; whatever they brought was at once devoured by the mad scrambling throng. And nothing would be traded for debased coin. Mercenaries sent to deal with the beggars joined them, plundered everything in sight. People shouted into houses: what price a guilder? Hardly had they registered shock at forty-six guilders to the mark when the rate climbed to fifty-five, sixty-three, seventy-seven. One mark was worth seventy-seven guilders.

The Mint: squatting there in the Old Town of Prague, a sprawling ugly low wooden structure with iron gates. Pickets from Wallenstein's regiment in the courtyards, patrolling the neighbouring alleys in pairs, powder-horn slow-match ramrod at the side, heavy musket on the shoulder. When peasant carts brought logs, the low wide main gate would open, and left and right behind the entrance flashed strong bronze four-pounders on carriages, powder-monkeys and gunners loitering by them, tending coals in a brazier. Equipped with his pass, every day the monster Michna slunk past the mobs and through the courtyard; a musketeer held his horse. The Serb, without baring his head, wandered up steps and along galleries, from office to hall, gallery, through the heat and fumes of the smelting-rooms, cheerful clink of the stamping-rooms, past stores of minted coins; into the strongly guarded stock room, weighing-room. Licked his lips, wiped away black whiskers that strayed into his mouth. He was very tense, spoke to none of the innumerable clanking workmen; masters and under-masters shrank back, his black-brown eyes were grim under the jutting balcony of his forehead.

The greatest speculator in the land, the mad *vabanque*-gambler Wallenstein, gaunt hollow-chested with a black goatee, flashy diamond chain on his hat, stood half an hour at a time by the stores of minted coins; if noticed he became uneasy, closed his eyes, disappeared.

People of the country, rejecting the new coins, sold abroad. So the frontiers were closed. Nothing was brought to market. An imperial edict was proclaimed in marketplaces: the value of money would not decline further; let no one be afraid. They mocked: "Emperor, emperor, in on the fraud. The aristocrats cook their porridge for him, for the emperor, the blind dog."

***

Oil Clouds

FROM Europe, from the coasts of Belgium and Britain in an endless line along the sea-lanes came black-tarred construction vessels, floating factories, oil-cloud ships rocking over the ocean. Icebreakers flanking them, and ahead. Soundlessly they cut the water. They divided north and south as they passed burning Iceland, encircled Greenland. And just as ice cast a barrier all around Greenland, so they barricaded the ice with their black deep-hulled structures. New arrivals streamed in.

When they reached their positions, greeted in silence by the crews of the Iceland fleets, they puffed the heavy smoke from their portholes, Holyhead's oil-breath, its white mass infused with coloured swirls, green blue red. The ships probed tentatively, first with this colour then with that. The smoke lifted slowly, the wind barely able to shift it sideways, new smoke blowing continually, building up, waiting like a horse outside its stable, maintaining an even height. The coloured smoke-masses climbed, their motion slowing until at a certain height they faltered, gathered, little by little spread horizontally like oil on a sheet of water.

At Scoresby Sound on the east coast, at the southernmost point, at Disko Bay in the west tests were carried out to ascertain the height of oil clouds of particular composition. The plan was that they should rise above the highest ice-fields, cover the entire continent as evenly as possible. Once the optimum mix of gases was identified, the ring of ships around Greenland set to work. Heedless of foehn winds or icy storms, they pumped out dark smoke clouds that gathered at enormous height and were pushed inland by more clouds coming behind. Clouds drifting out to sea were rounded up by lines of fliers with squall-bombs. The corralled gas-balls stuck tenaciously together. Ever darker masses settled in a plane, as they piled up ever denser became more firmly fixed in place. They were an unyielding space-filling thing intermediate between gas and solid. Falling rain could not penetrate the burgeoning banks of cloud. Water and snow gathered in hollows, emptied spouting onto the fringing lines of ships; had no effect on the elevation of the gas. Attrition from the edges remained the biggest problem. Squadrons of fliers and cargo airships were stationed at horrendous height, always in danger of being trapped by the rolling clouds, capsizing crashing. They had to set a constant barrage of explosions all around the gas zone to prevent the smoke from blurring fragmenting. The engineers' fear that the buoyancy of the clouds would gradually diminish with height, that the cloud-masses would begin to sink, proved unfounded. The enormous dark cloudbank over Greenland maintained its elevation; would support rafts as buoyantly as seawater.

The Iceland expeditionaries went about their aerial work in their usual grim dogged silence. They averted their gaze from the horror of the luminous Tourmaline vessels; not a word was said about them. The ships were stuck fast. The newcomers did not see these monsters as ships, so overrun were they with bright algal tree-like growths, occupied by swarms of birds. At their destinations the Tourmaline vessels had been clumped close together away from the rest of the fleet, as if quarantined. The immobile structures had long become overgrown; the growths had thrown bridges between them which were only rarely severed by shifting ice floes. Birds strutted and nested on the grey red bridges; molluscs and fish became caught up, sported and died. The resting vessels loomed into the icy air like grassy hills. As they lay there in the bays, at the entrances to fjords, they looked like steep hunchbacked islands. Sometimes the grey and red hulks were seen to twitch and shudder.

The Iceland expeditionaries laid great wide duckboards on top of the oil-clouds. And when they stepped on them they pulled in nearby boards, aligned these and pinned them together. Now and then a raft would wobble when they stepped on, slide sideways into a depression in the cloud, rear up, overturn. The castaways would scrabble in the grey pink violet smoke. They tried to work free of the gelatinous spongy boggy stuff, threshed about, paddled hand over fist towards the boards, could not extricate themselves. New masses of gas drifted in, bumped around them, over them. They were bedded in, cemented, flailed at the chest, the bleeding nose and mouth, were squashed as the head flopped wheezing sideways. At the start many of these aerial workers stumbled, lay sprawling arms dangling on the billowing gas. The murky upwelling nudged at their bodies, here stuck fast to a limb, tore it from the body, stretched the body with its scrabbling hands treading feet ever longer longer as it was drawn down. At the edges the fabric frayed; sometimes a suffocated black-faced flier or a twisted torn-off body part fell onto ice or into water. The aerial workers ran about, laid board after board.

A battle with the winds began. The northeaster with fog and thickly swirling snow tore at the outer fringes of the cloudbanks, blew ragged fragments away. Small groups and solitary figures were tumbled down to the distant land, perished. People stood on the flattened cloud, stumbled; it was worse than at sea. Were tossed with their board rafts up high, then down, from side to side. They had to make terrible haste to lay board after board on the vaporous foundation growing out into the landmass. Often they stood insensible up there, flung themselves in, vomited, were tumbled whirled around, carried by surging wallowing boards that sometimes sped apart as in a game, were piled atop one another by a knot of cloud, crashed together. At the edges they hung suspended over the immense icy land. Far below lay the watery mirror of the fjords, in the east rocky peaks soared with the rigidity of death almost up to their feet, jagged crests almost touching. The icy breath of old snow wafted up. Blue-white glaciers moved sluggishly down over the white plain, through the rocky defiles they had abraded. Scree and avalanche debris hung askew over rock terraces like giant carcasses.

Winds howled over the ice. The land lay dormant, like a blind man awaiting his fate. From every coast the layers of smoke came reaching out, yearning towards each other. The aim was to steer the billowing masses together, leave just one gap like an island in the middle.

***

In the south

AH the pain and love with which Conrad left Paris behind him! If only he had enough blessings to give this city, through which the Seine flowed in ever new meanders without ever being able to quit the city!

They travelled south. Warm climate. The air of the blue Mediterranean wafted over it, as yet there were no palm trees, just terraced vineyards, fields of roses, drooping bushes of yellow mimosa. Age-old ruins lay in the ground. He had come to a good place, all warmth and ruins.

And as the youngsters on the farm – together with the important agronomists who had become attached to them and people from the locality – proceeded to erect cabins (at first they lodged in nearby villages), Conrad sat with his wife and son in the only habitable cottage on the farm, wandered around and was like a parched tree that drinks its fill of rain. Ah, he breathed, how much time it takes to come this far! How old you have to be! How much must pass away, of life, love, suffering. And what remains at the end? This diversion …

He took part in none of the labour, busied himself, as he admitted with a laugh, only with breathing in and breathing out. The young colonists were content, said it's right for his age, we all have what we want, he has his peaceful strolls, warmth, air, of course no city, no wine to drink, no oysters, we have the soil, the labour, soon we'll have a roof over our heads, won't need to trek every day from the village, a roof of our own built by our own hands, eat our own bread, own fruit, drink our own milk, we'll have less meat, but there are brooks nearby, we can fish. They had learned a lot, they had no use for most of their stuff, it was superfluous, and that lesson – they swore at the time wasted, were glad it now lay behind them – they would never have learned on their own. How young this Conrad was, actually, when he made the decision, yes, he's one of our own, he saved us from being eaten up by the city.

Ah, thought Conrad, how lovely it was in the city, and how they did what they could there, Madeleine, Notre Dame, the proportions, the soothing, the decisiveness, the power, all of it, and yet people never found calm, how bitter it is for me to leave it all behind, ah, I am not their enemy.

They had set off in spring, the days rolled by, their toil showed progress. Birds flew about and sang in the nearby woods, others from the village came with the youngsters, they sat together in the evenings, played and smoked, danced peasant dances, sang songs with them, it all seemed wonderful and better than a summer holiday, and gradually they adapted completely to it. And why not, thought Conrad, why shouldn't they adapt to it. He went about in linen trousers and cap, sometime took up a shovel, knelt with them in the upturned soil, planted seedlings in neat rows. The earth spoke too powerfully to him. He wasn't up to contact with simple black loose soil, not yet. I have to learn it first, he sighed. It wasn't easy, went slowly. And yet something happened that made it seem the opposite.

***

Cataldino

THE first to decide was Cataldino, the builder and carpenter. The many logpiles were an enticement to him. The way the natives botched the construction of huts irritated him. And as their numbers rose into the hundreds and crowds surged around them, sullen, idle, awaiting instructions, and no soldiers appeared, he roused himself. He said: "Now it's my turn." He formed a team and set to work.

He had little time for idolatry, and even less for huts of branches and mud. First he wanted to build some big barnlike accommodation rooms, with a normal roof, walls and floor for the families, and then some individual roofed houses, little by little. And as he began to work, issue orders and curse, the other Fathers set themselves in motion. Their life-spirit revived. Theology and despair are just not enough. Emanuel together with Maceta and Cataldino still dreamed of their lovely New Jerusalem.

"It won't be a New Jerusalem," scoffed blunt Cataldino, "but they'll have a place to live, that's a start." Over his black robe he wore at his side a fat satchel from which poked an axe and a carpenter's rule. He was in his element and dreamed up something new every day. A hospital was already forming in his head. Meanwhile he erected sheds for fishermen and hunters. "Whoever gives more than he can is a charlatan. If you behave yourselves you'll have a church soon enough. But first things first."

And once they had dug the first turf and made holes for the first posts, news spread and the people no longer had to go out to implore refugees: "Come to us, you'll be safe." They came of their own accord. In what was once a camp, it was as if the work of construction set a whole great invisible engine in motion. The Fathers were dumbfounded. They observed the living tumult, the many separate desires that meshed together, the incessant movement, and felt themselves seized with it. And people even regarded them as the instigators, which they weren't at all! They hadn't even planned these huts! They joined in with a will.

The flood of refugees abated. Emanuel sent into the country and pulled in all the Fathers who could be reached. The young town, which they no longer saw as a camp, seethed with people, a thousand already, disciplined workers were sorely needed. But everything grew almost by itself, all you had to do was monitor and organise.

The Fathers discussed it, more bewildered than joyful.

Cataldino the sly sceptic said straight out: "We've exchanged roles, our dark friends and us. They set us tasks. We wanted to proselytize. We never get around to it."

Maceta, who had learned smithing, praised his people: "How they study the tools, how inquisitive they are about fire-making, smelting, every hammer blow interests them!" The other Fathers sang a similar song.

"The mouth must now remain silent," was the view of big Father Faber, who turned to fat everything he ate and yet was the first to volunteer at any heavy work, wheezing enthusiastically. "Now we're building Christianity. Building it of wood and clay, and in mats for sleeping, and in streets." Natives attached themselves particularly to fat Faber wherever he appeared. It was his mighty figure and booming voice. They could think of no animal with such a voice, and because he always kept strictly to practical work they understood him more readily. Here everything went according to his will.

Cataldino the builder swooned and rolled his eyes. "I hope we find some stone at last. Dear brothers, just imagine, a house of real stone on the Paraná!" But stone buildings did not appear so soon. They were not yet done with wood and clay, needed shovels, axes, nails. In his knapsack Maceta had a few screws of various sizes, which made a tremendous impression. He landed himself, foolhardy fellow, with the construction of a cedar cupboard. Hour after hour he had to take out the screws and let the people practice screwing into spare bits of board. The positioning of grooves for the little auger, the insertion of the screw, all this took up a whole day and formed, so he felt, a true bond between him and the people. The people were thereby won over to the Fathers' cause. They converted. A faith community? Obviously. It was all a matter of faith. The Fathers only had to keep their eyes and ears open to note how the natives mixed everything up into strange concoctions: screws with the wanderings of John the Baptist in the desert, nails and hammer with the Crucifixion. And the Fathers, who worked on buildings with axe, saw, chisel, and who learned the Indian language, sweated and taught, soon saw how necessity had led them along a good path which they would never have found by themselves. The dark people gave things funny names. This was no house, but a cave along the refugee trail, the heavy nail that penetrated the rough log was implored not to hurt and not to keep Jesus suffering on his cross, it was called "Have-no-fear".

★★★

THEME 11. BODIES

Paldan Ishe (from *Wang Lun*)
Tilly (from *Wallenstein*)
Time of True Humanity (from *Mountains Oceans Giants*)
Ambrosius Alfinger (from *The Land without Death*)
The Airman (from *November 1918*)

★★★

Paldan Ishe

ON the afternoon of the third day Paldan Ishe kept his brown eyes open a long while, gazing from beneath the mask of black pock crusts recognised Ch'ien-lung and moved his lips. He also recognised the six bishops who stood in beggar rags along the walls, not leaving the room for an instant, so that they might attend at the onset of death.

Ch'ien-lung bent to the sick man's ear. "I am desolate that you should be suffering in my country, Your Holiness." Paldan Ishe seemed to want to laugh. He shook his head and gargled.

Unperturbed by the enormity of the event that was about to pass, the parting of the Buddha from his most recent body, the old Emperor spoke. He asked often if the sick man understood him. Firm nods. With hard precision Ch'ien-lung related recent events, disturbances. Paldan Ishe's eyes grew lively as Ch'ien-lung whispered. The holy man was in his element among heavy downcast souls. When Ch'ien-lung was finished he saw the brown eye globes move, but the sick man's lips twitched, formed no words.

The Emperor rose, sternly threw back his head.

Next afternoon he sat again at the holy man's bedside. The six bishops stood unmoving in their beggar rags along the walls, waited. The Emperor whispered more urgently, repeated his account, grasped the sick man's knuckles, desired new advice, promised to build new monasteries for the Yellow Church in every province.

The sick man strove for words, smiled. Only his look spoke, was silent. Anger twisted the Emperor's face.

When the Emperor came next afternoon, he found the holy man sitting up in bed. Only four bishops stood along the walls, barefoot, browncowled. Two were supporting the holy man, who kept his eyes closed, unable to open them beneath the cushion-like swelling of cheeks, lids, forehead. The two shavenheads were supporting him because he had shown by signs that he wanted to walk. A heavy fug of incense shrouded the room. The Yellow Lord stood transfixed in the smoke. No glance met his. The holy man was turned with his face to the west. Ch'ien-lung's palanquin went hastily back.

On a seesaw of delirium, turbidity, bright confusion Paldan Ishe woke and dreamed. Fleshtrussing cramps, hollow swaying over chasms, a clear feathery brightness alternated. The great weariness evaporated. The white walls of the labrang rose up, roofs gleamed in dull gold. The late Dalai Lama appeared and walked quickly past under his umbrella. Master the images, meditate! Brief rest in white halls. People, so many people, on camels, in carts; plunging, sinking people. Courtyard gates, sedan chairs, gongs. Help across the sea, great boats, small boats. Gigantic, incorporeal, he dragged his luminous body leaving a phosphorescent wake, he was a pillar high as Heaven, revolving. No trembling beset him. He couldn't tell if it was his feelings he felt, if they were the feelings of others, many, countless others. Poised. Poised mysteriously between six mysterious syllables.

On the morning of the third day Amitabha left the body of Lobsang Paldan Ishe. The corpse stiffened in the position of a praying Buddha.

***

Tilly

INTO the crooked-ceilinged mayor's quarters strode Tilly, frail, in the dress of a Spanish captain, ostrich feathers bobbing tall over his little hat; he greeted the tall lean Bohemian, who laughed heartily and rejoiced with him that it was not too late to show the enemy their teeth.

The Brabanter, stiff, ghostlike in a white scarf, a pair of pistols and a dagger at his belt, short white hair, each strand laden like ears of grain with the thousands he had killed. His pale pointed face, bushy brows, moustache stiff as a brush: steeped in the mangled legions of a lifetime, they clung scrabbled at the buttons of his green doublet, his belt. Each one of his knobbly fingers represented the ruination of towns; each knuckle a dozen villages exterminated. Jostling over his shoulders came the bodies of butchered Turks, Frenchmen, Palatines; and one day he would appear before a judgement seat with all of these, together with their horses and hounds piled in a jumble over him, a horrendous burden beneath which his head and hat were lost to sight. Throats torn open red and raw, bellies pale and iridescent, veined, dripping onto the slit cringing sleeves and the buckling knees. Entrails winding, long tripes that tangled him, lolling and wobbling over the braced leather-clad legs, endless soft wormy rustling trail that made him jerk, wrench, wheeze as he walked. He trampled the earth like a mammoth, but held himself icily cold, ears inured to the screams of people, marrow-curdling shrieks of swine, horses shrilling whistling, as they all clung to him trying to suck their lives back from him from the tiniest little straw of hair; throats of horses reaching, nostrils quivering, dappled, black; shattered dogs snuffling at his mouth, his nose, slurping greedily at his breath.

He must have been emptied long ago, they were sucking

on a rotten tree, he rattled around in there and they could not bring him down.

At his back fourteen regiments of foot, and six mounted.

Facing him the Duke of Friedland, yellow dragon risen from the bubbling Bohemian swamp, covered in black slime up to the hips, leaning back on little knobbly hind legs, ringed tail pressed to the ground, broad bloated body rocking in the air, the long gaping jaw emitted blissful snake-fierce huffing breaths; the snuffling grunting induced shudders.

At his back twenty-four thousand men.

***

Time of True Humanity

IN London's underground research town, provocatively called the Greenlandeum, suspended over the heads of the teeming masses in strata of clay and marl, the most powerful brains among the ruling class of the time had come together and gathered about them every kind of raw material. Here in the district of Carthagon, working on plant energy, sat Atkinson, a cold gloomy man, said to be a eunuch by his own volition, a misogynist, a misanthrope. In Oceana, working with water, the Spanish Berber Escoyez, the water-creature who at the start of the Greenland campaign had advocated diverting the Gulf Stream and creating new sources of salinity in the sea. The heat of flames was studied by Nadeya, a manwoman from Atkinson's stable. In the district of Tel el-Habs, the Hill of the Prison, sat several senatorial personages who could only with difficulty be termed human. These were men and women who had taken part in the construction of the human towers, and like animals who had once licked blood could not free their thoughts from what they had seen and experimented with. They returned reluctantly from the ships and Scottish peaks to the sober paltry realm of humans, those two-legged whinging bare-skinned obsolete creatures.

The elite of Tel el-Habs no longer wanted to be embodied in human organs. Experiments they tried on slaves in their prison they tried on themselves as well. Tribord set aside his old name, called himself Mentusi. He stopped eating, spread animals and plants over his body. Mentusi said to the manwoman Kuraggara, who was once Mrs Macfarlane: "Meki and his generation did well to abandon fields and forests to the wild. What we can make of ourselves we shall make. They built great factories, facilities. We've dragged these facilities around with us for centuries. They require space and supervision. How proud we are of these facilities. Now they're superfluous. We must reset the point of attack. I'm all for ploughed fields and herds of cattle again. A dog can eat for me, as much as it wants, as long as it remains my dog. Did you see the stones and oaks and herds of cattle thrown onto the towers. They had to eat for the towers. I'll be a dog myself, if I keep guzzling what the factories brew up."

Polyps hung on the man of Tel el-Hab. His abdomen was bored through. He had sent his colleagues out into abandoned forests; they brought back foxes otters African zebras turtles. The age-old difficulty of marrying two species was overcome: Mentusi had worked it out while observing the construction of the towers. The Tourmaline webs mixed all species together. Just as he had scorned Meki, he scorned Marduk who had made trees grow: "Kuraggara, they were yogis and fakirs. Jokers! Let them admit it. Until the Greenland expedition we were nothing. The man who tore fire and rays out of volcanoes is my man."

Kuraggara held her sides laughing: "I'll try to have a turtle baby."

"Why not. Who can stop you."

They did terrible things there on Tel el-Habs, the Hill of the Prison.

***

Ambrosius Alfinger

AMBROSIUS Alfinger, a battle-hardened captain, was sought out by the Welsers and appointed governor of Maracaibo. He was to gather gold, and procure darkskins for sale in Coro's markets. Accompanied by two hundred Whites, halberds, muskets, arquebuses and a number of horses and bloodhounds, he struck out from Coro. The men had flocked together for war and adventure, rapine and murder. In the lands of the Whites, in Spain, Portugal, Italy and Germany they had nothing to lose. They were not bad men, they were what they were and could not be otherwise.

Alfinger came to the Perijá range. He had to cross it. His band began to go hungry. As they climbed higher, the sun burned terribly. They had no time to make themselves understood to the darkskins. When they found the first village they stormed into huts, shoved the occupants aside. Once sated they looked for gold. They chained people and loaded them up. On they went.

Ambrosius Alfinger was a wiry man, already over fifty. He wanted gold and slaves. But he saw only desolate mountains. He descended into the valley of Upar. He sent envoys to the dark men and women in the villages, he wanted to trade. He was afraid they would run away. And so it was that unsuspecting chieftains welcomed him, led him into their houses, he squatted there with some of his companions. Meanwhile others of his men looted the place. Screams penetrated to the chieftain's lodge, they stood up to investigate. Then Alfinger rejoined the others and together they cut down the chieftains and the rest.

Entering the valley of Upar was easy, leaving was hard. The Sierra de Tairona was their next goal. The path into the mountains seethed with refugees. A poisoned arrow from an ambush in the rocks above hit grey Alfinger, who always had a friendly smile and organised everything without fuss.

The poison was known as 24-hour poison, because it killed within twenty-four hours.

Alfinger had himself lifted from his horse, all men are mortal, they ate of the Tree of Knowledge and so are cursed. They waited for him to name his successor. But they had to lay him beneath a tree, erect a shade for him, then the dark man who was his interpreter sucked at the wound below the knee. Blood flowed, the knee swelled and turned blue. The leg grew heavy, and three hours later the lieutenant came to Alfinger and said: "If you don't name a successor, General, there'll be fighting among us and we'll all die tonight." The governor demanded hot water, threw in some herbs and drank a large jugful. He had them remove the shade, covered his head with cloths, lay out in the sun. The band's chaplain appeared, admonished him, pointed to the swollen leg. Alfinger received the last rites. He still had twelve hours.

Then he sent three envoys out to find among the darkskins a witchdoctor skilled in healing. One of the three returned to report that the country for miles around was empty of people, the other two had gone higher into the mountains. These two were pursued for a while by Alfinger's men, and killed. So for an hour he waited in vain. In these long hours Ambrosius Alfinger suffered agonies. He grew despondent, and did not speak. When the two envoys failed to return and his lieutenant told him they must have deserted or been seized by the natives, he regained his smile. He understood. Now he could sit up, drink another jug of hot bitter tea. His head was still unaffected. Alfinger stroked his long beard: "We were ill prepared. I had no idea they use poison in these parts. Else I'd have brought along a proper witch doctor, he'd have cut off my head and set it upon a horse." The lieutenant, a brave man, joked along: "But would they obey you, with horse-legs?"

"What about horse-legs? It's not my legs you obey. It's not my boots you watch." He summoned the dark-haired interpreter and asked if he had ever heard, among his people or elsewhere, that someone could be cured of the poison by cutting off their head and quickly placing it on a horse's neck. The interpreter stared uncomprehending at the lieutenant, but Alfinger spoke in earnest.

Then he asked the interpreter if he was prepared to hack off the leg with a sharp sword and an axe. When the interpreter gave no answer, Alfinger asked the lieutenant if he would perform this service. The lieutenant summoned the chaplain, and the chaplain admonished Alfinger not to cling to this life. Whoever dies here is surer of Heaven than someone dying back home, for he dies as a warrior for the Holy Church. Alfinger breathed easier: this was his view too, but he owed the Spanish Crown large debts, and maintained that a warrior shouldn't be allowed to die without a struggle, and once again desired the lieutenant to hack off his leg. The lieutenant was accompanied by two soldiers with arquebuses, Alfinger knew they would shoot him unless he died soon. The lieutenant waved dismissively towards the poisoned leg that lay exposed and swollen green-blue all the way to the hip, and said: it's too late anyway. The chaplain agreed, and set up a loud rapid praying. Now Alfinger named the lieutenant as his successor, in order to be rid of him. So the lieutenant, content, withdrew with his arquebusiers. Alfinger smiled his old smile, told the interpreter to lay an arquebus by his side, and whispered with him.

The interpreter soon reappeared at the place where the general lay and the chaplain prayed, accompanied by a mercenary skilled in ironworking. This man brought a crucible, a long stout iron bar, and tongs. He heated the bar in the crucible until it glowed red. Then he handed Alfinger the tongs. The chaplain followed all this nervously, peering over his book. Now he held the book close to his eyes, stopped praying, and his breath hissed. Smith and interpreter clenched their fists, eyes started from their sockets. Scorched flesh sizzled and smoked. Alfinger sat up straight and burned the flesh away from hip to knee. When he was done and threw down the tongs and iron bar, his face was rigid, and both thought him dead. But he pressed his back against the tree, remained upright, and his eyes blinked. An hour later he had tea brought and looked for the sun. It was about to set. His hand felt for the arquebus.

As dusk fell the lieutenant came with torches and a litter of branches. But Alfinger was sitting upright and staring straight ahead. The chaplain was crouched at one side and the interpreter at the other. Alfinger ordered that two mercenaries should make a fire near him and keep armed guard all night. The lieutenant obeyed. In the night Alfinger, set like a stone under the tree, had hot oil poured onto the wounds. The chaplain slept by the fire, it was morning before he took up his book again and stared in horror at Alfinger sitting there rigid, then made haste to resume his prayers.

Who was Ambrosius Alfinger? A White, a man, a hunter, no worse than others. Belligerence was his backbone, whenever he defeated someone he felt good. Fame, power and gold were his heart and blood. The dark people were sand beneath his feet.

On the way down from the Velez mountains he told the chaplain: "We must return to Maracaibo. Every day they pour oil onto my wounds. But the leg grows worse."

And as they marched in the mountains between Pamplona and Cucuta – Alfinger dry as a stick, armed men before and behind, bearers laden with looted gold as far as the eye could see – he had to be lifted from the horse. The bone had been scorched. He was carried at night into a cave. He ordered the looted gold to be piled at the entrance to the cave. His captains cursed one another, swords drawn. One captain, since he felt disadvantaged, wanted to attack the treasurer and take the king's fifth for himself. When they heard Alfinger calling for the loot to be brought nearer, they closed ranks and explained that the entrance was too narrow. The general demanded to be brought outside.

He could no longer stand, he held the loaded arquebus under his arm. As they carried his litter out of the cave by the light of torches, the bearers stumbled. The arquebus under his arm fired, the ball buried itself in rock. A chunk of stone came loose, and crushed him and the two bearers.

Next morning they pushed on in a forced march. Monks and chaplain positioned themselves around the king's fifth and Alfinger's share, carried by darkskins under the eye of the treasurer. The captains foamed like jaguars, and hoped for a defile where they could tip the transport over the edge after first looting it.

But the mountains fell away. The land became flatter and flatter, they sat on their horses and played guard over the transport.

The place where the tyrant Alfinger died was given the name Miser Ambrosio.

***

The Airman

IN the military hospital by the airfield, an airman lay in a private room in the Surgical Station. The slate at the head of the bed read, in Latin: abdominal gunshot. The wide eyes were dull. The tall nurse in white, as she rattled the dressings trolley from his bedside away to the window, leaned down to him: "Feeling better today, lieutenant?" He tried to smile, and she shrank back. There were deep folds around his mouth, the nose was thin, the face had a grey-blue sheen. His voice was slow and slurred: "Thank … you … nurse." His head moved side to side, his fingers played. "You want a drink, lieutenant? Are you thirsty? I'll bring you something." Oh God.

She hurried to the big hall, the Station nurse was recording temperatures on a chart. They whispered. The Station nurse, cold: "Well, good luck finding a doctor." She shrugged, continued writing. Then she left the pen lying on the chart and looked directly at the younger nurse: "But why do you need a doctor for that one? Just wheel your trolley into the room with a big smile. He already had the priest last night."

The dressing-nurse's eyes widened. The older one: "Anyway, where is your trolley?"

"Still in his room."

"I'm nearly done here, just three more beds. Then we'll deal with the empyema over there, he really needs it. The other beds are moaning about the stink."

The nurse hurried away. The older one frowned again at a thermometer: "You still haven't brought it down, Kunz."

In the private room it was just a day like every other.

Ever since the room was there and opened its windows, every morning started grey, bright, brighter. The sun shone in around eleven when the trees across the yard shortened their shadows. Then the sun slipped away, the brightness lasted another hour while the room's occupant breathed and suffered, it grew dark, darker, night came. Now one man lay in the bed, fading. There was the dressings trolley, when the nurse tiptoed back in – by the window next to the bed, looking out calm, friendly, full of hope from its white-clothed glass surface. In the basins and trays lay shiny sterilised knives, pincers, scissors, clamps, sewing things; tall glass jars stuffed tight with swabs. Below were plaster-shears and bandages, uncovered. Thus did the nice dressings trolley bide by the window, metal glinting. It had swung in on white legs with little red rubber casters. The tall blonde nurse stood between bed and trolley, to hide it. It was necessary for the nurse to stay here, she wouldn't run away, death was calling to her.

Not much had happened to the young man. He was observer on a reconnaissance flight, the machine gun of an enemy plane was playing in the area, one bullet, as it flew on its hundred-kilometre journey, landed up in his body. A second earlier, before he straightened himself in his seat, it would have found empty air. Now the leaden round zipped through the young man's belt, jacket, trousers meeting no resistance, nor did the soft skin, untouched as yet by any lover, offer a defence. The bullet embedded itself as smoothly as if it belonged there. It grew from the world into this soft body like the root of a plant into soft soil. Along its path it encountered the mirror-smooth peritoneum, and made a little tear. The long slender intestines were in motion, but didn't shrink back when the bullet came, it was too fast, cut a path through tasting as it went the thin porridge still there from breakfast; the bullet carried none away. It traversed the gut. This enormous vessel undulated mightily, in it blood from the heart pulsed and beat, the bullet nipped, planted itself in bone behind, a vertebra, and stuck there. Meanwhile, along with the man in which it sat and the airplane, it was much farther off from the little gun that had spat it out. When they landed they unstrapped the man and did lots of things to him of which he had no awareness. The bullet was extracted from its hiding place, every tear located and closed. The little surgeon, always ready for a joke, looked up as he rolled the bullet between two fingers, his hands tucked into pale tan gloves: "So whose turn is it today?" Two assistant nurses called out one after the other: "Me." The doctor, still burrowing away deep in the body (he had dropped the bullet into a discharge basin) growled: "So, we'll have to draw lots again." One of them sighed: "Oh, I always lose." The surgeon adjusted his head mirror, murmured behind the gauze mask: "You're not the only loser." The war lost, we're lost, this man here lost, so wash up, wash the peritoneum, saline infusion, maybe he'll pull through.

The tall blonde nurse in the private room stood stolidly by the dressings trolley, hands at her back. She'd seen enough dying in the east, in Romania, and in the west. But still happening, now when it's all over, still happening. She pulled herself together, touched the damp trembling hand on the blanket, and held it. In case someone should suddenly come in, she pressed a finger to the pulse (but there was no pulse to count); she held the patient's hand in both of hers, he never stopped staring at the window. She didn't know what she was doing, holding his hand so long, pouring impetuous emotion into her hands. What can I do, she thought, she feared, she wanted to share her breath with him. The war's over, it's all finished now. He looked up at the ceiling. She let go the hand, the emotion was too much for her. You won't die, I'll hold on to you, you mustn't, what's your name, on the slate she read: Richard, come, Richard, hold tight, she squeezed his hand, the patient became aware, his eyes flicked to her.

Just then the door opened with a bang, a big red-cheeked young man in striped linen hospital pyjamas rushed in, his right shoulder was thickly padded under the jacket, without pausing he belted out: "Richard, hot news, they're here, sailors. Everything with legs is running away." The nurse had turned around at once, the patient's hand still in hers as if she was taking his pulse. The visitor was at the bed frame, he stared at the patient whose wide eyes were still fixed on the nurse. He let go the frame, clapped a hand to his mouth, said "Oh, oh."

The nurse: "Please don't shake the bed." He ran out. She too left, on tiptoe, pushing the trolley.

The patient faded alone. Delicate tiny flora carried by the bullet from the air and from the jacket into his body proliferated inside him. They draped a sinister pall over the guts, dulling their sheen. Grey specks sank into niches around the intestines, which were still pulsating, rising, falling. The fungi strayed into the man's veins and let the warm stream of blood carry them merrily along, how blissful they felt in this sweet sap, so different from life in cold air, on cloth. Like an orchestra awaiting the conductor's signal, they set themselves in whirling motion. And now the human was a great hollow vault through which their music echoed. He lay limp, sweating.

Vines creep over the walls of the vault, they dangle into the space, it's a jungle and these are the Tropics, monkeys clamber, monsters with wizened necks, they crawl from the swamp, colibris flit with curved beaks, plants present their blooms, shoot out narrow red tongues. Now there's organ music, and sombre cassocked men descend the scales, they drag long trains behind them, they preach and exhort, it's a long dark song.

The grey daylight outside brightens. Hours lurch by. A day has set itself in motion, 10th November, Sunday. Little sunbeams slither across the bed.

Nurses come, support the airman's head, hold wine to his lips. His face (whose face) grows ever longer. His lips fall open –not he opening his mouth. They call out. They call to him.

But he's been swallowed by the jungle.

***

THEME 12. PERFORMANCES

Musicians (from *Wallenstein*)
Ribbons (from *Manas*)
Parade in Moscow (from *The Babylonian Exile*)
Dances on the Amazon (from *The Land without Death*)
The People's Tribune (from *Citizens & Soldiers*)

***

Musicians

THE CAMP near Pilsen. Around the walls wooden huts, tents, hollows in the earth, farmyards, gradually becoming villages that punctuated miles of stubbled fields and copses. Near the town, surrounded by swampland, fringed by trenches and booby traps, accessible only by bridges, the artillery – noisy smoking smithies, patrolling sentries, cannon on wheeled trolleys, here and there black heaps of cannonballs on straw, covered by sailcloth. …

In the cold morning sun, sleepy powder-monkeys carry huge tongs, longhandled shovels, logs for levers across to the artillery park. In little lean-tos fletchers at clamp benches twist sinew for bowstrings. Occasional tumults of barking, shrill human shouts.

Music: military march, slow tempo, across from the town wall, deep bass soldiers' voices:

To war with a laugh and a curse,
To war with a laugh and a curse,
We had neither money nor purse.
To Sevengates town we came,
To Sevengates town we came,
We had neither bread nor wine …

The ensign marched alongside the many-plumed captain, a long pole braced at his midriff supported the stiff cloth of the standard, on which was blazoned the captain's colourful coat of arms: fledgling birds stretching their necks up from the nest. The captain disappeared into a cottage, the company broke up.

Three musicians continued to play in front of the cottage, bells drum fife, legs lifting daintily, loose hose to the knee edged with long strips falling at the sides, pointed shoes with ribbons and buckles. On their heads big wide-brimmed tasselled hats. Children and dogs chased about them.

Over the drummer's right shoulder, the button-studded leather strap from which the drum hung by his left leg. As one hand lay slack against the glinting rim, tapping rapidly, almost automatically, now loud now soft like a gurgling nightingale, the right hand lifted elastically, whipped back and forth to make sharp reports. The left hand incessant; the right now and then joined in its long rim-rhythm as if pulled along, then rat-tatted so vigorously on the skin that the drum shook against the raised knee and transmitted the vibration to the drummer's teeth. He smiled, eyes twitching.

The bell-player was a mere lad. His left hand rested languidly at his hip. The flowing silk scarf fluttered out behind him. In his right hand he held the yard-long pole, at its tip the glinting star with its hanging bells. His eyes wandered over the children as if he played for nobody, seemed free as the air. He stood rock-steady in a graceful pose, nothing moved, not head, foot, rump, just the two eyes, their lids, the right arm. Even that stayed mostly pressed to his side, lower arm raised, wrist turning. With the slightest twitch or turn he could make the bells twitter clang boom, blare proud and enticing like the noise from the beaks of a thousand birds; and when he swung his pole high as if raising a standard, shifted his legs, he lowered his head, gazed defiantly at the points of his shoes. The fife took the lead; it rested on the bandolier over his right shoulder. The piper stood still, attending to the melody. His mouth, his nimble fingers gambolled, lifted, pressed onto the hollow tube. They excited it, soothed it, caressed it like a beloved pet. He gazed soulfully from dark eyes.

★★★

Ribbons

Ah, where is Savitri?
When was the last time, Manas, that a woman,
Any woman, placed her feet upon your toes,
And laid her tender tendril arms about your neck?
The skiffs, so many skiffs, skimming over the round pool.
Aai, aai from boat to boat.
You temptresses with shining hair, do not flit past,
Do not float past like leaves,
Pause a while to bring Manas peace,
Calm his eyes, his hands, and help him catch his breath.
There, outside the hall, the Victory Theatre, where they sang:
'Manas our jewel, we rejoiced when you rode out,
Now you are here again.'
How they dance, the women. They have no fear of Manas.
The men have run away.
The women – whose work is this? – have come out from their houses
And stand and try out steps and sing, move their arms,
Such grace in their shoulders.

Their bracelets tinkle, and some spin around.
How they throw out ribbons, spin around,
Throw out ribbons, wave the ribbons up and down,
Wave red ribbons, wave blue ribbons.
Dance, fling their slender legs
Stretch out their ring-decked toes,
And spin, sway, wave ribbons.
His soul, it was not calmed,
Was filled, his soul, with a longing deeper yet
Than the longing of some dead thing for life.
No dead thing can be so filled with yearning, such
  deep yearning,
Enormous thirst for life, can be so filled with love
As a living thing, as he himself for love.
His breast was seized by it, arms seized,
So deluged was he by the founts of love.
His eyes stayed open, the lashes forgot to blink.
The women danced, waved ribbons.
Manas' breath fled.
He was a sigh amid the waving ribbons,
A delight.

★★★

Parade in Moscow

Now in Russia Tsar Nicholas, Nikolai I Pavlovich, son of Tsar Paul and his second consort Maria Fedorovna, had died, and Alexander Nikolaevich ascended the Romanov throne. This happened in the Sixties of the last century. The Crimean War had ended unfortunately for Russia, and the whole nation from the pinnacle of Tsardom down to the depths of the popular masses were seized by a consciousness that The Time Had Come. But for what, wasn't clear. In his declaration on the peace treaty with Turkey, the new Tsar announced sweeping reforms. Even Foreign Minister Gorchakov couldn't help declaring in a round robin to other states that Russia wished to focus its attention on new reforms. …

The Minister for Public Works had Kremlin Square in Moscow cleansed of all the people, animals and rubbish that had gathered there over the course of centuries. A number of road engineers with their assistants and under-assistants paved the square with smooth flagstones, laid tracks all around and across the square, carpenters erected a rostrum, decorators laid carpets and nailed up flags, from the old imperial Terem Palace oxen escorted by a squad of cavalry hauled a wagon bearing the Imperial Throne. (But it was a facsimile, there was concern the real one might be stolen.)

And one morning, the approach of which had been predicted with certainty by the court astrologers, riding across Kremlin Square on a sturdy black horse came Tsar Alexander the Second and his glittering retinue. Guided by Rostovtsev, who was very nervous, he took his place on the rostrum. Shots were still being fired in all nearby streets, killing a number of stray dogs. Then Rostovtsev in his big general's uniform gave a rousing speech from a second rostrum, which had prudently been erected beyond pistol-shot of the imperial throne. As a result no one could hear him. He spoke of ruin, of cautious Progress and decisive Regress, of the power of ever-advancing facts, and the even greater power of the Tsar. When he concluded with a Huzzah! for the Tsar, those on the court rostrum thought he was announcing the arrival of Progress, and in self-defence let loose ten salvos in his direction. All missed the target, due to the fortunate positioning of the speaker's rostrum.

The main act began. On the court rostrum, George had taken a seat near Tsar Alexander the Second. He had been allowed up there by Rostovtsev and Gorchakov, the Foreign

Minister, as representative of an unfamiliar power, hence to be treated with redoubled caution. He smoked a fine cigar, which he'd bought in Constantinople, and had a small table at his side for the arrack with which he refreshed himself. He was the only one near the throne who smoked and drank during the ceremony. The degree of unfamiliarity led to disastrous consequences. During the ceremony, a great intimacy developed between him and the Tsar. George assured the Tsar he was here only because he was on the point of adopting the same interest in Progress and Regress as Alexander. He thought, when he heard of the enormous preparations being made here, he could use the opportunity to sort out his own business at the same time, he hopes this is in order.

Alexander nodded down from his fake throne, not sure if he should be jovial or fraternal, and so, from behind a handkerchief: He hoped so too.

Trumpet-blasts from every rooftop that was under surveillance. But they hadn't reckoned with Alexander Herzen. It was Herzen now who, flaunting the billowing locks of Idealism, climbed onto the heavily damaged speaker's rostrum. Since no one knew if he was part of the programme, and Rostovtsev and Gorchakov were just now shaking hands and congratulating each other on the splendid start to the day, and it wasn't raining, they let him speak. He spoke from the heart. He demanded fundamental, bold, radical reforms. All half measures meant stagnation, any thought of fantastic Utopias was far from his mind. "Freedom," he cried, "fourfold freedom: of the peasantry from estate management, of the courts from the government, of words from the censor, of our backs from the rod. This is no fantastical Utopia."

Couriers brought these words to the Tsar's attention. By mean of a cannon-shot he invited Herzen to sit down. The speaker's rostrum was shattered.

Then along came a procession representing modern

culture and its blessings. The Tsar was to be informed of all reforms in a non-threatening and at the same time enthusing manner; and if he wanted them, then reforms would happen in God's name.

The two commissars had achieved wonders in such a short time! Not only had they mobilised, from America to Japan, from Alaska to Newfoundland, everything that could be presented to the Tsar in terms of new inventions. Their untiring efforts had also succeeded in procuring, on loan for today at least, inventions that would not be made for another thirty or fifty years. These days, exhibiting an electric bulb or a dynamo will arouse little amazement, but if you consider that these items will see the light of day only decades later, your scepticism will need to be moderated. When the amazed Tsar caught sight of the colossal American and English machines, his hair stood on end. They had to remove his headgear. During the pauses, when the amazement abated, they put it back on. People counted this off and on activity as if it were the curtain at a premiere. He clapped his hands. Everyone copied him. The whole crowd clapped. The Tsar nodded over his shoulder to congratulate Gorchakov and Rostovtsev. They bowed low in their general's uniforms, each beaming and pointing to the other, as the saying goes, "twins wearing the same cap". George too was delighted, he drank to them both, they again pointed to one another, George murmured, "Well well, so much going on in the world." Admittedly, when the current transformer with a rating of 50,000 volts came along, Alexander II blinked doubtfully. He bent down to George and smiled: "Potemkin villages! But it's good." George: "Well well."

Alexander II and George took so much pleasure in each other's company as they exchanged views in this free and easy way, that after a while they changed places. George sat on the throne, the Tsar down below smoked, and drank George's arrack. Slowly and surreptitiously they changed their wardrobe too, one boot after the other made its way up or down, the purple robe went up, George handed over his nice comfortable jacket, made for him in Constantinople in the tailoring workshop of Kiku, so gorgeous it suited even the powerful Tsar.

First to appear bleating onto the broad square, seething with a huge mass of humanity, was a big flock of woolly sheep. These were escorted by shepherds. They carried a banner with the first point of the Programme: "Let the people be clothed!" Several dogs took care that the sheep didn't stray. … Behind them marched men making loud clacking noises with giant shears. They were the barbers of these sheep. It made clear to the sheep as well as the onlookers: now there must and will be shearing. Nothing will die, they only have to yield up their hair. …

Now a mass of common city dwellers and peasants was driven onto the square. Suddenly the cordon of soldiers blocking off the square parted, and all the poor chance onlookers from the farthest reaches of the square were driven by whips into the arena. They raised a frightful outcry. There were little men and little women, some with children, some too with horses and little peasant carts. The little people made a pitiful din, and had to be driven with violence along behind the perfume industry, because they thought now they were for it. Really it wasn't a quite comfortable sight, given the frequent rifle shots. Enormous laughter followed this procession, around two hundred and fifty people kept trying to break away, causing work for the gendarmes. …

Then the whole pack was driven headlong away from the square, and insofar as they engaged in fisticuffs with the gendarmes, were imprisoned and deported.

***

Two Dances on the Amazon

BESIDE the water lay a boat the men had left half finished. It rested on two wooden runners. They fetched palm leaves, in the afternoon burnt it away from the inside, fetched palm leaves, burnt it from the outside. They did this so their men could travel.

In the evening a thunderstorm broke. The old women kept the manioc mash until they were all back from fishing, grilled the fish. Then there was loud laughter, children kept by the fire in front of the clan house, young women and grown girls disappeared into the huts. They painted themselves a lovely black with soot, red with urucu, they oiled their hair, the almond eyes of the young ones glinted with pleasure, they hung necklaces of black seeds around their necks, tied threads of red cotton on arm and calf. Then one leapt from her hut, she was the first, she swung the dance-rattle, whooped, she wore a net shawl over her shoulders, a little red parrot sat on her head. The others ran out, they looked beautiful and happy. They formed a line one behind the other, arms crossed at the breast, swayed left, swayed right, sang a dancing song, filed past the clan house. The children and old women stood up.

Two lines in the dirt – this was a river, the young women leapt along the bank, they wanted to cross, they were the men. One rowed on the river, the back covered in palm leaves – the river spirit. They bowed down to him, he let them cross. They greeted the old women and the others. Then they faced each other, two by two, heads lowered, hands covering their eyes, man and wife, and wept greetings.

The dance ended, darkness fell. They laughed and ate, radiant in the firelight.

THAT evening they performed the great armadillo dance. There before the great fire the armadillo leapt. The hero was called Rairu, he danced close to the powerful beast, it grabbed him, he had to throw away his spear, the beast struck his shoulder, he had to throw away his bow and quiver of arrows, the beast butted him in the chest, he had to throw away his shield, he fled from the strong armadillo and crawled around in the dirt, circling and again circling, the armadillo danced around Rairu, first on one leg and whooped, then on the other leg and whooped. It drove him towards the pit trap, he tried to escape, it grabbed his head and pulled him into the pit, the pit collapsed on both of them, the big armadillo and Rairu.

The armadillo has disappeared!
The great armadillo has defeated Rairu!
The great armadillo has pulled Rairu into the pit!

And people clambered from the pit, greeted forest, river, sky, moon. The great armadillo had vanished into the moon. The young warrior women and their captives danced when the people sprang out of the pit. The women held spears, the men held shields, but they had to die.

Cuzumarra, fat warrior, squatted with the queen on a mat. Unseen by others, the spirit of the great armadillo came down from the new moon to him who was once Cuzumarra and spoke: "Well, Cuzumarra? Stand up! Or is even that beyond you now? Stand. And dance."

The queen squealed when he rose from the mat and pushed into the circle of dancers. The spirit told him not to heed their shouts, to take a shield from a dead man. He did so, and stood with the men.

A monstrous howl greeted the new moon that showed itself in the blue between palm leaves. One by one, men fell, Cuzumarra among them. Women thronged drunkenly towards the blood that sorceresses sprayed, the older women to regain their strength, the young women for their lives and children.

Frogs boomed from the swamps, thunder rumbled. The river flowed silent under pale moonlight. Through nightdark fields, masked dancers paraded with clappers, feeding the ground with blood from gourds.

***

The People's Tribune

AND now several wind instruments began blaring. Their mournful tone suggested they didn't really believe any of it. Karl Liebknecht, the new People's Tribune, emerged from the forest of red flags.

From where they stood, separated from the graves by a sea of people, they could look right at the speaker's face. And when this Liebknecht began to speak, it was at once a very different matter from those who'd gone before. Flagbearers hoisted their flags proudly and as one to greet their leader. The rumble from the throng of voices outside subsided, there were cries of "Quiet! Liebknecht!". The cry "quiet" rippled outward; everyone must know all the way to the Schlossplatz that Liebknecht was about to speak; now, without loudspeakers, across a whole web of streets, half Berlin was to be addressed.

The People's Tribune was lanky, he had a pale restless face, his eyes, bleary, turned from side to side without resting on anything; the dark moustache drooped uncombed over his mouth. Now and then the still youthful man ground his teeth together, in a kind of perpetual fury and outrage that prevented his thoughts from cohering. He seemed to be the only one at the cemetery who did not realise how the throng was hanging on his every word. He spoke loudly, with vigour, in irregular bursts, and at the same time croaked and often stumbled.

Shrill as a song of vengeance and victory was his opening:

"The Hohenzollerns hoped to parade victorious at the war's end through the Brandenburg Gate. But instead the proletariat intervened. The Hohenzollerns ran away, every throne in Germany was overturned. These gentlemen and their cowardly hangers-on are now nowhere to be seen. They have slunk into their mouseholes. They dare not, these generals, these cabbage Junkers, they dare not stand before us and account for themselves, with good reason, the exploiters, the bloodsuckers, parasites on the poor toiling workers from whose sweat they have lived and who have now shaken them off and squashed them underfoot. The time of mass murder is past, the game is over at last for the criminals on the throne; covered in contempt and shame, cursed and hated by the whole world, they have fled away condemned, pathetic, along with their blue eyeglasses, these incorrigible bloodsuckers. Even into foreign parts shall the hatred and curses of the starved, murdered, cudgelled people pursue them."

The People's Tribune wore a black frock-coat that hung on him loose and wrinkled. His nervous head, the hair on it drifting over his forehead and ears, turned with these last phrases up to the grey sky; it was to this that he had screamed his rage. Now the man ground his teeth and surrendered to his spleen. A curious unrestrained hatred had been set off, a mere dram of this hatred. Why did they listen to him with such enormous excitement? Because he was no orator, because as he spoke he was not addressing them, because he was only giving expression in their presence to his grief, but it was genuine emotion, a torrent of grief, and as the torrent swept downhill it carried them along, and who after such a war did not bear within themselves bitterness, anger and hatred. Ah, the powerless times are gone. We shall be raised once more to the heights of humanity.

Now Liebknecht crossed his arms and gazed into the

open grave at his feet.

Dark holes. Now it was not about princes and mass murderers. Now it was the turn of the dead, the fallen. He would sing a hymn to their courage. But he tendered them only a few words, his voice low, as if embarrassed to address close relatives in front of so many people. "There you lie, you have shown what you are. The blood that flowed from you is our blood. They shot you, they shot us. Everyone should know it, and that we feel the agony of these wounds. Accept our thanks, friends."

Already his eyes had lifted from the dark embrace of the grave walls, his eyes bored into the red of a flag in front of him, his arms travelled through the air.

"The agony shall not be forgotten. We know what the target was of the bullets that hit them. The awakened proletariat was the target. The murderers had not yet had enough. They flailed away on every front, they threw the people's property out of every window, squandered the people's energies, used everything up in order to triumph, in order to force upon the world their insolent wicked yoke. The whole world rose up against them. In the end, when everything was lost, they murdered you to save themselves. And even now they do not stand idle. They have accomplices and supporters where none would have expected."

Now he was yelling, he lifted his shoulders and cried out with arms stretched high; he seemed to be trying to lift himself off the ground: "Conspiracies are in train, to disrupt the dictatorship of the proletariat and place it once again at their mercy. After such defeats, after such crimes the murderers and assassins still have the gall to forge new schemes, and find accomplices. Their conscience has not awoken, and they know how to befog the consciences of those others who are in league with them. We shall block their path! Be on your guard! Comrades, colleagues, friends! Using every means, even by putting our own lives on the line, we must fight for the revolution."

The coffins were lowered, sailors lined up at the graveside, a triple salute rang out.

***

THEME 13. TROGLODYTES

Burrows (from *Wallenstein*)
Underground (from *Mountains Oceans Giants*)
Busy Mole (from *Manas*)
Strays (from *Citizens & Soldiers*)

★★★

Burrows

THEY crept out of burrows in the earth, mud-brown men, frightened squinting faces, grubby peasant smocks, their blinking eyes scanned the plain that fell away in front of them, the windbreak of green bushes; they signalled, whistled behind them. Children clambered up flinching at the light, afraid. Women with long braids, sand in their bonnets, shook dun skirts in the grey-white light of morning. The tall forest edge came alive; the undergrowth among firs and beeches was broken through; low whistles.

A double row of tiny white tents down on the plain, slender tall lances looming over low village houses; the stone cross at the foot of the slope overturned; horses neighing, a shot now and then; over a few shingled roofs a layer of dark smoke unmoving; at the other end of the village, little barrows moved slowly up the lane. To the left on the horizon, the church tower of Zittau. They were in the very farthest corner of Saxony, on the Bohemian border.

The men dragged spades and pickaxes out of the forest, dug an open grave, deeper, wider, bending mutely to the task extended it in a zigzag along the slope, hour by hour. In the forest cattle lowed, women washing, cooking at a fire; the smoke rose as scattered wisps dispersed by big cowhides stretched high in the treetops. Small bands of men slipped separately down the slope in the middle of the day, crept around the village, fell from both sides on solitary carts, struck down mercenaries, carried sacks to nearby hiding places, at evening slipped back up.

Trees felled, palisades erected. Cave dwellings, forest dwellings in Lausitz. Communities attacked by vengeful troops, killed, those who could flee crept among other refugee groups. From Lausitz into Bohemia wandering gypsy-like bands gathered, climbed scouting along the hilly country beside the Elbe, past vineyards, blooming fields of hops, rapeseed, beets. Open towns were unsettled; orchards plundered near Leitmeritz; on the meadowlands by Melnik lay the corpses of people dead of hunger; many women children stayed behind in the villages. They thronged the gloomy valley of the Moldau, aimless, driven on by misery.

★★★

Underground

THE masses of the western townzones were driven from the surface down under the ground; underground, the rulers could impose their total monopoly power. After refugees had set up simple temporary subterranean dwellings, the rulers, arrogant and gleeful, established factories devices weapons underground. Meki-factories in Hamburg and Oslo were destroyed by monsters: this provided the excuse to transfer all facilities away from the surface. Jubilation among the rulers where this occurred. Now you can show them what you are.

Masses of humanity dug themselves in against the rampaging monsters, were trodden down by these arrogant men and scarcely less masculine women. Like a tree, a forest with roots pointing upward, the cities grew down into the depths. Thick slabs of concrete and rock covered the locations of former squares and streets, or else these lay desolate. When centuries ago the Meki-factories appeared, people had abandoned ploughland and forest, let them revert to uninhabited wilderness, had concentrated in city-states. People clung to their devices like flies to a honey-stick. Now they abandoned even the old townzone sites. People lived as best they could, not like an anthill aimed up at the surface. They dug into the Earth, made what they needed piece by piece, by their own hands. Nestled in the Earth like a family of beetles deep beneath the bark of a tree; dug themselves in deeper and deeper.

Several months after the first stunning assaults, driven by Delvil's vengeful outbursts, those parts of London along the Channel, the districts of Colchester and Ipswich, later the southern suburbs Hastings Ramsgate Dover, had all vanished from the face of the Earth where they had stood for so many centuries. Streets of ruined buildings were invaded by wilderness and forest. The concrete slabs were left open to the air; mosses and patches of greenery soon covered them. Concealed openings had been built into the slabs for ventilation and the delivery of raw materials. Shafts as in a mine were driven between different rock strata. They were building a coral reef. They proceeded from many places at once, and converged in the depths. They pushed through sand, alluvial and diluvial rubble; forced back deep groundwater, cut into layers of impermeable clay. Calmly implacably they spread abyssally deep into the Earth, these new cities with their people, the life of London Oxford Reading Colchester Hastings Ramsgate Luton Hertford Aldershot. They sank into the beds of old forgotten seas, between marl and chalk, rummaged among the silent remains of thin-shelled mussels from distant epochs, fragments of cephalopod from millennia before. They pushed walls of earth apart where once at high tide myriads of conches, generation on generation, had played, crystal clear beings with strong paddle-feet that they moved up and down like wings through the foaming tide.

As storey after storey was dug into clay, as ever bigger caverns were excavated, and spoil – loose earth, blasted rock – was heaped up in the ruined streets of the surface, everyone lost any sense of fear. They were not fleeing from the monsters: they were on a grand new expedition. The senates called: "Away from the Earth," and they dug merrily down; the miracle of human capability experienced by the Greenland expeditionaries they now could experience for themselves.

***

Busy Mole

When the sun rose he moved up higher, to a deep
  limestone cave.
All four of them slept there in the dark, Kalongs on
  the ceiling, Manas in a corner.
The stars came out, flashing flickering.
Now Manas crawled out of the cave.
Doubting, whispering, chewed his lips.
    'Am I a demon?' And chewed his lips:
    'Hope the Kalongs don't see me.' His eyes glowed:
    'Maybe I shall move against Kailash.
    I want to tear Shiva apart.'
And shook from below like a mountain about to split
  itself asunder.
    'I don't know why I've been sent back, what I'm
      supposed to do on Earth.'
Struggled with himself.

He rousted the Kalongs from the cave. He dug himself
  in,
Dug himself into the damp soil in his corner,

He wanted to bury himself deeper and deeper,
And groaned gasped: 'I shan't walk the Earth again.'
The three dreadful Kalongs blocked the entrance to the cave,
Their bodies stood tall,
They stuck their snouts into the cave to see what Manas was up to.
But the cave had bends, with niches and protrusions.
They only heard his muttering and gasping at the back,
Shifting soil and stones like an industrious mole.
They bayed bleated. In there he was groaning:
'Manas escaped from the Field of the Dead,
Manas with the hands of a lion, teeth of a tiger.'
They squealed: 'Fists of stone.'
He laboured and roared:
'Manas stands in a cave,
Stands at the wall, digs in the corner,
At rock that's damp.
And roars and roars: I don't know why I've returned
Just to have wet hands from scrabbling at rock!
Just to see desolate steppelands!
Just to see stupid humans, I, who am become human too.'
They squealed:
'Come out, Manas. Come with us, come along now.'
He roared: 'I shall go with you to the Field of the Dead.
I need to tear someone apart.
I want to go into battle.'

And for whole long days Manas dug away in the cave.
Finally no words came out.
Only a low groaning and the crack of thrown rocks
Told the Kalongs he was still alive.
They dared not go back in.
But one night suddenly he crawled to the entrance,
Hollow-eyed, chin trembling, covered in mud from head to toe.
They snarled in his direction.
Arms dangling, dull-eyed, he blew air from him:
'But can I actually die?'
Stood, scraped shoulders legs against the rockface.
He kept asking the same question, they did not understand it.

In the middle of the night his face changed.
He seemed to see the cave, the night, the Kalongs.
He summoned Nishumbha to him, petted him a long while,
Then lay down on him, but would not let him fly.
He seemed to fall asleep there.
Then Nishumbha felt Manas growing heavy, heavier,
Manas squashing him in fury, in a spasm.
Nishumbha squawked fidgeted. Manas wheezed.
His arms were made of iron. He beat at Nishumbha's throat.
'Up, up,' he cried, always 'up!'
The other two Kalongs flapped closer.
'Up, up,' constantly from Manas,
Though he was squashing Nishumbha to the ground until he almost choked,
It was one wild stretching motion.
Then he relaxed. 'Up, up,' in Nishumbha's ear.

He was lighter now, Nishumbha crawled forward.
The Kalongs spread their wings.
'I want to go into battle.'
They whinnied: 'Where then.'
He breathed: 'Onward.'

***

Strays

IN the forest some lived in well constructed burrows underground. They had learned to build dugouts, and to camouflage them. Though as a rule military police and army patrols never ventured into the thickets, it happened now and then that a simple peasant who had some reason to avoid the open road would suddenly, all alone in the silent forest, feel the ground give way beneath his feet, and he would tumble flailing into a meters-deep abyss. And what kind of abyss? A man trap? No, not at all. He would tumble in among merrily squeaking piglets and horribly cackling chickens alarmed by the fall. And when the unlucky fellow had tried in vain for a while to clamber back out amid the animal chorus – a hard task, for the walls narrowed like a chimney as they rose, and widened greatly lower down, precisely the opposite of what someone trying to clamber out would wish – after a time, which might be several hours, someone would appear up above, a woman maybe, and then several men shining dark-lanterns down, and after some palaver they would lower a rope ladder and he could climb back into lovely daylight, mucky with soil and the droppings of hens and pigs. The people up there would watch him closely. Any who fell into the pit would likely know about the outlaws already. They would be stern or friendly, as the case required. No one would escape without massive threats of penalties. But mostly the mishap would result in new trading connections.

Once a butcher from Douai suffered such a calamity. He was an elderly man, who had little enough butchering to do. In the interests of his children, every couple of weeks he looked anxi0usly about for livestock that would take pity on hungry humans. Glum and empty-handed, he was walking one afternoon through the forest, he couldn't bring himself to return home like this, and took the diversion through the forest purely out of chagrin and professional antipathy to the military police who strove to maintain human beings in a state of hunger. Then he tripped. And something happened he had never dreamed of: he fell in among pigs. "Can it be possible," the butcher thought, "is this where people hide their goods and chattels? Is this still a human age?" It was pitch dark down there, at least for the moment. He was limited to ears and sense of touch. There were chickens down there too. But where were the people they belonged to?

Slowly his eyes adjusted, and he gazed with delight on the riches at hand. He didn't mind dirt and stink, to him they were nourishing aromas. But why did no one show up. The elderly man was reluctant to try climbing as the first option, but he worried that it might be half a day at least before the owner showed himself, the fellow would surely come to feed his stock.

And indeed, it had grown dark when finally, as he squatted in a fatherly way among the dear little pigs and the good little chickens, he heard voices above, then there was a shout, ah, they could hear something, and then a dark-lantern shone down. A man's voice said: "Aha, there he is."

"Just the one?"

"Yes. I say, what are you doing down there?" He spoke French.

"I fell in."

"What were you doing in the forest?"

"I'm a butcher from Douai, I lost my way, I was heading home."

"Butcher?" Now there was a burst of laughter up above. Someone called down: "So you meant to acquire our pigs on the cheap?"

"But sir."

"You're a burglar. We'll turn you in to the police."

"Let me out, sir, I'll explain it all to you once I'm up." The butcher was not at all frightened, he could feel the coins in the lining of his jacket. Someone called down: "Are you hurt?" The question seemed friendly enough, so he replied: "Yes, a little. My knee." A few minutes later, during which the lantern had been withdrawn, the question came:

"Do you have a gun?"

"No, just some money." Now the rope ladder was lowered. He clambered up happily and was greeted by a mighty salvo of laughter. This was triggered, among other things, by the dreadful state of his clothes. It seemed to him, as he looked around at the circle of ten men (a woman was also present) that he recognised one or other as locals. He apologised for having caused them any inconvenience, described his accident, when questioned replied quite openly that he'd been scouting the district for contraband goods, alas without success. He'd now like to enter into a business discussion with the good gentlemen. At this they grew extremely reticent. To cut a long story short, he was informed, after a confidential discussion out of his hearing, that he would have to stay here until tomorrow morning, around midday.

"Here? But where? In the muck?"

"No." There were enquiries about the amount of cash he was carrying on him; he named a considerable sum, somewhat rounded down. And in a satisfied friendly way he was informed that they could do nothing more about the situation without the presence of a certain two persons. And they led him for ten minutes or so through the forest, suddenly plunged down some earthen steps, and were under the turf in a room with board supports, tolerably warm but alas horribly smoky. Several other rooms adjoined, less warm but even smokier. They told the butcher that this room was a bit higher than the others, and so smoke was drawn into it. They were sorry they would have to accommodate him in the last room, which was the highest, where two others were already asleep. Well, he can console himself with the thought that who comes last eats last. The butcher complained: "You could suffocate in there." They assured him: "We all have the catarrh, but no one has ever suffocated."

Next morning, lightly smoked but nevertheless well refreshed by his sleep after a solid supper, he crawled together with his two companions in sorrow, the newest recruits to the band, from his bed of hay into the front room, a kind of communal living room. There wonderful coffee was served in real cups, and six of them were sitting lazily on benches around the table. The young female, not yet twenty years old, maybe eighteen, maybe even younger, fed the iron stove with damp lumps of wood, which were roundly cursed by all as the principal malefactors, i.e. smoke generators, but there was nothing to be done, they were delivered by Nature in that condition. They had red wine and cigarettes, provided on demand; the butcher noticed that the girl wrote everything down, it was run like an actual bar. Apart from an irritating cough, the butcher felt quite at ease.

The sense of ease was accompanied by the thought that his family must be dreadfully worried about him, the accident must have enhanced his value. He himself regarded it not as a deprivation of freedom, but as deferred business.

As first the oven alone, then the others, finally he himself began smoking, he grew curious about how they had managed so wonderfully to be done with the war, for he found their situation exceptionally pleasant. …

***

THEME 14. EXILE

Exodus to Saxony (from *Wallenstein*)
Mother of Pestilence (from *Manas*)
Cuzumarra (from *The Land without Death*)
Arrival on Earth (from *The Babylonian Exile*)
The Forester (from *Citizens & Soldiers*)

***

Exodus to Saxony

WAGONS creaked along roads to north and west past laden fruit-trees swarming soldiers; the Bohemian Brethren were emigrating to Saxony.

Seated on heavy nags, under wide high felt hats, sword at the side, squat stony men and citizens; on long-bearded faces could be read: political rights, and the King. Alongside came peaceable Free Confessors, who cradled themselves in their hopes; their Hus had been burned at Constance by the Council; who would join them? What would become of the world and the human soul without the salvation that Hus brought anew to Bohemia? Jesuits and the Emperor Ferdinand have stolen away the chalice and sword that King George Podiebrad placed centuries before in Thein church; they have exhumed dead heroes of the faith, burned them, thrown the ashes in our faces. They all wore long brown and blue smocks, big black floppy hats, vests with red lapels. Many of the younger ones stepped out bright in short jackets with rows of brass buttons and yellow hose, with studded walking sticks.

Behind those ready for martyrdom came the timid, cast down by fear, who wanted only to save their lives. Roads out of villages, town gates were thronged by the poor. As their benefactors walked by they joined the train; knapsacks, wheelbarrows, mule-carts blended with the broad stream of wagons and coaches. Here, at the start of their sorrows, they were strongest; the sight of them clouded the eyes of the well-to-do with bitterness; the poor were embarrassed. Peasants, backs turned to the migrant stream, already knew what was happening here: misery was teaching an alien sentiment, senseless hatred upon senseless hatred! They would blame themselves, punish themselves for memories of abandoned houses and fields. Thatched roofs, red-tiled roofs, barns sties herb-gardens lavender mignonette mint. Lovely gables with little columns, serrated dormers, shingled eaves with memorial tablets, terraces fronting the houses, pictures stored behind sea-squills.

In many places tearful adherents of the Old Religion thronged about the migrant stream: Catholics, priests in regalia, almost craving forgiveness. They walked blindly in the dust of the road, to which they were unused, buried in thought, in their hand the book, the Bible. The book, that terrible book, loathsome book! How often in their imagination had the Catholic priests, sorrowful and pitying, seen the most wretched people wandering with the book; what unspeakable misfortune had that book caused. Many thousands were moving out, from all classes of society, women and children too.

The migrants were taking all fertility with them. Women plump, young, careworn, little mothers, brown faces, proud, shrivelled; women on carts, beside donkeys, in coaches. Long gowns, headbands, colourful skirts, camisoles; embroidered doves in their hair, women from Pilsen in pinned white headdress. Those from the Choden land on the frontier, small bodies in red. They tramped through the waning summer, merged on highways; apple trees dropped round red fruit on them. In villages ahead, officials set watch in the church tower, for in a few places some rogue had rung the bells at their approach to stir the people up at the sight of the sad procession. Troops from the Holstein Regiment were posted to turn the wanderers onto side roads, divert them around larger towns down wearisome perilous lanes, over barren heath.

At crossroads, by roadside crucifixes, men appeared, ragged, looking like beggars, armed with dangerous clubs. They had been sent by old Count Thurn, fugitive rebel leader, now agitating in Saxony Brandenburg Holland. Mocked the wanderers to goad them on: "Where are you off to? Look at you! Did the Emperor buy your land off you? Must have paid a good price, seeing how fast you run to keep it from robbers. How much, how much?"

"Gypsies, gypsies," they yelled laughing behind them. Now many were overcome with pain and despair; shoulders grew weak, their knees knocked. Oh the road! After weary hours of walking the riff-raff straggled up behind them again, quaint figures on muleback, saluted them: "Praise be to Jesus!" The popish greeting was ignored in silence. "Are you heathens?" – "Have they cut your tongue out already?" – "Oh, pious people, these are pious. Dissenters. For whom the Jesuit gents weren't pious enough. See, there's Simeon from the Needlemakers' Guild. Did you open up your chests, Simeon, pack all your glassware in a sack?" – "Simeon, don't be proud, I'm a tramp too, master, my greeting is offered in earnest respect." – "The respectable damsel Faustina, look at her, on a wagon beside her father; taking herself off to Saxony to find a husband, hope she won't forget me." – "Honourable upright gentlemen one and all, aunties, cousins, God be with you. Lovely company along the whole highway. Welcome between our doorposts. You had the forethought to bring your own roofs."

Whips snapped at them from wagons; stones were thrown. They fell back: "The highway, the highway! Dear brothers!

Sisters! Little brides! Would you like to come with us, read palms, sell moonshine and gentian?" – "Auntie Walpurga, tender delicate creature, come down to us from the lady your mother. You're no infant now, fly into my arms. I stole a big cushion from an Italian, I'll tie it about your waist, under your skirt; you can earn hellers and Bohemian groats with me. What will you give me for my instruction?"

As they leaped around mocking and jabbering, waving their caps, smacking their legs, curses rained down from the mouths of the men who continued calmly walking, from those with sacks and sweat-dripping cheeks, from the old man behind the dog-cart. "Take your God-be-with-you and be damned, you rogue!"

"Master, well spoken. You'll have no troubles. You carry good fortune in your gob."

"Damned swinish ruffian." Now one stretched out on the verge, pointed his dirty bare feet in an affected manner: "So I am cursed, and I thank you for it. Look at me: your words have not improved me, master. They were no use: I'm no prettier, no sleeker, no more gentle than before. Do you know others?"

"Filthy tramp, treacherous dog, godforsaken thief." A merry swarm followed the angry outbursts at a distance, shook their heads: "Still no use, still no use." Stones flew.

Near Leitmeritz the valley of the Elbe broadened out, fruit heavy on the trees amid dense foliage; on the slopes grapes shimmered green, brown, blue, villages, villages. Beyond them long lines of mountains, isolated cones swathed in haze. The road became steeper. The pointed peaks of Radobýl and Lovoš to left and right; spruce forests. Gillyflowers grew wild – Mary's tears, shed on the path to Golgotha. Where now is our Mother Prague. Little springs trickled at the roadside; the small green-smocked man with the reedy voice and no left thumb who sits there red-haired, he's sewing his boot; he keeps a pot for the souls of the drowned. Higher and higher, sweet mountains, sweet forests, sweet springs. How the crags tower, try to box them in. No one leaped out at them, here only birds sang. Cool forest, needles underfoot, peaceful villages unmolested by Commissions, manor houses, green meadows, farms. Moments ago they slid their feet across lush ground as if to drink it in, were gasping at the sight of gorges and rockwalls below, now here a level plain stretches bewitched before them, wagons and animals men children women move into it as if sinking into nothingness, disappearing into an expanse that reaches from Heaven to earth and out to every side. Voices fell silent, colour drained from faces; barren wastes, hostile to humans, unapproachable by living beings.

They tiptoed cautiously around bluegreen clumps of swamp-pine, plucked bog plants that stabbed the fingers; marshy ground shook, they danced, stumbled. Looked behind them, began to grow frightened, no more dark forest to be seen. The air uncanny. Here and there poor people crept out of the earth ahead of them, carrying hammer pike bucket; grey dust, ore; strange caves, huge spoil dumps, enormous sinkholes. The ground began to fall away, the wagons moved more easily, wave by wave the ground descended, heathland, dark silent forests. Slowly they all came down with bated breath into an unknown region, over there.

They crossed the wide bare plateau sadder, more exhausted. Hateful Croatian riders pranced on little horses up ahead, came round behind them. Wild sheepskin hats askew on black locks that swirled high; they kneaded their brown mounts with their feet; their legs in dazzling white linen trousers and high boots jogged up and down. They rounded up the train with whips and pikes, circled them like sheepdogs. Incomprehensible orders were shouted by soldiers in a foreign tongue. A curse: you ducked. And yet fear of them faded the closer they came to the frontier down below. They saw with anxious unease how this was happening: how they were retreating from the high ground. Soon these riders will have vanished, returned to the beloved homeland, they will once again see the green meadows, while we remain outside.

Unconsciously they slackened the pace of travel; the Croats urged them on; sometimes an axle was deliberately broken, blocking the whole road. Several tracks marked the way, and they could have hurried on down, but instead the train piled up immobile behind the blockage. They exchanged glances of furtive sweetness, touched arms wearily, picked stones from the path, kissed the sparse dwarf pines, hearkened to the squawks of ravens as if they were songs from human mouths. Some approached the riders, humbly asked that they be allowed to rest a while here, little thinking how they were to find food. Some just lay down. The Croats became fiercer, started manhandling them; this region was repugnant to them. And the Bohemian refugees, as if disaster lay ahead, jostled against one another, were forced apart, moved on in misery, checking checking every downward step.

Until next morning a shocking mind-numbing distant sound of bells behind a little rise ahead, carried on gusts of wind. The riders uttered cries of joy, laughed at one another: Saxony! The first white wretched Saxon roofs!

★★★

Mother of Pestilence

Then down across the glacier,
Down from Milam, guided by Prurana,
Came the Mother of Pestilence, astride a panther.
Durga, Kali is her name.
Black and marl-daubed her giant body,
She had four busy hands of bone,
Carried drums, and slings to strangle with.

Behind her, riding donkeys, the Mothers of Terror,
Yellow-fanged fire-red naked women,
A pack before which every living thing falls sick.
They urged their skittish mounts down the glacier
  with switches.
Manas stepped from behind the stony rubble as they
  neared:
'Take me with you, great Mother of Pestilence.
Make me a demon. What are your demons.'
    The awful Mother saw him. 'A dead, a human
        dead.'
A black spirit draped itself across her shoulder from
  behind,
Sputtered at him. She shoved it back:
    'You are Manas, who came up to the Field?
    I saw you at the waterfall, and at Martoli Karak.
    Ganesha and I had to laugh to see you lying there.
    We laughed when the demons set you lurching.'
'You laughed.'
    'They are no friends of ours.
    And sometime we'll seize hold of them again,
    And do with them what must be done.
    But they handled you so marvellously.
    All of us who saw you laughed.
    How they lurched inside your body, how they
        leapt.
    And when Puto saw you at his tree, on the hill,
    And they gave themselves away, -
    Ganesha, what was it there?'
He, grey on his rat's legs, beat the snow with his trunk:
    'You asked me something?' – 'Yes, and?'
    'Who is this standing here?' – 'It is Manas, his soul.'
    Ganesha swung his trunk, trumpeted: 'His soul!
    Just look at his soul! It's past its best. Haha!'

'Ganesha, he'd like to know why we laughed,
You and I and all of us, when he came onto the Field.
"Sorrow, sorrow, I want sorrow."
And the demons took him when enough was enough.
And he lay there and Puto came.'
'Yes, Puto.'
Ganesha crept around Manas, swept clouds of snow about him with his trunk:
'That was their master stroke.
I fell in love with those three.
I thought to myself,
They are so lovely, those three, they leap so jauntily,
They really should be gods again.'
'Why did you laugh at me.'
'At you?' The gods exchanged a glance:
'What's your problem? Are you complaining?'
Ganesha leaped towards him on his rat's legs.
And Manas fled.
Ganesha all around him: 'Moaning, you're complaining!'
Bellowed out his trumpet-laugh, laughed, laughed,
Ran rings around Manas, hemmed him in.
Other spirits, attracted by the guffaws, came along,
Encircled them, asked questions, queried ghastly Durga.
Ganesha rolled in merriment on his back.
Durga cried: 'We must get on! Ganesha!
Come, Ganesha! Humans are waiting.'
He wheezed himself breathless laughing.
Down the glacier went the Goddess of Pestilence.
She drummed her fingers on the drum.

Ganesha floundered upright:
'He comes into the Realm of the Dead
And asks himself how dead someone is
When he is dead.'
And leaped along in Durga's wake.

★★★

Cuzumarra

WHEN the strangers from the land beyond the mountains came down the northern rivers and stopped at villages, they were received as guests, welcomed and cared for, given presents when they left. The village of women was richer than any they had seen in the north since their escape over the passes, but here they were escorted like prisoners. Below lay a wide, smooth lake, they had a good view of it, boats carried people to and fro, tall grass and clumps of reeds loomed over its mirror, the water gleamed very pale. The view opened up even wider as they were led around a bend in the hill, the lake lay behind them, in front the hill fell away gently, covered to its foot and beyond into the plain with fields and meadows, dotted with little huts and toiling people. Farther on there was scrub, then thick black forest like a frontier wall. But here and there breaches had been cut in this wall, and pale water, endless water glimmered through. Their hearts leapt into their mouths, they forgot where they were, they thought it was the ocean. They conferred and traded questions.

One of the spearwomen grinned, pointed to the pale endless water and said proudly: "Amazon!" It was their river. The strangers stared at one another, incredulous.

Then, without a word, they were led one by one into an empty longhouse. On the floor were sleeping mats with pretty patterns, several chairs lined the back wall, doubtless for chiefs, decorated with colourful strips of raffia. The chairs were shaped like animals, made of wood, you could see a black head with big ears, and eyes of little mussel shells. Fat tufts of gaudy parrot feathers hung motionless from beams. Stout wooden rollers carved with snaking lines lay in front of the chairs; they were neck rests.

By the time the strangers were all brought inside this big empty house, the last light of evening was shining through the door. They walked in, no women followed, they looked about, observed, waited. They knocked on walls, picked up chairs, beside the door they found empty arrow-stands. Outside, a big fire had been started to combat the swarms of mosquitoes that invaded the dusk. Smoke drifted through the door, red flames lit up the room where the strangers stood and moved about. A few women warriors crouched around the fire, chattering and laughing.

Two men entered the house. They looked like men of the last tribe the strangers had come to. They brought gourds with a pale strong-smelling concoction. Then they brought flatbread, bananas and roasted ants. Cuzumarra asked what tribe they were from. They made no reply. When he held up a gourd and asked them what the brew was called, they glanced fearfully at the lighted doorway, gurgled and pointed to their mouths. The tongues were stumps. The shocked strangers squatted on the mats, tried to eat and drink. They feared poison, but they were dying of thirst. They slept only for the first part of the night, were then wakeful, fearing attack. A thunderstorm rolled briefly past. The fire outside burned low. When Cuzumarra strode angrily to the door a woman stood up, then others, twenty women. They barred the way with spears. Cuzumarra stood still, said not a word. The air was chill. They poked up the fire. He went back into the house. The men wrapped themselves in mats. The companions spoke to Cuzumarra: "We have come far to the south. Who will listen to you here? These are Amazons, enemies of men. We are afraid."

Another: "They cut out the men's tongues. Why did you lead us here? Do you know what they will do to us? They won't spare you."

Cuzumarra could give no answer. Like them he complained: "We have come too far south. People did not listen to us. We should have turned back. Don't scold me. We must gather our courage. Perhaps we can sleep again."

"It's too cold. We prefer to sit and talk. We've been meaning to talk with you."

"Then talk."

"We had no courage, because you are the leader and we the led. Cuzumarra, we beg you, let us go. We are bewitched and cannot follow you."

He sighed: "What do you propose?" Now they'll say what he does not trust himself to say.

"We fled from the Whites over the passes with clothes and weapons. Our weapons we lost long ago. The forest stripped our clothing from us. Our skin is covered in sores. We have been too long away from our country, we have come too far south through this steaming forest, to this terrible river. It lies just over there, we feel it even in the night. It sends up cold mist. We have no more thoughts of home. We have lost everything, and everything has been taken from us by witchcraft. Sometimes we speak about the whiteskins and what they have done to us and our families, then we forget it again, laugh, and are different men. We follow you, Cuzumarra, but we no longer know why we follow. Help us."

Another said quickly: "We are bewitched. We speak of the whiteskins but without anger, as if they were just agoutis that dogs hunt in hollow trees, or dolphins. The Whites don't hurt us. Why do we no longer hate them, Cuzumarra? It was because of them we made this terrible journey, and now we laugh and drink and sleep."

Cuzumarra hid his face in the mat so they would not see by the light of the fire how he rubbed his forehead. "We shall turn back. We shall go back."

One said: "But I – I am not going back. Never."

Another said loudly: "I – I am not going back. I shall never go back."

A third: "I shall never go back. Never again shall we go back up into the mountains."

Cuzumarra listened in horror from under the mat, not showing his face, they were speaking his thoughts. "And you would betray your kinfolk?"

Next morning two elderly women came, stood outside the door and called to them: They would soon be brought before the queen.

They entered a big finely decorated house. On the mats many women sat with legs tucked under them, fists anchored at their hips. Some were young, some older. Along the wall three sturdy older women sat on the wide animal chairs and gazed sternly back at them. Nobody spoke. No one indicated that they should sit.

The woman in the middle had yellow circles on her cheeks. She asked Cuzumarra who they were. He replied. She asked what they wanted. He replied. When he spoke of the Whites she whispered to her neighbours. She bade Cuzumarra approach, stared at his ragged clothing, stroked the skin of his face, touched his golden ear discs. Then she turned to the companions. One by one they stood before her. She whispered about the strangers' hairstyle and skin colour. Cuzumarra was invited to speak to her in his own language. After he had done so the women engaged in rapid conversation. Finally the queen invited the men to take their place on the mats. Then everyone ate hot mash.

Following this interview they were allowed to wander

as they pleased through the village, alone or together. They were assigned an escort so they would know where they were welcome and where not. They saw the extensive village and its gardens, and on a nearby mound was one even larger, and across the river there were supposedly many more villages of women. They were allowed to talk to men, only a few had been rendered mute, most were crippled by the wounding of a leg, an arm or an eye. There were many children and nursing mothers. The men who were these women's lovers were nowhere to be seen. The women demanded of Cuzumarra and his companions more stories of their homeland and the Whites than had any of the northern tribes. And after Cuzumarra's first comprehensive account of the cruelty of the Whites, and the women, like the men of the north, had danced their spear dance and the women of the next village had answered their warcries, Cuzumarra beamed at his companions: "Are you content? Are you still afraid? They will lead us back. We have done what we had to do. The Whites will come down into this land and die in a trap."

They were not content. He realised with a shock that they really had no desire to go back. In the guesthouse where they lodged they turned on Cuzumarra: "What did you say to the queen? Again and again about the Tumbo and how they leaped into the abyss and about the defeat of our lord Tangasuku. We beg you, stop telling these stories. We believed them once. Now we don't believe them."

Cuzumarra thought them mad: "All right, so we tell the queens and the women that the Tumbo are still alive and we live in peace with the Whites and we deserved what happened." Cuzumarra grasped their hands and regarded them one by one.

"It won't do any good," they said, "to gaze at us one by one and hold our hands. We told you we no longer want to go back. We'll never wear the white shirt and coloured cloak again. You go to Cuzco, if you yearn for the Son of the Sun on his golden chair. We thank you for leading us over the passes. Otherwise we would have stayed the same as our parents."

"You are bewitched, my dear companions, can you not sense it?"

"Thank you. Once we were bewitched and now we are no longer. Cuzumarra, recall what they told us in the north and along the dark river? They said we must have been divided for the Whites to cast us down like that. They saw things more clearly than we did. For there is more to the story than what you tell, Cuzumarra: that the last great lord with his fivefold red headband had two sons and they allowed the country to fall into the hands of the Whites. Division was among us long before that, during the time when our parents and grandparents toiled and order reigned and leaders of five families and ten families were set over us."

Cuzumarra could not bear to listen, and wept.

★★★

The Forester

THE forester, relative of our old knock-kneed general, senior man at the garrison in the little town, was still in Strassburg. He wrote to his wife:

> "My own true girl, circumstances finally make it possible for me to write a letter to you." (This was not strictly correct; our depressed forester was, like many others, powerfully carried away by the mighty emotions of these days, and he did so like the taste of cider.) "For my friend, Sepp Kundt, will cross the Rhine today, although we had exchanged oaths that we would only take that final step together. But he

cannot bear to see what's happening, and I think of what you said, my true girl: stay in Strassburg till you know for sure if we have really and truly lost everything. Today is 24th November 1918, a holy Sunday, and tomorrow Kundt will cross the Rhine into our old Germany that you and I love so well, as is our sacred duty and all the more so in such a grave plight, but it was in Alsace that we found a position and respect and our daily bread.

In the two weeks since I last wrote I have not once been back to my forests. The first time all the roads were blocked by returning German troops, the railway was still operating and I sometimes stood glumly beside our train but, my dear Rike, there were so many familiar faces on it that I feared betrayal and so would rather stay on in Strassburg.

What abominations were carried out up to the 21st of this month by people wearing the Kaiser's uniform I shall recount to you when I see you. They planted the red socialist flag on the cathedral, and behaved in all kinds of swinish ways. Respectable Reich German citizens I got to know told me quite openly: if those are Germans and the Germans do nothing to counter them, then the French will have to come. In their hatred they have torn down every statue of the Kaiser and just left the empty plinths standing, and the things they write on them, my dismayed mouth cannot allow to pass my lips. Some people have bought up all the livestock in the country villages and slaughtered it in contravention of the prevailing decrees.

They were peasants whose minds are poisoned by the notion, oh the Frenchies will soon be here and then the livestock will be worth nothing. But who stuffed themselves with meat afterwards? Do you think, my dear Friederike, did even a mutton bone, a little slice of veal, ever reach the likes of us? Gracious me no! It was snatched from us by deceit, even when we were willing to pay. Where did it all go? To hoarders and black marketeers. Same thing with milk and potatoes.

Our Alsace has never experienced anything like it. Dear old uncle has taken me along a few times to meet with our officers passing through here, dressed in civvies and poor as church mice. I myself helped a few, and I've chatted to lots of them, because you entrusted me to do my utmost to enable us to return to our lovely house in the forest where our two precious gifts were born and we experienced so much joy. But that is all over now, my poor true girl. You have already taken that difficult step and are back in our old beloved homeland. I am unable for sorrow to tear myself away yet, and so have already suffered much grief. For we are already under French occupation, Friederike! I don't know if your newspapers are reporting on it, or if the red socialists where you are even allow newspapers to be printed, or if our enlightened Fatherland is to drown in lies and deceit.

Let me apprise you of the actual truth. We here in Strassburg are French! My pen, dear Friederike, is loath to write this, but it is so. And so now our dear city must become French, despite the nearness of the frontier. If only I were back there and could give the liars and the Frogs a good one on the noggin with my bullwhip. But I no longer dare to travel by train. Last night, when I thought of you, in my dreams I gave our duplicitous landlord at the Golden Crown and the chap at the post office, once my closest pals who have now declared themselves to be Frogs, as I shall tell you about later, both a stab in the neck with my hunting knife. May God the Almighty and Righteous drive home this blow so sincerely aimed.

***

THEME 15. STATE VISITS

Lama trek to Peking (from *Wang Lun*)
The Count of Pfalz-Neuburg (from *Wallenstein*)
State visit to Yapeyu (from *The Land without Death*)
Floored (from *Citizens & Soldiers*)

***

Lama Trek to Peking

MONTHS before his departure a stream of pious beggars, pilgrim men and women from every province and from Mongolia made its way towards Tashilunpo. Many who reached the gold-roofed monastery town began to trace out in their own fashion the route the holy man would take: they threw themselves full length on the ground, placed a stone at the forehead, stood by the stone, threw themselves down again and so measured the road with their bodies.

From Lhasa caravans wended southwest to Lunpo, onto the route the lama would take. Their passage could be traced. Countless prayer flags hung on strings from tree to tree, from post to post; they erected tumuli of stones with the six blessed syllables *Om mani padme hum*. On passes and mountains they laid the shoulder bones of sheep. They pulled out their own teeth and stuffed them as sacrifices in cracks in the cliffs, cut off locks of hair, tied them with strings and hung them to flutter beside bright rags.

Then the train filled the narrow streets as it left the monastery buildings with their crimson breastwork, the purple of their window bays, steep walls, the up and down of rock cut steps, the roofs and cells. The gold-gleaming labrang looked from black-rimmed windows onto the departing caravan, like a widow whose tears are frozen. Bright flags flapped, horns blared. Lobsang Paldan Ishe, Ocean of Wisdom and Virtue, had set off for Peking.

It was winter now. The enormous levy that accompanied the lama pope trudged ponderously forth. Treeless steppe stretched away endlessly. In the hard ground stood thorn bushes, wretched pines and spruce. Cold air blew. In a finely carved and painted palanquin with yellow curtains, four monks bore the holy man squatting motionless on tucked-in feet on a red cushion, shaven head bare. His ears were large, long. He wore a black silk gown embroidered in blue, with white fur sleeves. Leaves of the *Kandjur* before him.

In the broil around him novices, consecrated priests, scholars, magicians, medicine men, all handpicked. The train grew as it proceeded: it was joined by holy men from Mongolia and India.

All the gloomy sanctity of the temple went with the lama. Along paths used to caravans laden with brick tea and bales of silk, priests swung their fearsome tambourines: two human skulls, joined at the crown and covered in hide.

In the lama's palanquin, on his right, a wonderful skull goblet inlaid in gold, with a bulging gold lid. It stood on a triangular base of black marble; at its three corners the goblet was supported by little stone human heads in red, blue and black.

From time to time when they made a halt for prayers, trumpets of human bones blew that ended in bronze fittings with flared nostrils. The tone recalled the whinnying of the horse that carries souls to paradise.

In front of the itinerant men of learning who walked along in pointed yellow hats of felt with fleecy tassels hanging down behind, enormous yaks pulled huge, ineffably intricate prayer wheels on carts.

A small contingent of Tanguts and fifteen hundred Imperial soldiers guarded the train. They pushed on to the northeast, past the blue lake called Tsomawang where the god dwells on the lake bottom in a turquoise tent.

The icy summit of Kailash, holy mountain, towered vast above them. After many days they reached the snowfields and mountains that lead to Kokonor. Then the dreaded northerly gales set in. The holy train, descending to valleys, winding over ridges, met at every turn traces of white death, animal carcasses, human skeletons. Here on every pass supplicating pennants, bones were laid out for the terrible gods.

And the terrible gods gave escort to the pious travellers from Tashilunpo. Yamantaka, most frightful of spirit gods, shrieked voracious in a storm across the boundless solitude of the paths and fell on yaks, mules and men, he of the bull's horns, pyramid of nine heads, sixteen legs, thirty-four arms. Iron spears hissed from his flailing arms, he tore the flesh from human bodies, devoured their hearts, guzzled their blood, he who spread terror from the fastness he could leave through sixteen gates. He could do nothing to the priests and holy men: the Dragsed, women of Hell conjured by the magicians, gave him combat.

With prayers of thanksgiving they crossed into the province of Amdo, close to the frontier with the Imperial province of Gansu. Then they arrived at the marvellous monastery town of Kumbum, nestled in its valley. The house of the reformer of the Yellow Hat church, holy Tsong Kapa, founder of the Sect of Virtue, still slumbered under the lovely sandalwood tree. To the east a rampart of ice and snow.

The yellow god dallied here through the winter. The world had a new pivot. The streams of pilgrims and caravans terminated here. A Mongol chieftain on whose head Paldan Ishe laid a hand presented him with a hundred horses, seventy mules, a hundred camels, a thousand bolts of brocade, a hundred and fifty thousand taels of silver. For the poorest of the poor he laid his hand a thousand times a day on saffron-coated paper. The land lapped blissfully at this God who spent himself so lavishly on it.

***

The Count of Pfalz-Neuburg

The vacancy on the Electoral College has stimulated ambitions in a distant relative of the Bavarian duke.

HE stood at the balustrade leaning on his cane for almost half an hour, whistled through his teeth, ignored the chancellor, made vigorous gestures. Drew his cloak tight about him. In the chancellery, his voice a whisper, he ordered the astonished man to drop everything; in a week they would set off together on a journey.

Philipp Ludwig did not take formal leave of his sons; he gave out that he would join a hunting party with his neighbour, the Margrave of Burgau. The major-domo and all the court servants stood shaking their heads as he climbed into the carriage, accompanied by a retinue of five men. He had sniffily reminded the chancellor's deputy to keep an eye on "those wily peasants". He took along as much coin and precious items as could be loaded onto a baggage-cart; half a day's journey from town they were joined discreetly by two squads of horsemen he had hired as escort. In such state he crossed the counties of Scheyern, Pfaffenhofen. Then the axle of the baggage-cart broke outside an inn. Cries and laments from the count, trussed up like a calf, immobile under his fur cap, embroidered Italian shirt, padded doublet, lambskin stockings. He feared that word might leak out, suspicions might be aroused in Neuburg, his sons might smell a rat, the escort might plunder the cart. He snuffled his way out of his tent of furs with the stiff silent chancellor; should they dismiss the escort, they'd hired a goat as gardener; but then they'll be at the mercy of lurking soldiers and ruffians. He pressed a mandrake root into the chancellor's hand, he himself clutched two in each fist: "Hold it tight so nothing will happen." The escort had to wait forty paces back while the cart was jacked up.

Two days later they were approaching Munich. The Count Palatine, over-active, highly-strung, dared to emerge from his dungeon of furs, dripping sweat. From time to time in the carriage, his thinking not at all straight after much chatting arguing and sounding out, he would play his latest trump: that here in Munich one cannot proceed so informally, as if it's the private business of any Tom Dick or Harry; that one cannot show oneself directly, sending footmen and runners to secure lodgings from a steward of the Residence, arrange a visit, make a return visit, gifts counter-gifts audiences banquets drinks for the retinue, rides merry-go-rounds. Done so, such a grave affair could easily be rendered ridiculous, become bogged down in endless talk and courtesies. In short, he'd totally given up any idea of a personal consultation with Duke Maximilian, totally and completely.

So what should happen, the perplexed chancellor wondered; better perhaps to turn back. Well, continued the count, he'd totally abandoned the idea. Speaking personally. It was his opinion, a private matter for him alone. He wouldn't stop anyone from harbouring a different opinion or idea; on the contrary, everyone was duty bound to come out with it, make a case.

So close to their goal, the spires of the Holy Virgin gleaming in the distance, a horribly embarrassing fear had sprung up that the whole situation was beyond him; the Bavarian Duke was an intimidating person; he imagined with horror that they might lay hands on him, the venerable Count Palatine, somehow provide a disrespectful welcome. Even before entering the city gate he felt overcome with repugnance, a confusion of painful images; saw himself on a chair in the splendid ducal Residence, hard of hearing, unable to respond to the finer points of Maximilian's words; a nerve-wracking spectacle.

He had cushions placed under his back, the curtains closed, ordered a slower pace. This drought in Bavaria, he complained. Anyway, if it has to be, he'll observe Maximilian from afar, beard him, flush him out. He blinked at his tensely ruminating chancellor, that glum worthy figure: Perhaps you should go first, somehow? The man wrung his hands, the words hot in his throat: "What are we doing here, Serenity? Good Lord, this whole journey, the long journey; and Your Serenity must be exhausted."

"Yes, exhausted. In a nutshell, Chancellor. I'm exhausted. Even worse, completely useless. All I need is a bed. I am an old man." He asked the chancellor for his cushion too: "You're a clever man. Couldn't have a better companion. We'll take a little snooze."

As the furious chancellor counted off the minutes of their approach to the north gate of the city, the count lay in a half-doze, mumbled contentedly that whatever happened nothing should be rushed, anyone could see he was tired; the other should manage the rest of it. When his half-closed eyes met the chancellor's gaze, he repeated softly: "You take on the rest. You have my full authority."

"But Serenity."

"Chancellor, you needn't bother me with questions. I have complete confidence in you; as I've always had, though I might not often express it. In the decades you have served me, you've learned enough of my principles of government. You have long since secured independence – no, don't be modest –in matters of administration."

The man turned away, inclined his head, flushed, pressed a finger to his temple.

The count called for a halt, slept half an hour. Refreshed, he smiled as they rumbled on: "I really think, when I look at such a learned and well-bred man, that you could conduct the government of Neuburg entirely to my satisfaction. I couldn't wish for a better successor than you. How tired I am. But the whole house is feeble, rotten."

When the chancellor in his shock asked leave to walk beside the carriage – he hoped to gain time for reflection by slowing the pace – the old man reclining within looked at him, languidly raised his right arm: Is he squeezing the mandrake tight; that's the main thing, then nothing will happen, Maximilian no doubt has none, so the advantage is ours. Anyway, he knows something; the basic point is that the chancellor will act for him with Maximilian. "Face him calmly. Don't be overawed by his ways. You'll sound him out, it'll be easy. The day after tomorrow, or perhaps a day later, we'll go home, if the weather holds."

"And you, Serenity?"

"Us? We're a foreigner, a guest of the Count Palatine of Neuburg. Don't worry about it. We'll give you directives once we've restored our strength."

Again the man wrung his hands: it won't work, the count as his companion, it goes against all respect, for Heaven's sake, such confusion, tempting God's wrath.

"My dear chap," the count gave a good-humoured yawn, eyes closed, "bear up. We have commanded it, so you're free of responsibility before human or divine authority."

"But in Jesus' name, respect, respect for Your Serenity's rank. What will His Highness the Duke of Bavaria and his glorious court think of me when I claim to negotiate independently in the name of the ruler of Neuburg."

The count palatine heard this with satisfaction: it wouldn't embarrass him, at least not much, he'd set it all in motion, of course there'd be some embarrassment – "To Your Serenity's house, your relations, your ancestors."

"True, it is embarrassing. It does no justice to the house. But it must be. We command you to represent us to the best of your ability while we are indisposed."

The escort dismissed; admitted that evening by the watch at the Schwabing Gate; recorded by the clerk as Chancellor Sartorius of Neuburg together with sundry respectable attendants; they secured lodgings at the famous Sign of the Ostrich. The count tripped clumsily along beside his perplexed chancellor, inordinately complacent. He laughed out loud when he saw how every day in the church of the Holy Virgin the locals burned several hundredweight of candles to Saint Benno.

In the Old Court, in a room in the War Chamber, Privy Counsellor Jocher heard the Neuburg delegation out. In the presence of the great strong dignified man who accompanied them with overdone courtesy to the stairs, the chancellor could barely keep countenance.

"We shall await the decision," declared Philipp Ludwig. A rented chair carried him half the day through the town; the count could not stop laughing. How they put everything on show, hide nothing away: pictures ornaments tapestries, building upon building, four-storied houses, elaborate façades, churches full of treasure. "Hold your purse close," he whispered to Sartorius that evening in their bedroom. "What fools these are. Our nephew Maximilian has lots of money, lovely lovely money. But see: he doesn't deserve it. He throws it away."

From Duke Maximilian's surly monosyllables, Jocher was able to convey to Sartorius, who listened respectfully, a laborious explanation that consequent upon the proscription against the Palatine, the power of election of course reverted to the Emperor, who would delegate; if he were not to bestow the power on said outlaw again, then on a brother, or a specified close relative, and so on. It was all a matter for the

Emperor and Court Chamber, that august institution worthy of the highest regard; let no one doubt that his rights lie there and with His Elected Roman Majesty, as if in the lap of God.

Before they left, Jocher, having on his return visit at the Ostrich encountered the ancient simpleton who was Sartorius' travelling companion, sent them a smarter man who knew his way around Munich. This fellow, oaf that he was, the same afternoon ensconced himself without so much as a by your leave in the count's room, hurled the precious trunks down the stairs, and that evening, when the count returned and spluttered outrage along with the utterly bewildered and helpless chancellor, made fun of him in front of the servants, mocked him and ordered the trembling man to vacate the room. In his fury the Count Palatine ran this way and that down dark passages, after a lively exchange of words was deposited by the gallant outside the front door in his nightcap, candle in hand, clad only in a nightshirt. For the whole night he sat stunned in the porch. At first cock-crow the door was opened by women hauling cans and pails to the stables at the rear and shouting, shouting fit to raise the dead, and already he was back in his chancellor's former room, rubbing knees and legs and holding vigorous whispered imaginary conversations with the gallant oaf. But as the day went on the Count became adamant that he must save himself from any influence Sartorius might have picked up from the gallant; he'd guard his rights himself, had no wish to be patronised; and with that ordered an immediate departure.

They were accompanied by the oaf for two hours out of Munich, with merry chat and pleasantries. The fellow relished the opportunity to maltreat an ancient visitor from foreign parts. It came to nudges and pokes behind the chancellor's back; in despair he noticed much of this but was warned by signs and winks from Philipp Ludwig to keep silent. The wagon then turned aside into lightly wooded country; for hours he slept on soft palliasses beneath the tilt, having first eaten and drunk his greedy fill. Waking, he asked about the presents Sartorius had received in Munich. A little chest was opened on the grass verge; it disgorged a silver bleeding-dish, a tall majolica vase, a gilded bronze candle-holder in the shape of a lion. He turned the pieces this way and that, tapped them so the straw fell away. After supervising the repacking, and being lifted onto the wagon hunched in his furs, the escort riding close again, he ordered onward to Regensburg, the Danube. His eyes flashed:

"Do you think I was intimidated by that scoundrel? The response of my nephew Maximilian was quite agreeable enough. The duke's merely being elusive. Hushing things up is the tactics of this world, where claims of legitimacy are at stake." He giggled happily: "Go home, my nephew said. When one is old, there's nothing more fitting than to die. Neuburg is so lovely, has such lovely gardens, greenery, fields, so much livestock, no lack of cows for butter and cream and milk. The forests are full of deer and pheasant; trout swim in the streams, and pike and carp. Go home, and admire your diamonds." He rubbed his nose, mumbled: "A sly response from Master Max of Bavaria. Did Mr Sartorius discover anything remarkable in his city of Munich?"

"Sufficient, Your Serenity. Riches in all their variety."

"And what did you think of it?"

The chancellor kept silent, he was pleased to let his master preen himself.

***

State Visit to Yapeyu

A SOLEMN day in Yapeyu on the Paraná.

It was reported from Tucuman that a royal Visitor, the counsellor Francesco Alvaro, was on his way from Cordoba and Assomption. Yapeyu was the permanent residence of the Superior of this province. Montoya wanted to receive him in Yapeyu, below the confluence of the Ibicuy river. With Montoya came the Bishop of Assomption, who was just then making a tour of the reductions.

Montoya, no longer the young man brought by Torrez to Father Emanuel, was broad and stocky, beardless; the other Fathers too, who stayed put now and taught and directed, had done away with their wild vagrant beards. Montoya's hair was grey, white at the temples, his angular face was lean. A fanatical severity permeated his being. The eyes under the strong brow ridge gazed out suspicious and restless. He rode, escorted by a company of native cavalry, beside the new Bishop of Assomption whom he had fetched, Felix, a lanky, venerable and handsome man of his own age.

Bishop Felix, an Italian, sat on his horse like a knight and enjoyed the gentle landscape. He lifted himself in the saddle to gaze behind and to the side. They passed dense groves of bamboo that accompanied the river's course and concealed the low growth along deep roadside ditches, in which water stood. His face, grave and calm, framed by a dark brown beard, exuded benevolence, the melancholy black eyes greeted the landscape along the bank of the Paraná. Rome, Florence, Ferrara were far away, he had given up Classical studies in order to hear no longer the hideous din of European wars. He dreamed of the magic of a southern landscape, of a great peace.

He had a particular reason to seek out the much discussed reductions of the pugnacious Jesuits. He was tracking down his nephew, young Gonzales da Santa Cruz, who had lodged with him in Assomption and then vanished in the direction of the settlements. What could have led my unruly secretive Gonzales, my prickly relative, to transplant himself here? Despite his youth he could have been my vicar apostolic, could have stayed for good in Assomption, where he was born. Of course, then I'd never have come to ride through this remarkable world. It's like another planet.

On the hilly grassland some miles from Yapeyu, they saw grass moving, feathered heads bobbed up and down in the grass, they were mounted Indians, a strong contingent. Felix turned in shock to silent Montoya, who had seen them already, and nodded calmly: "We'll stop and wait for them. They want to welcome you."

Then the vanguard of the horsemen, a cavalry company from Yapeyu, was with them, formally welcoming the episcopal visitor. The whole troop caught up with them at an open place back from the riverbank, strong riders armed with lances. They unfurled flags, paraded with their mounts in tight formation this way and that. Then they halted, sprang from their horses and threw themselves to the ground before the bishop. Montoya whispered: "They await your blessing." Felix, absorbed in the astonishing scene, raised a hand and spoke some words. At once the bodies were back in the saddle and forming up. They surrounded the guest and his escort, banners fluttered at their head, trumpets and drums sounded.

As they rode the bishop drew Montoya close, they had hardly spoken for most of the journey, the bishop, usually jolly and talkative, had no idea once initial courtesies were done how to approach this enigmatic man. To think of his fine brisk Gonzales among these sourpusses. Felix turned his handsome bearded face to Montoya: "Well, my dear Father, what is this? These are your people?"

"A company from Yapeyu."

"There are more of these?"

"They sent one company ahead first. No doubt another awaits you at the gate."

"My God, all armed and have horses and are trained?"

"Of course."

"My dear Father, I'd heard of it, I just never imagined it like this."

Montoya cast a casual glance at his companion. It worked away in Felix as they trotted on slowly. I'm being received by a military power, an actual state, how alarming. These lads of old Ignatius are an outrageously assertive bunch. They even have flags. What do they gain from it. Quite incredible. Back home they have no idea, the eyes would start from their heads. "Tell me, dear Father Montoya, do the other reductions have such horsemen, and armed?"

"Of course."

"But it's dangerous. I assure you, when I saw them approaching, my heart pounded."

"Dangerous for whom?"

"Why, for the towns of the Whites."

"They obey us. For the rest we never have to give them orders. We just tell them what's good for them. And they persuade themselves that it is so."

"But if they were to fall upon our towns?"

"It never enters their heads."

"It just occurred to me."

"Our natives have no desire to know the sinfulness of towns, and sensible townspeople do not fear them. Anyway, why should lions and tigers fear the shepherd."

The bishop was shocked. "Who are the lions and tigers?"

"Not our people."

"Our townspeople? Are our townspeople so wicked?"

Montoya's face flickered, without looking at the bishop he said: "Not any more."

The second cavalry company fell in at the gate. Through

the gate, bearing insignia of their rank, came dark men, the corregidor, town officials of various grades. Father Vinzenze Griffi, who exercised the office of priest of the settlement, approached the bishop's feet. And behind him, to Felix' great joy, was his good Gonzales, he came forward to kiss the hand of the bishop, who had dismounted. The bishop took him by the arm and gazed into his face: "Nothing changed. Exactly as you were." But he saw that he had changed. The bishop had little time to surrender to his thoughts.

The people of the settlement had taken great pains to welcome the bishop and prepare the town for the royal Visitor who was to come with him, or a little later. They had brought flowers from the fields into the church, erected triumphal arches in the streets and woven garlands. And how they decorated the arches and garlands. They went fishing and hunting, caught the most splendid fish in the river, organised a drive for jaguar and deer, trapped fowl. They hung trophies from the river on fishhooks among the great palm fronds of the garlands, and these were the pride of the fishermen. They disembowelled the jaguars and deer, tied the great carcasses to the poles of the triumphal arches. Amid the green foliage they tethered colourful fowl, hummingbirds and parrots on long strings. The garlands shimmered with whole flocks of such birds. They carried huge masses of foliage into town, spread a carpet all the way from the gate to the church. Flowers, fruit, fowl in front of every door.

And so, preceded by a vanguard of cavalry, amid blaring music, the bishop entered sundrenched bell-loud merry Yapeyu. He was buffeted by cheers from the people lined up in dense crowds on both sides of the street, behind him rode Superior Montoya, Father Griffi, and his Gonzales. The Italian bishop had never dreamed of such a sight. He wondered, as he distributed blessings left and right, how this reception and his journey should be described, reported to Rome. Really you can only praise it, but it's surprising and a little bit illicit. Native infantry, and a troop with actual arquebuses, brought up the rear. The music was silenced, they neared the church, the cavalry moved aside for bishop, clergy and town officials. Organ sounds swelled towards them. As they entered they were enveloped in the lovely clear tones of a children's choir. Women knelt in the church, flowers at their breast, you could hear them sobbing as the bishop prayed at the altar. The Te Deum rang out.

As the bishop left the church and was led to the house that would be his for the visit – it was no different from the other houses, but they had spread soft fabrics and linens on a cot, placed skins on the floor, set up a table and some chairs – he became aware of large bowls and baskets outside many of the houses, filled with maize and other seed. On enquiring he was told: these are for sowing, they've been put here so they too can receive the blessings he bestows as he goes through the town. And then the little creatures gambolling about the posts of the garlands like small and middle-sized dogs, but on the other hand not like dogs in their catlike slinking, they jumped at him as he went into his house, and the bishop saw he was expected to smile and say a friendly word. He smiled obediently and asked Montoya what these creatures were called. Young jaguars, he learned.

***

Floored

DURING the night of 7th November, the German Army Command sent a telegram to the commander of the Allied troops seeking an immediate armistice. They received the reply: German plenipotentiaries must present themselves at the French advanced posts on the road Chimay-Fourmies-La

Capelle-Guise.

At ten that evening they crossed the Allied lines near Haudroy, were taken by truck to Soissons, and early on Friday morning reached the Forest of Compiègne, the HQ of Marshal Foch. He had them admitted at around nine to his railway carriage. He was flanked by a French general and two admirals, one English and one American. The German spokesman, a civilian, thought it necessary, given the severity of the situation, to broach a few remarks; the Supreme Allied Commander waved him aside with the words: The guns will not fall silent before this treaty is signed. (He himself did not believe it would be accepted.) They were given a seventy-two hour deadline.

At one o'clock a captain with the German delegation was assigned the task of conveying the document with the utmost, utmost despatch to the German High Command by car, by plane, by whatever means possible. Every hour meant more deaths. Germans fired wildly when the captain came speeding along in his car, big white flag waving, bugler outside on the footboard sounding a signal, no one could hear it amid all the firing. The delegates wasted five hours casting about this way and that, and then took the desperate decision to break through somewhere even if it cost them their lives. They charged ahead, and had luck. But they climbed out amazed when they reached the German trenches. Nothing but a few machine guns here and there along the parapet, and a tiny handful of troops firing like men possessed, among all their dead comrades.

Saturday passed into Sunday at Compiègne, no reply came. French railway workers showed their newspapers to the negotiators standing around waiting: headlines big as fingers: the Kaiser has abdicated, the Crown Prince as well. It is now 10th November, tomorrow at 11 o'clock the seventy-two hours will be up.

At eight in the evening a radio telegram reaches the Great Headquarters: new conditions are demanded, my God, they've wasted whole days on this, what on Earth will happen. At last the redeeming word: at half past ten a radio message to the Armistice Commission: "The German government accepts the Armistice conditions presented to you on 8th November. Reich Chancellor Ends." The German officers must meet with the French interpreter officer, who asks: who is this Chancellor Ends? He is known neither here nor in Paris. The head of the German delegation, a stolid man of middle height with straw-blond hair and gold-rimmed pince-nez, the journalist and parliamentarian Erzberger, has to repair the damage and explain: it just means Reich Chancellor. Ends means end, full stop. And, he adds, probably that's what will happen to this chancellor. Which is of no concern to the interpreter.

At five in the morning they signed the treaty.

At this point the Americans had three and a half million men under arms; in the New World a further one point four million, deployment ready, were now demobilised.

The Battle of Metz was supposed to begin on 13th November. Eight fresh US divisions were already standing ready to the north of the fortifications; General Castelnau with three French divisions to the south was to advance on Saarlouis and Saarbrücken supported by six US divisions.

From the Forest of Compiègne the Allied Supreme Commander was able to inform his generals: "Hostilities along the entire front are to cease at 11 o'clock French time on 11th November. No Allied troops are to cross the lines achieved on this day at this hour without further orders."

And when next day the negotiators crossed back over the enemy lines with the signed document, they saw that revolution had arrived, the Kaiser was no more, and in Germany there was no proper government. In those four difficult days the whole world had changed. Even the telegram they had at last received had been composed by no government and no Reich Chancellor. In the general confusion it had emanated from the Supreme Army Command.

Because everything was happening so monstrously fast.

★★★

THEME 16. HOSTILITIES

Viennese Welcome (from *Wallenstein*)
Set to! Set to! (from *Manas*)
Franz walks into a bar (from *Berlin Alexanderplatz* tr. Eugene Jolas, amended by C. D. Godwin)
Beauty Contest (from *Babylonian Exile*)
Room for the Night (from *Citizens & Soldiers*)

★★★

Viennese Welcome

NEAR the broad empty cathedral square, at Bishop's Place beside the Heiligtumstuhl – the Relics Stand – stood the mansion of the merchant Hans Federl, an excessively rich and eccentric Bohemian of ill repute. Someone else had been lodging in this house for several weeks past: the Jewish Primate of Prague, Bassevi. Jews no longer dwelt within the city: a renewed imperial decree had expelled them outside the walls, to the Lower Werd. With his imperial letter of protection, the man from Prague had to be tolerated.

The mob swarming around Wallenstein's cavalcade roared and heaved as extravagantly splendid and costly baggage piled up before Bassevi's house, the door of Wallenstein's coach opened to let him off at the steps, and the escort rode off into the neighbourhood. More and more came thronging to the Federl mansion; the sweeps, those sooty urchins, sprang again into action, set up ladders against the house-front, six, ten, twenty, stood black and grimacing, bleated droned yelled songs mocking the Jews, made ready to climb up to the roof. It was an outrageous insult that Wallenstein flung at Vienna, given that he had, so everyone said, an invitation to the imperial court.

And shortly after the slovenly city guard – they had an understanding with the mob – had driven back the rowdiest of the people, there appeared beneath the Relics Stand the stout figure of a city counsellor with his gold chain of office, on a lofty steed. With studied grandiosity he dismounted at the now cleared steps, allowed himself to be led into the reception parlour. Invited by Bassevi himself to enter the refectory, he remained stiffly under the chandeliers, fixed the smiling little grey man with a penetrating glare, and declared that as far as he knew he had nothing to discuss with Bassevi, rather he had business with the newly arrived colonel of Prague, who enjoyed the Emperor's favour. Nevertheless – the Jew bowed his regret – he is occupied in the back rooms with calculations; not astrological, but simply to do with business; from long acquaintance of the guest's humours, at such times it is not advisable to interrupt him, even in the case of such an illustrious visitor. Whereupon the counsellor found it apposite to repeat that he desired to be announced.

But before Bassevi could open the door behind a curtain heavy as a carpet, Wallenstein emerged with long steps, his gaze directed at the floor. It was his habit to cut a wide path when he was thinking, shove chairs aside, press lips together, sometimes purse them to a snout, wander among the furniture. He would make lively grimaces, utter emphatic words, hiss, laugh, stand still, rummage in a cupboard, smack the table whinnying, leave the tassels of the curtain hanging on his brow; often in the course of his wanderings he would sit wherever he happened to be. He came through the door like a storm, his eyes played over the two men without apparently noticing them. Bassevi signalled with his eyes to the Viennese gentleman, then led him out of the way, and when he saw that Wallenstein's course was aimed again at him, pulled two little tables and a small stool to one side against the wall, all in complete silence. The counsellor, straightening his sword belt, harrumphed when the door opened, and when the colonel swept around him, harrumphed and shuffled his shoes. He was scandalised by the visitor's utterly unconventional dress, the swinging arms bare and hairy, around the chest only a low satin vest, a narrow coat of mail peeping out at the armpits.

Then, amidst the scraping foot-tapping rustling that filled the narrow little room came the strangled irritated voice of the fat counsellor: "Noble sir, noble and worshipful sir. Our beloved friend." Who stood a little while very close, head inclined over him; to the man's terror uttered growling grinding animal noises, pressed him against the bare wall, tugged at his sword-belt, which came apart, once left once right, let go. Four big steps, the curtain swayed behind Wallenstein, the door slammed shut.

When Bassevi tried to help, the reeling man lashed out, caught him in the throat. Bassevi said nothing, not even that his house lay under the Emperor's protection. The counsellor cursed as he pulled himself together, spat at the Hebrew.

★★★

Set to! Set to!

Re-embodied by his encounter with Savitri, Manas is back in the world, but at this point is sheer physicality (or Id). He doesn't yet recognise his mentor Puto.

BUT through the green walls, from far away
Rang out a clashing and smashing, slamming and
  hitting.
It rang out *rum*
Rum dum. Rum and *rum*.
Manas took it in with open ears.
Dreadful threats and slamming hitting,

Crashing and then silence and more crashing.
He had legs, so must run as fast as he could into the crashing,
Slamming hitting smashing pelting clattering, *rum dum, rum dum.*

Out of the forest. An open rocky ridge.
Such rattling cracking.
And over it the blue sky, thin white clouds
And a blooming silence on the ground,
Big butterflies bobbing, bright-dappled.
But on the high slope – a wilderness of scree, wide field of rubble –
There moved, among boulders and scrawny cacti,
An ash-smeared scrawny man with club and slings and shield.
Facing him, above him, at his side three demons,
Little darting storming figures that twisted as they leaped,
Came crashing up against his shield, tripped him,
Came aiming for his mouth.
Already he had spun around, lifted up his club against them.
They stood, leaped apart, man and demons.
Demons darted, trailing smoke, high above him,
Pelted stones down onto him.

And Manas stood and stood there on the ridge.
Behind him pine trees raised green candelabra arms,
The power of speech had left him.
They were fighting in bright sunshine.
His face screwed up in glee, in glee, as they lashed out and huffed and crashed.

Manas laughed.
His eyes gleamed with glee and craving.
He flared his nostrils like a beast. He trembled with desire.
His breast did not want to rise,
And he giggled, his throat, his breast, in glee-craving.
He uttered grunting happy groans, soft cooing laughter,
Like the clink and clang of tin when lightly tapped.

His face was twisted as he stood there, Manas,
And his legs stepped out, his mouth bliss-blessèd.
'Have I seen this before?'
Rum, rum dum.
Both sides were pelting stones and staggering, oh ye gods,
Staggering head over heels among the rocks,
Came up again, ye gods,
Stretched themselves long, and dived down, clashed,
Head over heels, four heads together.
Was he thinking this, was he seeing it?
Chuckling cooing breathless Manas
And laughing, laughing full-throated, from his deepest breath,
As he watched the demons leaping, and the ash-smeared man.

And as they swooped, the demons heard the laughter,
Were offended, looked at one another as they flew
To see what was amiss:
'What's the rascal laughing at?'

They thought it was Puto laughing.
Then the laughter kept on coming, and it came
from the pinewood,
Where something living stood, skin gleaming,
shook its fists at them.
'Why are you laughing, wretch?' screamed
Chanda, the one with fangs.
'You're risking your skin.
Watch out, we'll be coming after you.'
He called across: 'But who are you lot? Why are
you fighting,
What's all the noise about? How you leap!
I can't keep my eyes off you. I'm looking at you.'
And began to shout as he made his slow way down:
'Get on with it, you lot, set to! Set to!'

***

Franz walks into a bar …

FRANZ now peddles racist, pro-Nordic papers. He's not against the Jews, but he is for law and order. For law and order must reign in Paradise, which everyone should realise. And the *Steel Helmet*, he's seen those boys, their leaders too, that's a great thing. He stands by the subway exit at Potsdamer Platz, in the Friedrichstrasse arcade, under the Alexanderplatz station. He shares the opinion of the cripple, the fellow with one eye, the man with that fat madam.

To the German people on the first Sunday in Advent: Destroy your illusions once and for all, and punish those who lull you to sleep with their juggling wiles!

Dreske the stutterer smiles at the floor: "Well, Franz, blessings upon you, as the sky-pilot says, on your new path in life. When we march out to Karl and Rosa next January, you won't be with us then, will you?" Let him stutter away, I'll sell my papers.

When they're alone the proprietor smiles at Franz. The latter stretches his legs comfortably under the table: "Henschke, why did they beat it, that gang? On account of my armband? I guess they've gone for reinforcements." That fellow won't let up. One of these days they'll kick him out of here. Blood must bubble, blood must bubble, its currents muggy and thick.

Henschke tastes his filling, I must put the goldfinch nearer the window, the wee creature needs a little light. Franz helps him, drives a nail into the wall behind the bar, Henschke carries the cage with the fluttering thing from the other wall. Franz stands on the chair, hangs the cage up, steps down, whistles, lifts an index finger and whispers again: "I hope no one will come near her now. It'll get used to it. It's a goldfinch, a she." Both say nothing, exchange nods, look up and smile.

In the evening, sure enough, Franz is kicked out of Henschke's. He comes tripping along at nine, takes a look at the bird, its head is under a wing already as it sits on the perch in a corner, how come a little creature like that doesn't fall off when it sleeps? "Wonder if all this smoke is good for it, little lungs like that?" "Never known anything else at my place, there's always smoke, actually it's not so thick today."

Georg Dreske, young Richard and three others sit at a separate table. Two of them Franz doesn't know. There's no one else in the room. When Franz came in there was a big row going on, lots of loud talking and swearing. As soon as he opens the door they lower their voices, the two new ones keep looking in Franz's direction, lean over the table, then sit back impudently in their seats and drink one another's health. Bald Henschke busies himself at the sink; contrary to custom he does not leave the place, but manages to fuss and bustle around.

All of a sudden the conversation at the next table grows

very loud, one of the newcomers leads in the chorus. He wants to sing, it's too quiet here, there's no piano either. Henschke calls over: "Why should I get one, the business won't pay for it." Franz knows what they want to sing, the "Internationale" or "Brother to light and liberty".

There they go, it's the "Internationale".

Franz chews, thinks to himself: they mean me. If only they wouldn't smoke so much, when they sing they don't smoke, it's bad for the little bird. One of the newcomers calls over: "Well, comrade, did you like the song? "Me? Fine, you've got good voices." "Why don't you join in?" "I'd rather eat. When I get through eating, I'll sing with you, or else sing something by myself." "All right." ...

Later: "What about our song? We got no music, you're a man of your word, ain't you?" I'll give em one, I'll keep my promise. First I'll whet my whistle.

Franz orders a fresh mug, takes a sip, what'll I sing? Calmly and slowly it flows forth: "I once had a faithful comrade, Never better could there be, The trumpet echoed wihidely, He firmly marched besihide me, There step for step with me." Rest. He sings the second stanza: "One ball winged by Death came flying, Is it sent for me or thee? Torn away from life and dyhying, At my feet he's lyhying, He seems a part of me, He seems a part of me."

He sings loudly, solemnly. Towards the close the fellows across the room have conquered their amazement, they howl with him and beat on the table, scream and start acting the fool. But now Franz remembers what he really wanted to sing; he blares it into the room: "There comes a call like thunder's peal, Like billow's roar and clash of steel, The Rhine, the German Rhine so free, Yes we shall all your guardians be. Firm stands and true the watch, the watch on Rhine."

Now they grow silent. Henschke steps out from behind the bar, sits beside Franz. One of the men swings his leg over a chair, buttons his coat, tightens his belt, a tall erect fellow, now the apple cart's upset all right. He goosesteps towards Franz, who'll get a crack on the head if the man ever reaches him. With a hop he straddles Franz's table.

Franz leaps up with flushed ears, the men at the other table do likewise. Franz grabs his table, tips it over, the newcomer, plate, mug, mustard pot all fall plump on the floor. Franz squeezes himself back by the window, here goes, if those fellows only don't touch me, boy, if they only don't touch me. I mean everybody well, but there'll be trouble if that fellow's silly enough to touch me.

"Fascist! Bloodhound!" the tall fellow roars at Franz. "Gimme the armband! Quick about it!"

***

Beauty Contest

WE report on the final evening spent by Conrad and the Prinkipo Nanny-goat in the main salon of the hotel. A contest was in progress to choose the Turkish beauty queen. It was not Irene but Conrad who, to her slight chagrin, chose this entertainment. She was annoyed that he offered no word of encouragement to her, the beautiful though not exactly young Nanny-goat, to take part in the competition. Strangely enough, no one else encouraged her either. The game, she decided, as with all these shows, was rigged. Since I myself, stuck in the library in Zurich, am unable to attend the magnificent show, I shall let the Turkish newspaper speak; it reads, immediately before reporting on how to keep food fresh, in the following terms:

Plesire Nasib Crowned Beauty Queen
Presided over by high officials, the selection

committee, of which the poets Hoopoe and Po-dagra are members, plumped in their second secret conclave for Plesire Nasib, following a majority vote in the first round for Miss Miao-tzu.

Since Miss Miao-tzu had attracted the most votes in the previous round, the announcement that the selection committee had awarded the title of Miss Turkey to Plesire Nasib aroused loud controversy in the crowded salon. At the very moment when a megaphone brought down into the hall invited Plesire to step forward as the Turkish beauty queen, the writer Cocka-too, recently elected to Parliament, leaped from his seat, climbed on a chair and protested loudly against the unjust decision, meanwhile encouraging Miao-tzu, seated at the next table to the chosen beauty queen Plesire Nasib, also to stand on a chair. He said that if anyone in the hall should be selected as beauty queen, it should be none other than Miao-tzu. These words were greeted by applause, causing adherents of Plesire to protest in their turn. Meanwhile the megaphone announced that no one should oppose the decision of the selection committee to which belonged such famous figures as Hoopoe and Po-dagra.

But Cocka-too would not give up the fight, and asked the guests assembled in the hall if they wished to set aside the committee's choice and call on Miao-tzu to accept the crown. At that moment, as tempers in the hall seemed to be reaching boiling point, both dance bands struck up at once, and while certain heated persons

> tried to continue their quarrel, the first couples, among them the new beauty queen Plesire Nasib with the film director Crook-shank, came onto the dance floor. The evening then passed quietly, apart from a vigorous difference of opinion between two gentlemen which threatened to degenerate into physicalities but through the intervention of two ladies was settled amicably, and social decorum gradually returned, electoral fanaticism having abated.

We have nothing to add to this excellent description.

***

Room for the Night

THE ancient bellhop at the little hotel near the cathedral grinned silently through the gap in the door into the room where his boss Anton Erbe sat on the high office stool at his desk over an opened accounts book, pen behind his ear, doing nothing. Herr Erbe was so idle, or so deep in thought, that he didn't even turn his head to the door to hear more clearly what it was the man had been mumbling for a good while now. Herr Erbe had acquired the habit of contemplative sitting and doing nothing while in the prison from which he had made his escape only this past Saturday.

At last Herr Erbe, a mild-looking man with a pince-nez, did turn his head because of the draught, and saw Hubert grinning through the door and moving his lips. Herr Erbe thought: either I'm deaf or he's mad, because I can't make a word out. Now Hubert nodded energetically several times and rasped that his voice was gone because he'd swallowed some food the wrong way. He croaked: "Here's another one."

"Another what?"

Instead of answering, Hubert pointed his right thumb back over his shoulder. He was pushed aside, and a tall elderly gentleman came into view. This gentleman, who had a small suitcase in his left hand and a knobbly walking stick in the right and in consequence did not remove his hat, is our major.

"You are the owner of this hotel? I would like a room."

Herr Erbe asked with a meaning look: "To whom do I owe the pleasure?" Whereat the major fixed him with a glare of command and asked pointedly: "Is this place a hotel?" The hotelier nodded. "Then I would like a room."

"I only ask because you seem acquainted with Hubert. You've stayed here before."

"Who is Hubert?" When Herr Erbe removed his pince-nez and pointed to the doorway, the major put down his little case, and stepped up to the desk: "Now I really would beg of you, my dear sir, I need a room."

"Just because you're acquainted with Hubert, there's really no need to shove past him like that. The man's been in service with our hotel a good thirty years." At which the major picked his case up again, then thought of the hard night he had behind him, and pulled himself together. "Well, do you have a room?"

"But of course. We can always find one, why not. Certainly the only question is, two nights or three?" Not waiting for the major's response – he really wanted to respond to this civilian familiarity with an about-face – Herr Erbe came out from behind his barrier, pulled a little wicker chair forward from the wall, into which the major despite everything slowly deposited himself, and then talked calmly down to him from his lazy office chair: "You see, here's Hubert, he's not all …; he'll take your suitcase up right away, second floor, Hubert, the twin-bedded room, it became vacant just yesterday, a couple from Vendenheim spent their honeymoon there, happy young things, ah, if only we were still so young. You must know

Vendenheim? Beautiful country, Alsace. I had to leave for a while, a year and a half, a long time for me. But you must come from Prussia, or Bavaria?"

The major forced himself to stay calm, he was an irritable man, the hotel he'd been staying in became too noisy, he recalled the horrible night with running footsteps and laughter just overhead. He squeezed out a sentence: "You were – deployed east."

"No, not that, I was never a soldier actually, nor a tar, I have my hernia and I'm already too old and fat for war. What they did with me, because they failed with everything else, was stick me in prison. And for what, do you think? I was never tried according to law. But there I had to sit all the while. Always investigations. And if the war hadn't ended I'd still be there, being investigated. They meant to aggravate me. And they managed it, I lost twenty kilos. That's fine, Hubert, nothing more for the moment. I sat there in Fadengasse, that's the investigative holding centre here in Strassburg, I was to have a hearing on 30th October, then it was put back to December."

The major cleared his throat, he thought of the night and let it wash over him. He huffed in sympathy: "What was it about?"

"What it was about, colonel? I wish I knew."

"I am a major."

"I beg your pardon, major. But I expect it's all over now with majors and colonels. Yet the title remains, the title lingers on, it won't be forgotten. What was it about, yes. It was the same with all of us. One is Alsatian, and that's a mistake. If one is Alsatian, whatever one does one falls under suspicion. Suspected of what, you don't know and never find out, but it hangs over your head. You don't try too hard to lose it, you'll never lose it, no point wracking your brains to think what the suspicion is about, others will find it, one fine day."

The major gave himself a shake and favoured the man with a response: "Well, let's be frank, after what we've seen these last few days and what's been happening here, there was good reason to suspect certain things."

"Don't say that, major. No one should say that. If you see it rightly, it's a treadmill … Take this situation, for example," (he obliged the impatient major to remain seated and listen, whether he wanted to or not) "I don't know you, and so I'm reserved towards you and wait to see what you are. That dissatisfies you, you expected a cordial reception, maybe you have a high opinion of yourself, and you may well have good reason, but I don't know you. And so you become even more reserved and surmise that I don't like you. And then I think out my part and wait a bit longer. And then, because nothing appears from my side and I don't say anything, you surmise I have hidden motives. And now you yourself have hidden motives and I for my part really do have hidden motives and I think to myself: you're not exactly on the level, either. Cordiality is anyway quite out of the question by now."

"Well then."

"And so we've grown suspicious. And there's nothing to be done about it. You're an object of suspicion because you're not frank, and you remain suspect. I for example have a wife from Nancy, she's a second cousin. We've always read French newspapers, it's her habit, and we've always kept in touch with our relations, even with the war. So they start sniffing around us, when the war's not going so well. We left old newspapers lying around, and then during the war we had newspapers and letters from relatives via Switzerland. For sure I could have done without them, but my wife, she's adamant, she says: but why, just because it's war why shouldn't I read my newspapers and read letters from my sister that anyone can read. I tell her: Girl, it's not on, it arouses suspicion. She says: I feel a quarrel coming on. I give in, and why should I break with our relations."

"Was your good lady detained as well?"

Mild Herr Erbe laughed on his high office stool: "No. My wife acted very sensibly. After they'd snooped around a couple of times, the police, she packed her little bundle and said: Anton, I won't stay here, they mean us no good and I mean them no good, but they're stronger, come with me! And I, stupid idiot, out of sheer obstinacy, said no, and so off she goes to her sister via Switzerland. And when the first letters from her arrived I was well and truly suspicious, openly collaborating with foreign powers."

The major cast a quick sharp glance: "In your place I'd have taken to my heels as well." Herr Erbe spread his arms: "Why? Why, major? Run from whom? This is my hotel. Business was excellent. I'd done nothing to anyone. But they hauled me in as anti-German, a traitor, and so I had to sit there from spring of 1917, a year and a half, major. They found nothing to charge me with."

"Mistakes were made," the major muttered, yielding to his fate.

The mild hotelier raised his head: "My wife's still over there, she'll not be coming until the French are here. Not a minute sooner. I'm using the time to feed myself up, otherwise she'll have too big a shock when she sees her old man. Today's Wednesday, on Saturday they fetched me out of Fadengasse, it feels like a whole month already. I wept, major, when they opened the cell and said we could go, we could leave, go wherever we like, and they were all standing there, crowds, Alsatians, they all felt as we did, and they cried and hugged us, strangers, but everyone friends, and they led me back to the hotel in triumph with music and singing, back here where my good old father used to live. Now, major, why do I tell you this? Because you must take it with you back home, back to Germany, so they know it too. I'm peaceable and good-natured, my wife thinks I'm too much so, but that's another chapter. Here I never gave cause for suspicion, I was no friend of Germany but also no enemy, and certainly not a traitor. And when I emerged from the investigation cellars in Fadengasse and there were dozens of others like me, and I stood in the street, here outside my hotel – well, damnation."

Herr Erbe gritted his teeth and stared before him, brow furrowed, he spoke softly. "At that moment no Prussian had better let me lay hands on him, but there were none to see, suddenly they were all gone from the street, and then I realised they were right to call me anti-German. Now I was. Still am. But I've nothing against soldiers."

The major kept quite still. Herr Erbe cleaned his glasses, replaced them carefully on his nose, settled the earpieces one by one, wiped his forehead. The major waited a while longer. Since Herr Erbe did nothing but stare into space, the major stood up. Erbe said: "The room is at your disposal." The major, his throat tight, said: "I am most grateful," and let Hubert lead the way. On the stairs he gave the bellhop money for newspapers, any would do, local or foreign.

***

THEME 17. SWANSONGS

Hai Tang's pilgrimage (from *Wang Lun*)
After the monsters (from *Mountains Oceans Giants*)
From the dream he never returned (from *The Babylonian Exile*)
Into the eddy (from *The Land without Death*)

***

Hai Tang's Pilgrimage

Ch'ien Long basked. Officers, generals, high officials, advisers who had taken part in the suppression of the rebellion received titles of honour, estates. On the day of the Thanksgiving Festival, the Emperor inscribed in a firm hand in the inner hall of the Confucius Temple: "Had Confucius been here, he would not have proceeded more thoroughly than I."

While corpses still rotted in the quiet streets and in the houses of Linching, Hai Tang the general's wife travelled on a great ship of mourning, surrounded by her women, along the coast to her southern homeland. She wanted to travel alone. She told Chao Hui, when he sold his house in Shanhaikwan, that he should take a concubine, have a son by her.

Soft autumn came. The ship glided along the southern coast. From the towns music shrilled. Harvest processions thudded in the fields. Junks streaked playfully over the dark water. Hai Tang still as death on the broad heavy ship. She did not journey directly to her home; the ship anchored off the island of Putaoshan. Hai Tang wanted to go before the merciful goddess Kuan Yin, secure for herself the prayers of the most pious monks.

Sunny jags of granite peaks. Dreaming tucked-in

landscapes. Slender fan palms with clear voices. Camellias a hundred thousand. Transpiring ponds, floating lilies. Between hedges, behind stony paths, a temple at the foot of the cliff. Stretched out sky.

Supported by two women. Hai Tang rustled along the path in grey voluminous clothes, grey veil over her face. They went through the entrance hall, across the vast terrace and the platform in front of the prayer hall. Hai Tang's eyes tolerated the reliefs on the steep breastwork of the terrace, extolling childish love. In front of the altar the eternal flame smoked in its carved wooden niche. Curtains, patchwork carpets, standards, drums, incense.

Goddess Kuan Yin huge at the back. She sat there by the wall in a white robe, left hand delicately raised; her face was golden; she wore a crown of five lotus leaves; her blue hair was fastened with a diadem. She sat on the marble plinth slender of hip, strong legged, head leaning slightly back; violet bib; white silk flowed over her narrow shoulders. The eyelids beneath black brows were lowered, but the yellowish lashes, thin, slightly parted lips seemed to flutter gently. In such mildness she kept her silence, in such absorption she heard and gave. Tablets and banners praised her. "Kuan Yin, great friend. Her merciful boat conveys all across. Her grace is vast as the waves of the sea. She arose for everyone. A mother's heart. Her golden body will not perish."

Monks in brown robes pressed foreheads to the ground before her. Murmurs, tinkling, a soft chant. Hai Tang crumpled her veil, breathed gustily and smiled, gazed away over the monks.

It was late evening. The island was vanishing in the darkness. Bearing lanterns a hundred monks left their cells and chapels in procession along stony paths. Hai Tang had donated a vast sum in order that they should pray for her to the goddess. She sat at the bend in the path under a boulder of granite. The procession murmured past, arms crossed, cowl after cowl. She paid the monks, an endless stream. Proud, triumphant she surveyed the boundless throng: she must succeed in overpowering the goddess. Peace, peace was what she wanted. Wang Lun had taken both children from her, vengeance had failed and even had it succeeded would have been of no use. Peace for herself, peace for her dead children, endless ever renewed floggings for Wang Lun! It grew calm in her as the torches vanished amid chanting into the temple. She gulped the warm air. The goddess had better look out, now the monks were crowding in on her, struggling with her, for Hai Tang. Her maids got to their feet. Hai Tang returned to the ship for the night.

The next evening she sat once more under the boulder of granite. The torches swayed past. In the darkness she turned her triumphant face, contorted with hate, towards the dark temple. She shook her arms over the heads of the monks.

On the third evening she sent her maids away. The murmur of the procession filled the paths. Hai Tang stared into the dazzling torchlight. She fell down, screamed, tore her breast. The goddess was stronger, the monks could not prevail. They could pray and pray and pray. Who had the strength? Who could save her?

Then it seemed to her the monks were back already. There was a rustling. A gleam played over the ground. In the light of the newly risen moon, slender-hipped Kuan Yin walked past her, mother of pearl white. The diadem on her curly hair flashed grassgreen when she turned her inclined head. She smiled, looked at Hai Tang said, "Hai Tang, leave your breast alone. Your children sleep beside me. Be calm. Do not resist. Oh, do not resist."

Hai Tang looked again into the green trailing moonlight. She sat up, pressed shovelled hands over her cold face. "Be calm, not resist. Have I the strength?"

***

After the Monsters

Blooming fading human beings of flesh and blood dwelled in the rumpled southern lands of Europe, on western ground with its massifs, young lowlands, on the level black blanket of the Russian tableland. The Earth moved mountain ranges highlands depressions under and around them. Great rivers drained clear water, filled lake basins. Brown and green plant-beings sprang from the ground. Forests and thickets grew along the Danube, along the Dnepr and the Don. Dense forest and swamp from the Atlantic coast to southern shores. Wildflowers grasses birds cooing sobbing dying in them. Animals crawled swam with bodies naked scaled furry over the levels, forever grabbing swallowing emptying themselves. Until they had again the ground in full, the water eager for transformations, the gnawing air. Hordes of humans in peace and death, wooing and bride-winning, through volcanic eruptions and floods. Holding fast to one another, fading away with tears, generation after generation, mother and child mother and child, lover and his beloved. And always the gases of the air yearning for the lung, the tiny cells, the nuclei, the soft protoplasm, forever inhaled and breathed out again. And when the heart stood still, cells separated and dissolved, they were new souls, decomposed Protein Ammonia Amino acids Carbon dioxide Water, water transforming itself to vapour. Greedy for sorrows and pleasures, always inclined to wander, soul-unions in snowy landscapes, on the vast heaving sea, in the roaring storm, stone-folk raising the ground up into mountains. Black the ether overhead, with its little balls of sun, sparkling heaps of sintering stars. Breast to breast the blackness lay with these humans; light gleamed from them.

***

From his dream he never returned

It was frail Conrad, gazing from sun-bright eyes, who (countering the old sinister wicked untruths of George, his shameless miserable destructive thoughts) at a ceremony under the tree calmly and as if it were nothing expressed what he felt as a certainty.

How radiantly the world is ordered, like all that lives, that carries within it this order and helps to construct it whether it will or no. (We are not the flock of lambs he showed me in the forest of St Germain. The wicked beast wanted us to be that. Mysterious world. We must help God. I begin to see, to live, only now do I stand at the very beginning of everything. Blessed, blessed my life!)

Wonderful and beyond all thinking is the conduct of the world. She is there. No one should scream at her or reject her, if she does not reveal herself today and tomorrow to our eyes. We ourselves must not withdraw from her, must be pleasing to her in friendship and cordiality to every single thing. Then she can grow from us as well. Ah, how much, how wonderfully much can the human being accomplish, you saw it in the cities, but the weightiest and most mighty, the true sole mover, is cordiality.

This light must be raised ever higher over the terrible darkness. That it never be extinguished, that we never sink down to be devoured by the ghastly lurking powers!

"A great orchestrator permeates this world, sees all that happens. Righteousness is still the rarest of all that happens here. Friendship, love, longing, knowing permeate the world and must endlessly wrest her free from the rigidity and cold wintry Death into which Violence wants to cast all things. These shake what is above down below, and raise what is below up above. How good for all of us that we are so very small and weak, have become such poor – no, rich – people, we can keep ourselves well. Woe to the hard, the violent, the blind, their path shall be endless until they have atoned and faded away. But nothing greater or more lovely can be granted them than to atone. Not only are they absolved and freed, they can become, in whatever garb, kings or architects."

No Sirrush slept outside Conrad's chamber, only his white cat. One evening she became uneasy, scratched at the door, never stopped the whole night. Within, old Conrad, hounded from his high Babylonian seat, sent into the world to atone, sunken into the earth, had lain himself down to sleep.

He dreamed blissful dreams, flew around lots of people known and unknown, spoke amiably to them, he flew around flowers, encountered the tree he loved so much. The tree fluttered its leaves, they understood one another. Then Conrad in profoundest gratitude opened up his breast and gave his life to the tree. He sank down over the sacrificial pit and into it dripped some of his blood too.

Then he was still spritely enough to fly higher. Then a wide black-blue heaven came, filled with star-flowers that held a mighty attraction. Oh how strongly those twinkling stars called to him. Their mighty choir received him like a shout of joy. He sang to them. They replied. Again he sang. He gave his whole voice to the greeting. The bliss was too much.

From this dream he never returned.

★★★

Into the eddy

They reached the sea at two places. As successor to the old man, those in the north chose Nimbiarapony. And when they retreated a little way inland to regain strength, and were in the region of Botas, a sickness came upon them and most died. Nimbiarapony led the remnant back to the Mbaracaya hills, to the river Iguatemi from where they had set out. He wanted to gather new people. Young people trekked with him through the wide lands of the Paranà. Forests, bush, grasslands and rivers exulted. The chief died on the Ivahy river. They searched through the forest, lamented and called out to him who was supposed to lead them. They scattered. None came back.

In the north the chiefs Necguei and Avavucu went with the Tanygua people. They stood on the shore. And when they despaired and turned back they came to the forest of Caingang.

The Caingang women gathered genipa berries and pineapple. The Caingang men went naked, wore wooden plugs in their lips, had shaven skulls, a big mat lay across the left shoulder. And when the strangers went through their forest they put on warpaint, set jaku feathers on their head, stuck feathers on their body, around the neck they hung bird bones, deer's hooves, monkey teeth. They attacked the migrants. They were tree climbers, hunted snakes, they carried axes to break up rotten trees and look for larvae and fat beetles. They took aim with their axes at the weary bands lost in the forest.

On their bodies the Caingang had painted jaguar skin, new moon, fish scales and bird footprints.

Two hundred Tanygua remained alive. They danced and sang and were happy. They crossed the Itariry river. There they saw railway sleepers laid across the graves of their ancestors. They cursed the Whites and went to the shore and danced on. Soon not a single foot trod the ground of this earth.

The storm blew Sukuruya's head feathers back, her long black hair fluttered, she gazed into the land.

She heard people calling, their laments without end, their rejoicing without end, their songs, their prayers. She saw the dance of the migrating tribes. Her proud face lit up. She went down, hid in a bush, spied on the sorcerer's dance on the shore. She saw old Nanderikini. We come to the sea, we traverse the scrubland of Yaboticaba, we approach the house of the great ancestors. What would my children eat? O Great Father, make an end of it.

Sukuruya swung her club. She whooped at the forest edge. Deer, tapirs and herons came. They followed her, they stepped along with her. They tried to dance as the people had danced when they called to the Great Father. There is a land where no one dies and there is no evil. Spades turn the soil by themselves. Fruit comes by itself into houses. Spirits came rustling, rustled in hordes around them.

On the riverbank, Sukuruya swished as a snake. She jumped into the water. Thousands after her, into the eddy.

***